MW01417099

"Kelly Foster Lundquist examines an archetype and emerges with a magnetizing story of a relationship that defies category: shifting, cryptic, tender, marked by contradiction and care. In vital, kinetic prose, *Beard* maps the fault lines between love, desire, and performance, the roles we learn to play whether we're conscious of them or not. A bracing, fresh testament to becoming, no matter who we are."

—**Paul Lisicky,** author of *The Narrow Door*

"*Beard* is everything I want from a book: hilarious, moving, surprising. Imagine the humanity of Gail Caldwell mixed with the absurdity and wit of Amy Sedaris. Kelly Foster Lundquist's memoir of her complex marriage is timely and timeless. A true feat of storytelling and personal revelation."

—**Nick White,** author of *How to Survive a Summer*

"Moving between memory and myth, Lundquist weaves personal narrative with the charged symbols of queer iconography—glamour, disguise, survival. What does it mean to carry someone, or to be the one carried? What remains when the performance ends? An incisive, beautiful meditation on intimacy and identity, *Beard* reminds us: not all beards are false, and not all truths are spoken."

—**Juliet Patterson,** author of *Sinkhole*

"Lundquist beautifully renders her fragile first marriage and all its earnest striving with honesty and grace. She has given me everything I want in a memoir; *Beard* is smart, funny, richly detailed, candid, revelatory, thoughtful, meaningful, and moving. And, in the way of all great works, it leads us to higher truths."

—**Michael Kleber-Diggs,** author of *Worldly Things*

"Out of the heartbreak of shame and fear, Kelly Foster Lundquist crafts truly beautiful and searching family portraits as she simultaneously chronicles her own deepening intellect, her capacious, hard-won sense of compassion, and her commitment to authenticity."

—**Lia Purpura,** author of *All the Fierce Tethers*

"In breathtaking prose, Lundquist renders visible the 'beard,' an experience so often presented as little more than a footnote in someone else's story. A love story, a treatise on seeing and overlooking, and an exploration of what it means to know oneself and be known by another, *Beard* is a tremendous achievement. I will be recommending it to everyone I know."

—**Chris Stedman**, author of *IRL* and *Faitheist*

"*Beard* is brilliant and bristly and heartbreaking and funny as hell, despite the fact that this book turns out to have very little to do with actual facial hair. Lundquist debuts here as a wry, cunning Rumpelstiltskin, turning the straw of human suffering into literary gold. The queerest thing of all turns out to be what all of us need: love."

—**Harrison Scott Key**, author of *How to Stay Married*

"Lundquist's *Beard* announces the arrival of a powerful voice in memoir. It offers an unsentimental, unqualified account of two people discovering themselves around and through the tether of their marriage. *Beard* reminds us love is a living, growing, changing force—that it calls us to be the best version of ourselves even in the most difficult moments, and that understanding and forgiveness are not idle acts. They are radical, nourishing, and necessary to thrive with dignity. Lundquist's work to unpack this story for herself and for us is a gift."

—**Charles Jensen**, author of *Splice of Life*

"Lundquist turns the well-worn trope of the 'beard' inside out, delivering a memoir as sharp as it is tender. With wit, precision, and unflinching honesty, she shows how easy it is to be both the punchline and the truth-teller. Ultimately, *Beard* is a memoir about the longing to be chosen, the betrayal of self-erasure, and the bittersweet process of rewriting the stories we once believed would save us."

—**Ryan Berg**, author of *No House to Call My Home*

KELLY FOSTER LUNDQUIST

Beard

A MEMOIR OF A MARRIAGE

WILLIAM B. EERDMANS PUBLISHING CO.
GRAND RAPIDS, MICHIGAN

Wm. B. Eerdmans Publishing Co.
2006 44th Street SE, Grand Rapids, MI 49508
www.eerdmans.com

© 2025 Kelly Foster Lundquist
All rights reserved
Published 2025

Book design by Marke Johnson at the Made Shop

Printed in the United States of America

31 30 29 28 27 26 25   1 2 3 4 5 6 7

ISBN 978-0-8028-8473-2

Library of Congress Cataloging-in-Publication Data

A catalog record for this book is available from the Library of Congress.

Ten percent of the royalties from this memoir will support PFund Foundation, a community-led grant maker funded by and for LGBTQ+ people. PFund Foundation's mission is to build equity with LGBTQ+ communities across the Upper Midwest by providing grants and scholarships, developing leaders, and inspiring giving. The foundation is a hub for engagement and advocacy across the Upper Midwest so queer and trans+ people and places have sustainable financial resources to do their important work. Learn more about this critical resource at www.pfundfoundation.org.

For Devin,

for the trying and the telling

The author in a yearbook photo

beard: *n.* [1960s+] (US gay/lesbian) a [partner] used as an ostensible lover or even [spouse], as a disguise for one's real [sexual orientation]. [gambling jargon *beard*, a go-between who places bets for another person, thus protecting their identity].

—*The Cassell Dictionary of Slang*

beard: *noun.* In [outdated] binary terms, a partner of the opposite gender meant to cover up one's sexuality. E.g., "*Harrison's just her beard. She dates him to make people think she's straight.*" See also: Closet, Fish Wife, Lavender Marriage.

—Chloe O. Davis, *The Queens' English: The LGBTQIA+ Dictionary of Lingo and Colloquial Phrases*

Author's Note

I have a very good long-term memory, the sort of memory that's been tested and diagnosed by people who test for such things. However, I also have ADHD. What that combination means is that I can recount with verifiable accuracy that I ate my first Taco Bell Enchirito (three black olives on the top) on Benning Road in Jackson, Mississippi, during a televised rebroadcast of *Young Frankenstein* in 1981. And yet, I can also drive past a building and say, "Oh, that's new!," only to have my daughter respond, "Mom, you say that every time we drive past it. That building's been there for six months."

Which is to say, if I'm interested in something—like Enchiritos and Mel Brooks—it sticks like glue. And I'm profoundly interested in all the events recounted here. I have also consulted years of journals, emails, letters, yearbooks, photo albums, DMs, and all sorts of other material to ensure as much factual accuracy as possible. However, my memory—precise as it can sometimes be—is as liable as anyone else's to be limited by my point of view and self-protective shame. I've therefore done my best to rely on those who were present for these events (most significantly, my first husband) to affirm the veracity of my version of them. Some names have been changed and others withheld.

Introduction

When I tell this story as a joke, I am its punch line.

Leaning in close, I might start with this bit: "The night before my first husband got outed to me back in 2003, I was in Chicago's Boystown neighborhood dressed up as Liza Minnelli for Halloween."

If the person I'm speaking to laughs—particularly if that listener happens to be a gay man with whom I share a set of cultural preoccupations—nineteenth-century American literature, musical theater, twentieth-century Hollywood, sitcoms of the 1970s and '80s—I might feather in more detail. Having leaned in, I might open my brown eyes wide. I might gesticulate expressively: half Norma Desmond, half Sally Bowles.

"I was getting my PhD in queer theory."

"My dissertation was on Walt Whitman's Bowery masculinity."

Then perhaps this little nugget: "We were at a bar called Cocktail with two gay friends of mine the night after Halloween when a barista who'd recently seen my husband out with another man walked over to say hello."

If the person to whom I'm speaking laughs even harder at this, I might say something like, "My ex and the man he ended up with had rhyming names: Devin and Kevin" or "After we divorced, my ex returned to school to get a degree in interior design" or "For our first birthday present as a couple, he asked me for a pink oxford shirt from Old Navy and a tube of Sun-Ripened Raspberry Hair Gel from Bath & Body Works."

If it's the right sort of moment, and perhaps my listener happens to be a couple of cocktails in, that might end up making them giggle so hard they tell me to stop talking so they can catch their breath.

My friend Carlos lay down on the floor of a fine dining restaurant where we both worked the first time I told him about it and kicked his feet like a child being tickled.

I've gotten actual spit takes. One of my friends even peed his pants.

Just a little pee, but still.

Part of what makes it funny is the fact that, despite what now appears to be a preponderance of evidence, I truly did not know either that my ex-husband was gay or that he was cheating on me before that post-Halloween night at Cocktail in Boystown.

As an English professor, I'm professionally qualified to tell you this serves as both situational and dramatic irony, with a garnish of verbal irony. I get why people laugh at me, why I have prompted them to, and why I have laughed so often at myself.

It's easier to be the one telling the joke than the one being laughed at, and beards are such an easy punch line.

The first time I registered the beard as a trope, I was watching *Saturday Night Live* with my then-husband Devin when Rachel Dratch appeared on the screen as "The Girl with No Gaydar."

She has Dratch's trademark goofy grin, somehow both crooked and hyperbolic. Her eyes are wide when she stumbles into a bar full of what are meant to be legibly gay men—lisps and limp wrists, teacup poodles, leather chaps, and rhinestone dog collars abound—and marvels at the number of hot, unmarried men in the room.

The seemingly "smartier, savvier" women who accompany Dratch to the bar, possessed with more presumably reliable gaydar, roll their eyes at Dratch's inability to accurately decipher the pulsing Morse code of that particular room.

On the night Devin and I watched that skit for the first time, we were two years away from our apartment in Boystown where I'd be holed up studying Judith Butler and Foucault by day and drinking pitchers of diluted cosmopolitans at bars with names like The Manhole by night. But I got the joke: gay men were always so obviously gay that any girl with a faulty "gaydar" was goofy at best.

Seven years after watching that skit for the first time, divorced and teaching at a community college in California, Devin sent me an email asking if I'd been watching *30 Rock*. Tina Fey's Liz Lemon reminded him of me, he said.

As luck would have it, I had just finished rewatching an episode of *30 Rock* called "The Head and the Hair." In that episode, Lemon informs a suspiciously handsome man she's just begun dating, "If you're a gay man looking for a beard, I don't do that anymore."

My ex-husband was right.

Liz Lemon was like me.

A year later, I caught another episode of *30 Rock* in which Lemon makes a splash on a daytime talk show by coining sassy catchphrases to chide women for putting up with bad behavior from their men. "Deal-breaker!" is the one that sticks.

During audience Q&A in that first episode, a "plain" young woman approaches the mic with her "hot" fiancé. Her hair, face, and baggy linen dress are all shades of beige. She wears matronly gold hoop earrings and no makeup.

The fiancé, on the other hand, looks like he could be Tom Brady's cousin: all steely jaw and broad shoulders and well-coiffed hair over a collared, checkered button-up artfully arranged just outside the neck of his form-fitting sweater.

When the two of them get their chance to pose a relationship query to Lemon, the beige woman reports that her fiancé keeps arguing with her about their wedding plans.

Emboldened by the talk show audience's approval of her hot takes, Lemon interrupts her, "Nope. Your fiancé's gay. Look at him. Look at you. Classic case of fruit blindness."

The message is clear: beige girls only land boys who look like that if the boys have something to hide.

Not long after this episode aired, *Parks and Recreation* introduced the conservative character Marcia Langman, a proto-Karen. As spokesperson for the Society for Family Stability, Langman objects to a marriage between two male penguins at the zoo and calls for the resignation of the show's protagonist, Leslie Knope, for officiating the wedding. In later episodes, we meet Langman's presumably closeted husband, whose sexuality is ostensibly made obvious in bits like having him ogle a banana sheathed in a condom.

One of (several) Langman punch lines: She's a frigid bigot who deserves to be hoodwinked by him.

Another mid-aughts beard plotline arose in later seasons of *The Office* when Angela marries "The Senator," who then ends up having an affair with Oscar, her longtime coworker. Partly because both Oscar and Angela were more prominent characters than Langman, this relationship got depicted with a bit more tenderness and warmth, but certainly, we are meant to understand that Angela deserves to be fooled because she's as morally rigid as she is vain.

If beard jokes abound in sketch and situational comedy, it's no surprise they also pop up in books written by those same comedy writers.

In *Modern Family* writer Cindy Chupack's 2007 essay about her first husband's remarriage to a man, she writes, "What woman today doesn't have a guy-who-turned-out-to-be-gay story? Admittedly, it's a smaller and stupider subset that has a husband-who-turned-out-to-be-gay story."

There's the scene from Tina Fey's 2011 memoir *Bossypants* in which one of her musical theater friends from high school comes out to a room full of people, and his coming out is noted by all but "scone-faced Patty," his Catholic school girlfriend who is described as "a sweet, quiet girl with short curly hair and a face as Irish as a scone . . . the only person at the party who didn't get what Brandon's deal was."

More recently, there's "The Actress," an *SNL* short featuring Emma Stone, all beiged up in a Kohl's sweater and matronly haircut. The joke of the sketch is that Stone—the beard in a gay porn scene—continues to ask the director questions about her character's motivation. Exasperated by her persistent attempts to give this character nuance, the director finally tells her, "She doesn't have a backstory! She exists to be cheated on!"

In the first season of Apple TV's homage to musicals, *Schmigadoon*, Ann Harada plays Florence, the wife of the titular town's closeted mayor, Aloysius Menlove (pun intended). Oblivious to her own ironic wordplay, Florence sings the song "He's a Queer One, That Man o' Mine," which contains the stanza "My man is gentle / As soft 'n' sentimental / As any lace adorn'd a valentine / He's a queer one / That man o' mine." But then later, when her husband finally and very publicly comes out, she tells him, "Of course I knew you were a homosexual! I'm not stupid!" The implication: if she hadn't known, she *would* be stupid.

There's the line in Rebecca Makkai's 2017 novel *The Great Believers* about a beard whose closeted and sexually restless husband ultimately causes her protagonist's death from AIDS: "Dolly was short and plump, her hair tight in curls. If Yale was right about Bill being in the closet, then he'd chosen his wife predictably: plain, but put together; sweet enough that she likely forgave a lot."

In all-too-rare contrast, Tony Kushner's beautiful depiction of the beard Harper Pitt in *Angels in America* helped me be brave enough to name what was happening in my first marriage and to leave it with more grace and love than I would have otherwise.

Still, the trope of the beard persists.

She is short (I'm 5'3").

She is plump (me too).

She is sweet (usually).

She is plain (as I sometimes feel).

She is dumb (as I have often felt or been made to feel).

Beards can be shaved, washed down a drain, swept with the meaty flesh of a palm into a bathroom garbage can.

We exist to be cheated on.

No trope exists in a vacuum.

If the beard's beige serves as camouflage, gay men have got nothing for cover. In pop culture the queerness made legible on their bodies is flamboyant, meticulous, preoccupied with its own aesthetic. They are depicted as indifferent to, if not repulsed by, the bodies of the women who love them. Never mind that in real life they may have conflicted feelings about their sexuality or it might take them years to decipher that code for themselves, let alone for anyone else, or that even today there remain countless reasons to hide your sexual identity, even from yourself.

I'm as guilty of the presumption of queer legibility as anyone. When my brother came out to me a year after my divorce, I blurted out, "But you've never said anything mean about my clothes." As if one of the central prerequisites for being a gay man were professing catty opinions about fashion. In my own defense, during my first marriage and sojourn in Boystown, derisive comments about my wardrobe were not infrequent.

It's easy enough to consign both beard and queer partner to these tropes because the pattern-desperate brain, hungry for control, likes to believe we'd know if we were missing something.

It's messier to reckon with sexual fluidity or the complexity of desire. It's messier still and much less comfortable to own the fact that we can lie and be lied to.

Here's the thing: not all beards are beige.

One night in 1956, Elizabeth Taylor threw a dinner party at her home in Los Angeles's Benedict Canyon. She and Montgomery Clift had been best friends for nearly six years. He kept his own sexuality (he was either bisexual or gay—accounts differ) tightly under wraps because of the way both the public and the studio system punished queerness at the time. But Taylor was well aware of Monty's sexuality. She had asked him to marry her three times anyway.

Each time he said no.

But they played along when, between Taylor's marriages, their studios encouraged the press to play up rumors of their supposed romantic connection.

That night in 1956, they were filming *Raintree County* together. After a long day of filming, a group gathered for a meal at Taylor's home. The dinner party consisted of Taylor and Clift; Taylor's second husband, Michael Wilding; Rock Hudson and his wife, Phyllis Gates (also a beard); and actor Kevin McCarthy.

It was foggy that night in Benedict Canyon, and after leaving Taylor's house around midnight, Clift struck a utility pole with his car, leaving it an "accordion-pleated mess." His famously symmetrical face was pulped.

McCarthy, who witnessed the wreck, raced back to Taylor's house to get help. In her hurry to get to her beloved friend, Taylor left her house without shoes. She crawled through the crumpled car's rear window and lifted Clift's rapidly bluing head into her lap, cradling and kissing it.

All the while, he pointed desperately to his neck. The impact had knocked several of his front teeth into the lip of his trachea. He was choking to death. One by one, she reached into his mouth and extracted the teeth. She saved his life. Clift survived, but his famous face was never the same.

In my most self-aggrandizing moments, fleeing the beigeness I fear most, I ponder the end of things with my own personal Monty Clift: the way I taught him to make mashed potatoes the night before I left, or how we are both alive now and well because of when and how I ended things. I picture myself as Elizabeth Taylor, some violet-eyed savior wearing Maggie the Cat's white slip. Monty's head nestled safe into the pillow of my *Butterfield 8* breasts, the whiff of White Diamonds in his brutalized nose as I pluck each ragged incisor clean.

He breathes free.

He walks away from the wreck, and so do I.

But sometimes I also wonder: what if *I* was the teeth?

Chapter 1

ON THE NIGHT WE MEET, WE DRAW GOD ON PAPER.

Seated in a circle with about twenty other summer camp staffers—most of us students from small Christian colleges all over the Southeast—we are instructed to draw the image that comes to mind when we imagine God. It's late May and we are deep in the piney woods of northeastern Mississippi. A resin-scented breeze blows across a lake just outside the windows.

The water glitters with the light from unobscured stars and a half-waxed moon. I can just make out a line of pine trees reflected black against the lake's dark water. I find myself looking outside often as I adjust to this second summer of working at this Christian camp—one of hundreds of such camps across the country where kids come to swim and hike and learn about God. Most of these camps are run by evangelical nonprofits and share conservative social values even if they differ on the finer points of theology.

For the next nine weeks, the college kids in this circle will each be responsible for as many as ten campers at a time. Ranging in age from eight to eighteen and grouped into grade-specific weeks—elementary, middle, high school—the campers will arrive with their parents or church leaders on Sunday afternoons and go home on Saturday mornings.

In between, their days will be filled with everything from

waterskiing to Ping-Pong to rock climbing to arts and crafts—and Bible study. A lot of Bible study. There will be morning devotionals for the whole camp, personal quiet times, small group Bible studies, worship services, special speakers, one-on-one conversations about personal relationships with Jesus Christ, evening devotionals. And at the end of the week, staffers will check one of three options on a 3 × 5 notecard dedicated to each camper: made a decision for Christ, still uncertain of personal salvation, or already a Christian before they arrived.

I didn't know about the 3 × 5 cards when I was here as an eight-year-old camper myself, but I suspect they checked "already a Christian before she arrived" on my card. My father was a pastor when I was born and still preaches on occasion, despite a later career pivot into community mental health work and a theological shift that led our family from an emotive, nondenominational evangelicalism to a more cerebral and reserved Presbyterianism.

Sitting in this circle eleven years later, my faith is flagging for reasons both acute and chronic. Children I knew died. My first boyfriend broke up with me days after I'd suffered a suspected ectopic pregnancy. It turned out to be a ruptured ovarian cyst, but for the next two years he managed to find every possible way to humiliate me—not on purpose, but in practice. Unlike the people who grew up being told God would keep them safe at night if they just had faith, I'd been told God could either protect or kill me at the roll of his immortal dice. Either way, he'd be good. Either way, he'd be wise. So I'd lain in bed watching shadows, wondering which way the dice had turned for me, trying to love what could kill me and still be good.

CHAPTER 1

In this circle, many of the worship songs, the prayers, the earnest confessions of my fellow camp staffers sometimes feel embarrassing to me, childish, facile. More than that, because of those shadows I slept with, I have no easy answer for the questions I know I will be asked this summer. Still, I want it to be easier to hate this place and all it represents. I want my protective sarcasm to be the only feeling I've got. But I like and respect many of these people, and have only just met the others. No matter what, like them or not, I want them all to like me. I want everyone to.

Last year I worked here in the camp's kitchen and snack shop, where I woke just after dawn to dump cups of orange powder from a container that read "Compare to Tang" into equally orange Igloo coolers. I used industrial can openers to pry into vats of diced tomatoes we baked until reduced with andouille sausage and vats of red beans to be served over rice. In the afternoons, I blended dozens and dozens of milkshakes and "blizzards" stuffed with the candy of each camper's choice in stainless steel malt cups until my forearms throbbed with the effort.

From that salty, sweaty vantage point, I longed to be part of the crew of actual camp counselors—the ones who drank the milkshakes and didn't spend hours cleaning them up. And here I am: finally, a counselor. Not only that, I'm a counselor who was particularly asked to return. So, I won't give in to my own cynicism. I can be soft and silly too. I can—we all can, as I will tell my campers despite my doubts—be reborn. I can be singular. A singularly hopeful, faithful person.

"Take a few minutes. Think, but don't overthink it. What do you imagine when you imagine God? You don't have to be an artist. Just do your best," says our group leader.

I glance around the circle. We are lovely young people: our muscles taut, our skin already burnished, our hair thick and glossy, our teeth white and friendly. Despite our location in a predominantly African American region of Mississippi, we are a mostly white group. The logos on our clothes—Patagonia, Columbia, North Face, J.Crew, Gap—suggest we are comfortably middle-class or aiming to appear so. The smell of pine trees competes with Davidoff Cool Water and various Victoria's Secret and Bath & Body scents: cucumbers and melons, freesia, pear, and rose. The faces around me feel like brightly lit rooms in houses I drive by at dusk. I wish I could walk in and be welcomed.

We're supposed to draw God on butcher paper taped to folding tables just outside the room, and several folks get up immediately to do so. Others, like me, linger for a bit in their chairs. I close my eyes. I take a few deep breaths.

God.

God.

G-O-D.

My mother sings in the church choir and has spent the last ten years teaching at a small Christian elementary school. I sang in the church choir for years myself. I've built houses in Mexico as part of a Christian relief effort and taught Bible school for "at risk" kids all over the urban South. But I've got no picture of God.

There's only darkness on the surface of the deep. A formless void.

I conjure tangible God-adjacent things that bring me comfort: "Abide with Me" on a pipe organ, my youth director's wife taking me to breakfast before school at McDonald's every Thursday morning for all of seventh grade, my grandfather's

CHAPTER 1

mischievous smile when he would show me the chilled Reese's Peanut Butter Cups stowed in his refrigerator, the feeling that he is still with me despite his death seven months ago.

Sitting in a room feeling like an awkward outsider, the thought of my grandfather and other kind adults reminds me that there are people who love me. Who even like me. Who don't see me as snarky or too quiet or not good enough.

We've been given only fifteen minutes to draw. Other staffers have already drawn their images and returned to their seats.

Finally, an image comes to me. It's not complete, but it feels truer than anything else: I think of my mother's steamed carrots.

In my maternal grandmother's kitchen, butter and lard form flaky biscuits, crispy chicken, minute steaks in velvety gravy, cornbread with pork cracklings. When I picture childhood mornings spent there, both my grandparents are tapping cigarette ash into beanbag ashtrays on their gold-flecked Formica table. Merle Haggard warbles on an AM country station. At the stove, my grandmother is cooking hot link sausage she stuffed with peppers and fat before my grandfather smoked it in his black barrel smoker. The hot fat of the sausage lingers on my fingers and my mouth. I can't ever wash it all the way off with the Irish Spring soap she keeps at every sink.

My mother's parents don't go to church, and they swear when they drink. My parents worry about me when I'm with them. The searing grease, the acrid tobacco, their angry words all corrode and calcify. I sometimes fear them the way I fear the wages of sin.

My mother does too.

Her rebellion and bid for salvation both played out on the plates of steamed vegetables with no butter or salt that she served her own children. Flaccid disks of squash, browning florets of broccoli and cauliflower, and worst of all to me, astringent orange disks of carrots, offset occasionally with a teaspoon or two of honey, which only made them worse.

That was what health—somehow the opposite of sin—tasted like. That was eating what you ought.

Suddenly that's how I imagine God—my ultimate "ought"—in this room of glowing young people: God is a bowl of carrots I don't want to eat.

I jump up from my chair and sketch out a rough blue bowl brimming with what looks like orange coins with little black squiggles meant to indicate steam rising from them.

I return to my seat and make eye contact with the handful of people I know in the room. Then two volunteers bring the butcher paper into the room for us all to share what we drew and why. We'll go in a circle, and I relax only slightly when I realize I'll be last.

There are pictures I'd mostly expect: A blue brook along a green hill ("he makes me lie down in green pastures, he leads me beside quiet waters"). A shepherd's crook ("the Lord is my shepherd"). An overflowing Central Perk–sized latte cup (it runneth over). A cross with a sunset behind it ("he causes the sun to rise and set"). Mirrors with no reflection ("I want my campers not to see me but to see God").

The themes of invisibility and obliteration continue in various forms: windows, black holes, treeless fields.

Finally, it's my turn.

"Ummm . . . my picture of God is this blue bowl with steamed carrots in it. I don't really like carrots, but my eyesight is bad, and I've always felt like it was my fault because I won't eat carrots. I guess sometimes I feel that way about God, like

CHAPTER 1

I should want to eat him more than I sometimes do, and it's my fault I feel far away from God sometimes."

A moment of absolute stillness, then laughter, slow at first, then hysterical. People are slapping their hands against their thighs and wiping tears from their eyes.

They think I was making a joke.

I'm rocked. But I know from years of theater training how to respond when an audience laughs. I wait it out. I turn my neck and broadcast a smile around the room. I shake my head as if I'm embarrassed; I am embarrassed, that part isn't acting. I even laugh a bit. While I'm collecting myself, I look around the room longer than I've allowed myself to do all night.

In the corner farthest from me, in a faded orange baseball cap and several days of thick stubble, is a boy I know only by reputation. His name is Devin. He's from Oklahoma, and he was friends with my roommate from last summer. He'd had an on-again, off-again relationship with our camp nurse, who's been a counselor herself in previous years. They are seated together on a loveseat in the corner of the room. She is laughing.

He is not.

He's looking at me in a way that makes my cheeks grow hot. His eyes are brown. He knows that I wasn't joking.

Devin looks like Montgomery Clift, whose biography I've read so many times my hometown librarian used to laugh at me when I returned to check it out. His jaw is square like Clift's. When he smiles to acknowledge my gaze, it's with the same self-assured, sideways grin Clift used on Shelley Winters in *A Place in the Sun*.

I smile back, then realize the laughter has died down. The camp director looks at me a little sadly.

And for the millionth time in my life, I wish I'd just pretended. I wish I could have said the thing I knew I was supposed to say and meant it. Wanting to want God is the beginning of actually loving him, I have been told all my life. And I do, so very badly.

I want to want steamed carrots.

I want to want God.

Chapter 2

The next morning, our work begins. Before the first campers arrive, staffers will weed and paint and ride around on four-wheelers spreading poison powder onto fire ant hills.

For my first assignment, I am paired off with the guy in the orange baseball cap who knew I wasn't joking. We are each given a pair of gardening gloves and four large wooden pallets overflowing with bright flowers—impatiens, nasturtiums, pansies, and violets.

The camp director shows us how to gently crumple the thin plastic of each container to release the plant and then to slide a single finger into the wiry white cluster of root ball to open it for the soil. If he was troubled by my God-as-carrots performance at the icebreaker last night, he doesn't seem so this morning. Like so many of the other people who are here, he seems more certain about life and God than I feel, and I wish I could be more like him. I smile more than usual and try to project confidence and calm.

Soon, it's just me and Devin and our gardening supplies. I remember that my grandmother recently told me that impatiens like shade, so I suggest we plant them closest to the building next to us. Devin agrees. I will learn later that like most of my family, his grandparents and parents also grew up on farms and kept thriving gardens he's been raised to help maintain. We start digging small holes for each plant.

We work quietly for a while until he breaks the silence.

"I think maybe we were on the same ropes course element last year," he says. "I remember you made a joke about how you were ascending like Jesus, and then when you came back down, you were like, 'Nah. I changed my mind.' I thought it was really funny. Do you remember that?"

I mostly remember that a cute boy had laughed at a joke I'd made that day. So, Devin had been that cute boy.

"I do remember that!" I say. "Also, I heard about you from Shanda and Kathy last summer—all those Oklahoma folks talk about you all the time like you're famous! I know they're all really glad you're here."

He smiles and waves off the compliment in a friendly way.

We continue quietly planting until he says: "I really liked what you said last night in the circle about God. I hate having to say stuff like that in front of people. Especially when I don't know them. I never feel like I say the right thing."

"Oh my gosh! Me neither! I felt so dumb last night."

I'm so grateful for this outstretched hand of sympathy that I narrate my entire internal struggle from last night. He responds with a similar story about his own drawing, which was so nondescript even he barely remembers it hours later, and I have already forgotten it. But it comforts me to know I wasn't the only one in the room who felt conflicted.

Eventually, we start talking about our lives outside camp: our college majors (mine is English and his is business), what our parents do. I learn he's got a closet full of VHS tapes of *Party of Five* and *90210*. He learns about my *Godfather* obsession. I don't mention my boyfriend back home. He doesn't say anything about the camp nurse he was sitting next to last night.

Once the plants are in the ground, we stay seated in the shade and keep talking. We linger so long we are late for lunch, which we eat together. He laughs from his belly and asks thoughtful questions. I sometimes struggle to talk to boys as handsome as he is, but it's easy to talk to Devin.

After lunch, still paired up, we stuff hundreds of envelopes with fundraising letters for financial supporters of the camp. Devin and I sit at a folding table with a return counselor named Missy. I don't know her well, but I talked to her a few times last summer, and I really like her. We discuss future plans and hobbies while we stuff letters. Devin and I realize that we share a love for the soap opera *Days of Our Lives*. We are doing impressions of the temporary demon possession of recurring *Days* protagonist Dr. Marlena Evans, when a fellow counselor snaps our picture. All three of us are laughing so hard at our own growling demonic voices that our eyes are wet with tears.

"Somebody's tickle buttons got pushed!" says a staffer sorting through mic cables a few yards away.

Eventually we join a larger crew outside and walk the two-mile perimeter of the camp picking up trash people have thrown out their windows and sorting it into piles in the bed of a battered old Dodge truck we call The Blue Cheese.

As we approach the camp, we stumble upon a hedge of wild magenta roses and Devin sings a few bars from a song about blood roses that I instantly recognize.

"I didn't think anyone else here would be a Tori Amos fan!" I exclaim.

"She's definitely weird, for sure. But I really do like her," he replies.

And then he picks a rose from the hedge and holds it over his forearm like a waiter brandishing a wine bottle.

"Want it?" he giggles.

"Why, thank you. Thank you," I respond, doing a bad impression of a 1940s screen siren. I sound a little like Katharine Hepburn, but only enough to grate on most of my friends' nerves.

I stick it behind my ear, anchored by a mass of heavy brown curls, already kinked by the early summer humidity.

Devin surveys the effect on me and smiles.

We arrive back at camp with about thirty minutes to go until dinner. I haven't stopped sweating all day, and all of us want to take showers and put on clean clothes for the night's training. We'll be reviewing the staff manual with a focus on page 8, the section that addresses the prohibition of counselor-to-counselor romances. They're not allowed (until the campers have all departed at the end of the summer). And still, to my knowledge, there's never been a summer when at least two or three couples didn't start dating or even get engaged not long after camp ended.

I am thinking about page 8 and my shower when Devin asks me if I'd like to come to his cabin before dinner to hear a live Tori Amos performance from the RAINN concert a couple of years back.

"Of course!" I say, and instead of turning toward my own cabin, I accompany him to his. I don't mind that others are watching us.

The thing about not having air conditioning in Mississippi is that all the fabrics in our cabins always feel damp, no matter how dry it feels outside. Even in early summer, the interior of every eleven-person cabin feels like an unfinished basement—

CHAPTER 2

dark with a sharp note of mildew in the air. When Devin motions for me to sit on his bed while he gets the CD out, his sheets feel almost dewy against my skin.

Soon, there's a trill of minor-key piano runs at the beginning, and you can hear the audience scream when they recognize the first bars of "Silent All These Years." It's a sloweddown version of the one I'm familiar with from her *Little Earthquakes* album.

There on Devin's bed, the rose he picked for me still tucked behind my ear, the tangled heft of my hair barely contained beside it, I monitor the progress of the late afternoon clouds by how the light on Devin's face goes gold then gray then gold again.

He is so perfectly beautiful. And funny and kind.

He understands me.

He knew I wasn't joking last night.

It's been months since the boy I've been dating on and off has known what I meant without me explaining it. He can be very kind but is increasingly withdrawn or depressed. And yet when I was the one who felt depressed recently, he told me he refused to hang out with me unless I watched *Willy Wonka* and cheered up first. Even on days when we are getting along, if I asked him to listen to a song I loved, chances are strong he'd start talking over it or make fun of it.

I've known Devin for only a day, and more than the fact of his square jaw or the ease of speaking to him, I can just tell.

He would never talk over a song.

The sun is gold, and he is gold, and maybe if I am near him, I can be gold too. It's only the beginning of the summer, but I let myself daydream about a future with him—going to movies and staying up all night talking about them or chatting at diners or catching trains in the big cities we both hope to end up in or listening to music on endless road trips. I know it's silly. But all my life, I've been waiting for some cinematic spiritual connection, and this already feels like one.

Why couldn't it be?

Tori Amos sings a line about mermaids. And I think of T. S. Eliot's line about the mermaids: "I have heard the mermaids singing, each to each. // I do not think that they will sing to me."

What if I'm a mermaid too?

It's this question—echoing a lyric from Amos—that I ask myself as I walk away from Devin's cabin ten minutes later to get ready for dinner.

But when I enter my own cabin, I get a glimpse of myself in the mirror, and my stomach lurches.

I look awful.

I'm wearing glasses that make my round face rounder. I'm so sunburned that the bulb at the end of my nose has doubled in size. The rose in my hair has shed most of its petals and twigs are tangled everywhere. I look like some kind of chubby Druid priestess in an oversize T-shirt and baggy men's Levi's.

I feel ridiculous.

But Devin invited ridiculous me back to his cabin. And in twenty minutes, he will walk past all the thinner girls here with sleeker hair, to sit next to me with a plate of Salisbury steak and mashed potatoes.

So, what if?

What if I'm a mermaid too?

Chapter 3

My resemblance to Judy Garland is uncanny.

I've been hearing about it since I was a kid.

Same auburn-brown hair. Same forehead. Same wide-set brown eyes. Same eyebrow shape. Same upturned nose. Same distance between our noses and lips. Nearly every casting director I encountered as a child actor took one look at me and said, "Oh my god! You look just like Judy Garland!"

I could never sing and dance like Judy, or act as well as her, despite the years I took lessons and acted in local theater, TV, and movies that often filmed in my Southern hometown. But there were so many moments watching Garland onscreen when I'd think, "She looks just like me!"

Like many actors, Garland looked young for her age. She was already seventeen when she played Dorothy in *The Wizard of Oz*, a character meant to be preadolescent. And she spent much of her adolescence playing jovial "girl next door" roles, often alongside Mickey Rooney. In the Andy Hardy series, she listens patiently as Mickey pines for more "conventionally" beautiful girls like Lana Turner.

Of Garland as a teen, cultural critic Anne Helen Petersen writes, "In a studio filled with glamour girls, Garland was always the ugly duckling—unsexy, ungainly, and always too fat or too skinny, or so the studios, and the press, told her."

In the old film magazine *Silver Screen*, Garland once told a reporter that she'd overheard a friend of one of her castmates saying about her, "She'll never be an actress! She just thinks she can sing. She's too fat. Imagine her being a movie star!"

Once she gained a few pounds after sneaking a month's worth of chocolate malts from the MGM studio canteen. Louis B. Mayer, the studio head who initially mandated Garland's use of amphetamines and barbiturates so that she could keep her weight down, reportedly took her aside and told her, "You look like a hunchback. We love you. But you look like a monster."

And thus, she returned to her old lunches of three mouthfuls of chicken soup, and the weight fell right off.

Once when I was in eighth grade, my acting coach explained to me that because of my "large features," I could expect to be cast only in "best friend" roles. I ignored this warning and showed up, weeks later, for an audition asking for a "young Ellen Barkin" anyway, only to have the casting director tell me that I didn't have "the right face" for a lead-girl role. The role ended up being Reese Witherspoon's big break.

Years later my college roommate, Lauren, became the Lana Turner to my Judy Garland. She was all swan. I was mostly duck. Or at least that's how I felt.

Lest you think I'm exaggerating, Lauren's eventual writer-husband used the pseudonym Grace Kelly for her in his first book. All of us old friends found the moniker perfectly apt and the book won a huge award and sold lots of copies.

If we had been in *Ziegfield Girl* together, Lauren would have been the romantic lead, and I would have chastely

CHAPTER 3

hopped off to pretend-sip a chocolate malt with my sexless adolescent crush.

Imagine that you're in college and you look a little or a lot like Judy Garland, depending on the day. After years of food restrictions and constant training for track and field, you've put on thirty pounds, and most of it seems to have gone to your upper arms and face. On some level you know you aren't that far off the norm, whatever that means. If you lose those thirty pounds, maybe forty, you'll be a size considered ideal. That's not all that much in the grand scheme of things, but it's indicative of how powerful the standard is, that this relatively slight variation feels as though it consigns you to secondary status.

Beyond that, you've got cystic acne so deep you've begun taking Accutane to manage it, which means that now your facial skin keeps peeling off like wallpaper. You are attempting to be less complicit in global child slavery by never buying fast fashion, the only fashion you can afford, but what that means instead is that you are mostly wearing ill-fitting men's pants purchased at thrift stores with an alternating series of silk tops from Express and Limited.

Now imagine that you are this version of Judy Garland, with scarred and peeling cheeks and old bell-bottoms and a red silk blouse that accentuates rather than disguises an uncomfortable new layer of belly fat, and imagine that every day, three times a day, you walk to your college cafeteria next to your own Lana Turner.

You know that Lana Turner's dad is an asshole and that her mom has been diagnosed with terminal cancer and that she farts loudly in your room and that she sticks the antenna from your cordless phone into her nose in moments of reverie and that she snort-laughs and that she pees her pants when you watch that one *Wings* rerun together where William Hickey says, "Maybe it was Las Cruces!" and then you both recite it together at the same time. Maybe she's as lonely and lost as anyone, but it won't always seem that way.

You know all of this, which is to say, you know Lana Turner is only a regular person—a kind, funny, ordinary, smart person you like and love. But then you leave your room beside her and not a single boy you pass, not even the nerdy ones who are waiting to talk to you about how they stayed up all night playing *Diablo*, looks at you first.

Even the Bible offers its own take on the Judy Garland / Lana Turner distinction. In the book of Genesis, it was love at first sight when Jacob—future patriarch of Israel—spotted Rachel herding sheep. Since he didn't have any money, Jacob worked for Rachel's father for seven years to earn the right to marry Rachel. But then the father tricked him and said: First you have to marry Rachel's older sister, Leah. Work another seven years, and *then* you can marry Rachel. Among the few things we know about Leah is that her "eyes were weak" and that Jacob "hated" her for being plain.

Eventually, Leah and Rachel together with their handmaidens would mother the twelve tribes of Israel.

My takeaway as a child? Better to be a Rachel than a Leah. Rachels are loved; Leahs are tolerated. My roommate was a Rachel. I was a Leah. Despite the love of my family, nothing—church, school, auditions—contradicted this belief. You could only do so much with what God gave you, and what God had given me was Leah equipment with Rachel aspirations. I was a Judy Garland with Lana Turner dreams.

CHAPTER 3

It shouldn't have mattered.

"Charm is deceptive, and beauty is fleeting," read the Bible verse I taped to my adolescent mirror.

It's what's inside that counts, said every well-meaning Bible study teacher or TV special or school assembly speaker ever.

But the same youth director who read me the Bible verse about fleeting beauty also admonished the girls in our youth group that our pastor's stunning wife—America's Junior Miss in 1977—should be a model to us for how to continue to be attractive for our future husbands, who would stay faithful to us only as long as we stayed fit and well groomed. He was one of a hundred other voices, some even less subtle, telling me how very much looks mattered. At the same time, I was also told I mattered because I was made in God's image, whatever that meant. God was faceless, which is what I most feared becoming.

For better or worse, looks mattered. Looks mattered when I was auditioning for a role. Looks mattered when I eventually gave up auditioning for roles. Looks mattered in every story of every happily married grown-up I ever heard. *What did you first like about her? Her legs. Her mouth. Her eyes. Her face. Her hair.* Eventually they would get around to personality or character.

The reality was that in the white evangelical South every bit as much as in any film audition, a particular kind of symmetry got you in the door and kept you on the stage or in front of the camera or in the relationship.

Were there exceptions?

Of course.

But only enough of them to prove the rule.

Or at least that's how I felt when I was seventeen years old and desperately afraid my face and my body explained away my worst feelings. I thought that if I could just "fix" them, the magic that beauty bestowed might make me magic too—might make me brave enough to act again, might make me like boys who were kinder or healthier than the aloof ones I kept chasing.

Even if appearances never mattered, even if facial symmetry was insignificant, even if it was only ever truthfully what was inside that counted, here's what no one ever acknowledged: In pursuit of the gentle and quiet spirit that women like me were exhorted by our elders to cultivate, it is every bit as easy to ravage your body until it's gentle and quiet too.

In 1954, Judy Garland mounted a huge comeback after years of struggles with addiction and depression—struggles that originated in her studio-mandated use of diet pills to maintain optimal physical symmetry—in *A Star Is Born*. Many critics consider it her best film and her best performance. In it, her golden energy crackles through the screen like she's a lit match. The performance earned her an Oscar nomination in 1955.

Everyone thought she would win. Her performance was too magnetic, too charismatic, too emotionally raw to lose. She was a shoo-in. Even the Academy of Motion Picture Arts and Sciences was so convinced that Garland would win the Oscar that they dispatched a film crew to the hospital where she'd just given birth to her son, Joey, so that she could give her acceptance speech there live from her bed.

But as it turns out, there was never any need for cameras. Judy Garland lost to Grace Kelly.

Chapter 4

When camp ended, I left a note under the windshield of Devin's car that said in part, "If we ever end up in any sort of institution or sanitorium somewhere, I'd like the room or rocking chair adjacent to yours, so we can keep talking." That summer we'd spent every free moment in rocking chairs that faced the lake. Just the two of us talking, the flowers we planted weeks earlier at our feet. On nights there were no campers, we'd often stay up until 1 or 2 a.m., sometimes all night.

When he flew back home for a couple of days to sing in a friend's wedding, I made him a care package of some of his favorite things, purchased from the Walmart in town: grape Nerds, Spree candy, Celestial Seasonings Orange Spice tea, a Tori Amos CD with her cover of Springsteen's "I'm on Fire." When summer break came, we took that CD and a bunch of other favorites to Atlanta where one of the other counselors had invited us to visit her family home. We rode the seven or eight hours there and back, just the two of us in Devin's car, stopping at three or four Cracker Barrels along the way so we could play the peg game and eat chicken tenderloins with sawmill gravy.

In our final staff meeting, we were asked to place colored pieces of paper with our names on them around the room, and we were asked to write affirmations on each person's page. Devin and I both got words like "real" or "authentic" or "funny." On my page, Devin wrote: "No words needed."

I was touched by this, but I was also waiting for the confession that he liked me as more than a friend. It was clear he did. Anytime we were in a room, his eyes found me. When he told me he liked my shirt or my hair, he'd brush my face or my shoulder and let his hand linger there. If we were seated, he'd lean into me and place his arm around my shoulder. We hugged often.

But we never kissed or even held hands. We had never said anything that might have transgressed the holy code of page 8. And while I was drawn to him, always aware of where his body was in the space around me, physical contact with him felt different than with other boys. I craved his attention, but when I tried to picture actually kissing him or doing anything more—historically a pretty easy thing for me to imagine about boys I liked—my imagination faltered.

Nevertheless, as my family pulled into our driveway the day my parents picked me up from camp, the phone was already ringing. And when I heard Devin's voice on the other end of the line, my desire to be near him was an ache that stretched from my solar plexus to my spine.

It is November and I'm back in Jackson, Mississippi, for my junior year of college. Devin is almost halfway through his senior year in Tahlequah, Oklahoma. We've talked often—most days, often all night—for months. We've exchanged letters and mixtapes. And in just a few weeks, he is coming to see me for the first time since camp ended.

CHAPTER 4

There will be a staff reunion at camp over our winter break and two of our friends will be having a page 8 wedding we plan to attend, but he's coming a few days before the reunion and the wedding so he can see me. We've said nothing about dating, but I am never not thinking about him.

My friends all say it's just a matter of time until Devin asks me out. But maybe to hedge my bets or maybe because it's something I can control, I have been dieting and exercising like it's my job. Maybe I'll emerge taut, thinner than he is, from a fleshier chrysalis. Maybe seeing me in person will be the stimulus that prompts him to act.

On this fall day, my friend Amanda and I are eating lunch at Amerigo, our favorite Italian restaurant in Jackson.

I watch as she pricks a large peach shrimp with her fork and rotates it slowly against the curved base of a big white bowl, picking up as much angel hair pasta as the fork, loaded already with shrimp, can handle. When her teeth pierce the small bundle, a glossy line of scampi butter rolls down her chin.

She giggles, and then wipes her face with a thick cloth napkin, two shades whiter than our white tablecloth.

I've seen Italian restaurants on TV, though I haven't traveled all that much outside Mississippi, and they look a lot like Amerigo. Purple clusters of plastic grapes hang on shelves above the windows. Chianti bottles with straw bases sit on wall shelves—old lines of white candle wax running down their sides. On the wall, there are art deco posters with bright food and mustachioed figures in white chef hats dancing. Perugina. Campari. Amaretto di Saronno. Each of them advertises in a stylized black typeface. Speakers overhead play a catchy mix of Rat Pack favorites: Dean Martin. Frank Sinatra. Tony Bennett.

Between the bar and the hostess stand, there's a wall of wine bottles horizontally stacked at an angle, their corks facing the wall to keep them wet.

This restaurant could be anywhere, I have often thought to myself when eating here. *Manhattan or Boston or Baltimore or London or even Italy itself, for all I know. We could be anywhere that isn't Jackson.*

Tonight, Amanda and I will make dinner with the group of guys who live in a pink house with our friend Spivey. We'll laugh at a new show called *South Park*, seated beneath wall shelves filled with beer bottles the boys have collected over years of hiking out west. The bottles have names I recognize from maps: Lagunitas, Sierra Nevada, Russian River. I've never been further west than a church ski trip to Colorado. None of the girls I know take trips like that.

I will smoke Winstons with Spivey and our friend Greg and this new student we all call "Daniel the Artist." They all look at me differently since I came back from camp, and I've heard they also talk about me differently when I'm not around—instead of mentioning my nice personality, how cheerful or friendly or funny I am, they now say things like how my butt looks shapely in a new pair of boot-cut jeans I've taken to wearing over to their place.

Spivey says those comments are mostly due to my increased confidence and the way it makes me carry myself, but I suspect the dry salad in front of me today at Amerigo's and its effect on my butt is the real reason.

I have ordered a Caesar: no Parmesan cheese, no croutons, no dressing, with three lemon wedges on the side, which is, as it sounds, a plate of undressed romaine lettuce spritzed with acid and dusted with table salt. Amanda has ordered the scampi with angel hair.

CHAPTER 4

After Amanda cleaves yet another plump shrimp with her teeth, she dips a pinch of pillowy focaccia first in the plate of basil oil next to it and then in the saline pool of scampi butter pooled beneath her pasta. She pops the bread into her mouth. Flakes of salt and chopped rosemary on her long, thin fingers.

"Foster, you gotta eat more than that, you know? You want the rest of this? I'm getting pretty full," she offers.

"Honestly, I'm not that hungry," I lie. "But thank you."

She raises a skeptical eyebrow, but lets the subject drop.

Eventually, she lays her fork and knife in a neat diagonal against the top of her pasta to indicate to our server that she's done.

"I could maybe take that home in a box, but microwaved shrimp is awful. Way too chewy," she says.

At least three uneaten shrimp, still warm, are left in the bowl over maybe a cup and a half of buttery pasta.

I imagine pulling the plate over, my tongue beneath the first bite of shrimp, pools of its velvet sauce coating the inside of my cheeks. Sauvignon blanc and garlic. Lemon zest and shellfish stock. Crushed red pepper. Parsley. So much butter. Creamy, though, not at all greasy. Perfectly emulsified. Not even cold yet, but about to be tossed into a large black garbage bag in the rear of the restaurant.

Even so, I don't take the plate.

I gnaw, instead, the green spine of my last leaf of romaine, and when the server takes our plates, Amanda stacks the still-full basket of focaccia and basil oil inside her pasta bowl. Then nothing remains on the table but my mug of steaming lemon water (I've been told it aids in digestion) and the syrupy dregs of her sweet iced tea.

Amanda doesn't lift weights or run or refuse dessert. She can eat whatever she wants and it never shows on her long, thin frame. In the three years she's been my best friend at college, I have mostly followed her lead, delighted to never refuse dessert too. We often leave campus in her Camaro, searching for foods that make us feel like we have traveled farther than Jackson.

We pull large green pickles from the barrel at Olde Tyme Deli and imagine ourselves at a kosher deli somewhere in Brooklyn. Other days, we pool our meager work-study stipends so we can split an order of Olde Tyme's brined potato salad. On nights when our friend John works at Bennigan's, we park ourselves at a booth where he brings us bowls of loaded potato soup and Monte Cristo sandwiches. At Swensen's, we get cheddar soup and grilled cheese to dip in it. At India Palace, we split a single lunch special and stuff a side order of garlic naan with palak paneer and cilantro and mint or tamarind chutney.

We giggle with full cheeks.

But that was before Devin.

I haven't giggled once since we arrived. I've been too busy trying not to think about what that pasta would feel like against my tongue. It's been months since I ate butter on anything, much less a mayonnaise-based salad or a cream-based soup or a fried sandwich or even a bowl of greens softened in clarified butter with cubes of soft cheese.

Devin is coming in just a few weeks.

Every day is dress rehearsal.

I remind myself of this when my cravings for anything more unctuous than canned tuna in water or baked ramen or lettuce with lemon overwhelm me.

Just wait until he sees you.

When, over shared cigarettes behind his house, Spivey speaks admiringly of Amanda's body, he says, "She's got fat in all the best places, you know?"

CHAPTER 4

And I do know.

What he means is that, especially in the pair of loose silk pants she is prone to wearing on our early morning walk to the American Novel class the three of us are taking together, her breasts and ass jiggle wildly, but nothing else does. And when she pulls her heap of red curls into a messy bun with her slender arms, she's like a marble statue covered in freckles. Fat in all the best places.

I've always been an athlete, and for most of my life, that's meant I was sturdy. I've been a sprinter since seventh grade. I even joined the basketball team so I could add extra cardiovascular training to my regimen, so I didn't get out of shape between track seasons. I ran "suicides" up and down the basketball court and the football field. I pulled a seventy-five-pound tire by a chain tied round my waist. I did push-ups and pull-ups and leg lifts. I ran wind sprints and forties and bleachers. I jumped boxes and rope.

Back then, I ate only grilled chicken and baked potatoes with salsa instead of butter, or half of a whole-wheat pita pocket stuffed with cucumbers and fat-free sour cream. I had plenty of company among the other athletes. Our coach approved.

But toward the end of my junior year, our track team had begun to disintegrate. Half our relay team had graduated. Our coach moved to a different school. I began dating my first boyfriend, and his mother served me a second dinner with sweet tea nearly every night after I'd eaten at my parents' house. Slowly, I allowed myself to eat what I wanted. I ate more and more and more. Flesh on flesh on flesh over bones.

I am back to bones now.

I taped a verse about resurrection from the Old Testament book of Ezekiel to my dorm-room mirror ("Thus says the Lord God to these bones . . . you shall live"). Between Ezekiel and the thought of Devin's imminent visit, I burn off lettuce and the little else I eat in twice-daily visits to the gym.

If I'm flagging in the fifth mile of a run or struggling to get to my hundredth deadlift or wondering if five hundred crunches are really worth it, I say to myself, "These bones can live. Devin is coming. Just wait until he sees you."

It will take years to register that the sinews and flesh Ezekiel also mentions will fail me as my bones become more visible. I will fall victim to every respiratory virus within a one-mile radius. I will land myself in the hospital repeatedly, my throat in danger of closing, in anaphylaxis my doctors say has begun to happen as a result of my body eating itself. I will not have a regular period again for six years.

At night, I force a pillow between my newly knobby knees so I can sleep without pain. I roll one hip out further than the other in bed and trace the ridged V of each hollow socket. My hips become a matching pair of worry beads. I run my fingers up and down them aimlessly when Devin calls at 10 p.m. to see how my day went and to tell me what happened in class. Up and down my hips, bump after bump. It soothes me.

I buy my first size 0 pants a week after lunch with Amanda at Amerigo.

I'm at the Gap with my mother and paternal grandmother, and I am pretending I don't see them watching me. Lingering in my dressing room, hidden from their sight, I don't have to hide my excitement when I effortlessly slide up the zipper on a pair of size 0 olive-green chinos.

Look! It's true! You can make yourself into anything at all, it seems clear to me for one contented moment.

CHAPTER 4

After the mall, my mother takes us out for Krystal burgers, the South's answer to White Castle.

When I was ten, dad and I used to come here before my acting classes. I could eat five of these little burgers back then—no problem—just a little griddled slider with maybe a sixteenth of a pound of beef in each. Minced onions and two pickles. A shot of mustard on steamed white buns. Not much else to them.

Today I opt out. I tell my mother and grandmother I had a big breakfast.

But I can smell the beef cooking, and I can see on the edges of the burgers my mother and grandmother cradle the bits of salty debris the buns have absorbed. In the back of my throat I can feel the snap of their pickles, the sharpness of mustard, the sweetness of melted American cheese, the bumpy caramel paste of griddled onion.

But I also know if I can just get out of this room and back to campus, I can wear those pants in the backseat of Mom's car to dinner, and that will be just as good as any slider ever tasted.

Instead of eating, I make small talk. I tell them about my American Novel class, and about *The Jungle* (if I can disgust myself, the burgers might not sound so good). I tell them how my brother Colin is going to stay with my friends at the pink house next weekend, and how we're going to make pasta for them and watch scary movies. I tell them about my philosophy classes and the people I still see from camp.

My grandmother, who only ten months prior buried my grandfather, and who spent the fifty years of her nursing career tending sick people, interrupts me.

"Kelly Gray, what's your body going to pull from if you get cancer? You've got no fat left on you."

I look at my mother, wondering what to say.

She doesn't speak.

She's just watching me.

I tell my grandmother I'm really good. That I'm feeling energized and strong. I tell her that I haven't gotten sick in three months, not even when my roommate had bronchitis.

I don't mention that it's been two months since I had a period.

"You're too dadgum skinny," my grandmother mutters.

"We just love you, and we want you to be okay," Mom says, in a bid to offset my grandmother's bluntness.

"Will it make you feel better if I eat a Krystal?" I laugh, throwing up my hands in mock exasperation, trying to ease their unrest, these women I love who both love me.

"YES!" they say, almost in unison.

I stand up to order a burger and my grandmother unclicks her purse to hand me a dollar.

I get a single Krystal. No cheese. Probably not more than 150 calories, I automatically calculate. Maybe not more than ten fat grams, maybe even five. Not so catastrophic in the big scheme of things.

But when I take my first bite, all I want is five more sliders. The entire burger is five bites at most, but I extend the experience as long as possible. Each bite a minute. Chewing slowly, then setting the tiny sandwich down in its paper box before I raise it up to my lips and then set it down again.

After we've finished our meal, I sneak off to the single stall bathroom. I hate throwing up more than I hate exercising, so instead of purging, I place both my hands flat against the wall and angle myself just so. I do body-weight push-ups against the wall for about three minutes, which is about as much time as I can stay in here without arousing suspicion.

CHAPTER 4

The tabulations continue. If, at 103 pounds, I do three minutes of push-ups, I burn about thirty calories. That's a little less than a quarter of the calories I've taken in, and as long as I burn more than I take in, I'll continue to fit in those size 0 chinos.

I flush the toilet even though I never use it.

I wash my hands, shaking my hands ostentatiously once I exit the bathroom to let my family know there's nothing to see here. Just a regular trip to the bathroom.

Twenty minutes later, they drop me off at my dorm. I kiss and hug them each from the back seat, grab that blue bag by its string, and swing it cheerfully out the car door. I wave goodbye and watch them recede against the horizon line of Peachtree Street. When my mother takes a right onto Riverside, I know they can no longer see me.

Instead of walking up to my room to drop off the bag, I walk to my own car and drive in the opposite direction of my mother to my gym.

There are calories waiting to be burned.

Devin is coming.

Chapter 5

SIX WEEKS AFTER ZIPPING UP THE SIZE 0 CHINOS, I AM SOBbing in a soft chair in Devin's cabin at the staff reunion. January is hours away and it's very cold, especially now that it's almost 4 a.m. We've been talking all night, have been talking for weeks, about whether or not we will decide to date. The only difference between this conversation and the ones we've been having on the phone or over email is that the last few have taken place in person in between large group gatherings—between going with a group of camp staffers to see *Titanic* and Devin's introduction to my family and my childhood best friend—in the car, in the mall food court—partitioned off from the others.

I do not know it yet, but the bronchitis I've been nursing for weeks is about to bloom into double pneumonia. My breath is a wet growl. I can feel a fever building.

In the four days since Devin arrived, I've eaten three oneinch cubes of grilled chicken, half of a half of a twice-baked potato, two cups of black bean soup, half a slice of frozen pepperoni pizza, a single scoop of mango sorbet, and two lemon-dressed plates of lettuce. Devin's physical proximity is an adrenaline surge. I'm genuinely not hungry, and the little I've eaten, I've barely kept down.

In this small, dark, wood-paneled room, once again seated across from me on a bed at camp, Devin is looking at me.

CHAPTER 5

He is exhausted and crying, and so am I. But we know that if we don't resolve this tonight, we might not speak again once we leave camp. I informed him weeks ago that I can't continue being his friend since I have romantic feelings for him. He's told me he also has romantic feelings for me, but that he's nervous to date me for a litany of reasons he's spent the last few weeks enumerating. But nothing adds up.

Every time I get up to leave because, sad or not, I need to go to sleep, he grabs my hand and says, "Wait. Just wait a second. Please. I need you to hear me. Please."

And I've stayed.

I've listened to his case. He says long-distance relationships are so difficult. I say long-distance relationships work all the time.

He tells me he's on new OCD medication that might negatively impact his behavior. He shouldn't make any major decisions while he's in the adjustment period. I tell him (truthfully) that most of my friends are on some kind of psychiatric medication. I can handle them, and I can handle him.

And that's what I feel more than anything else. No matter how fragile my body feels, I feel so strong right now, so ready to hurl myself off any precipice as long as I fall toward him. If he falls, I can carry him. I can carry anyone. I pull tires. I run bleachers. I jump boxes. I am strong enough for any of us.

Shifting on the edge of the bed, adjusting his legs, Devin brings up another reason we shouldn't date: He's only one semester away from graduation, and after that, he's pretty sure he'll be moving from Oklahoma to Nashville. It's never a great idea to begin a new relationship with such a major life change on the horizon. I point out that Nashville is actually much closer to Jackson than Tulsa. It's only a morning's drive, and I can happily move to Nashville after I graduate. Plenty of good grad schools there. I've already ordered brochures.

Then he points out that he's still figuring out who he is and what he wants out of life. That's not the best time to date. I'm also trying to figure those things out and why can't we figure them out together, I ask. I tell him my parents are in their fifties and they tell me all the time they are learning new things about themselves. That's normal. That's life.

Finally, he argues against loss.

"If we date, and it doesn't work out, I will lose you for good, and I cannot lose you," he says. "Being able to talk to you is the closest I ever get to feeling like myself. Some days, knowing I can talk to you is the only thing that keeps me from just feeling like I'm in chaos. I really, really don't want to lose you."

I'm leaning the now-sharp edges of my shoulders into the worn orange stuffing of this armchair. Each time I imagine what it'll feel like to walk outside knowing I have ended my friendship with Devin because I'm in love with him, I start to cry again. If it occurs to me after these weeks and hours of repeated conversations that any person I have to argue into a romantic relationship is probably not the right person for me, I won't remember it later. Mostly I think of Meg Ryan in *When Harry Met Sally*. I think of Meg Ryan in *Sleepless in Seattle*. I think of Sandra Bullock, Renée Zellweger, Julia Roberts, Drew Barrymore, Gwyneth Paltrow. Would they take no for an answer? Would they stay just friends with someone they loved and who they knew loved them back if only he could just admit it and stop being so commitment-phobic? I've even got Meg Ryan's haircut to complement my size o frame, complete with a healthy serving of Bed Head products over my zigzag

CHAPTER 5

part to make it extra spunky and adorable. Head to toe, I am my own best argument.

Look how cute I am! Just look!

When he repeats for the second or third time that he can't lose me, I put my hand up to silence him.

"I know. I get it. So just don't fucking lose me. I'm right here. I feel the way you breathe right before we hang up the phone. I know you feel that." I list all the ways he's woven himself into my daily life—the songs I hear, the movies I watch, poems I write, poems I read, ideas I've got about the future, things that make me laugh or cry or pause—he's in and over all of it. I've even noticed myself writing the number 8 differently lately—instead of one unbroken swoop, like a figure skater might do, I now place two separate circles one on top of the other just like he does. I tell him so. "I don't want to be lost. And I don't want to lose *us*."

He is crying while I talk but then he's exasperated when I stop. He raises his voice as loudly as he dares, realizing there are other cabins close by and everyone else is sleeping.

"But what if you don't know who I am AT ALL? What if you don't really know all there is to know about me? What If I'm too much? What if I can't . . . ? Like, you know what? I hardly ever like poems. I think most people who write poems are pretentious assholes, besides you. What if I'm not who you want me to be? What if you've just made that up because you wanted me to be that? I mean, I'm really judgmental. I care way too much about what people wear. I care way too much what I look like. It takes me hours to get ready some days. I can be so shallow. I judge people. I really do make fun of people. I always need everything to be a certain way. And I judge people," he says for a third time, and now he's losing steam again, and I'm just perplexed.

None of this is new information.

He speaks up one more time, this time barely audible: "I'm afraid you can't actually know me. Not really."

Once again, I respond that I know him better than anyone, but even my seemingly endless energy for litigating my case has begun to flag. I'm honestly not sure if I've been prosecution or defense in this fight, but both are ready for court to adjourn.

"No," he says wearily. "No, you're so right. You really do. You really do know me."

Then he stops talking, and he just sighs into his hands.

What he could say here—and does not—will set the course for the next ten years of our lives, but we don't know that yet. He is carving glyphs I've got no Rosetta stone to help me translate. He knows I haven't registered what he's been trying to say for weeks, for months, for years even before he met me. Whether he can't or won't is perhaps irrelevant. He doesn't. Given the choice to tell me straight what he tries to say sideways, he allows the obfuscation to stand.

And for the next seven years, I will be hypothesis, control, variable, petri dish, slide. I will be major and minor premise of the syllogism he needs more than anything to be true.

> *I love Kelly.*
> *Kelly is a woman.*
> *Therefore, I can love being married to a woman.*

He takes a deep breath.

"Kelly, I'm just so sorry. I just don't know what I want."

Even in this moment, I know this is the truest thing either

of us has said all night. I also know that no matter how spunky or adorable I can be, "I don't know" is a closed door I can't open.

"I don't know" is the same as no.

And "I don't know" isn't enough for me.

I stand up to walk out the door. "I can't do this anymore. I really do love you. But this isn't enough for me. I'm so, so sorry. I'll see you in the morning," I say.

I grab my black velvet peacoat from the empty bed next to his, where his half-packed suitcase lies open, shirts and pants and underwear all rolled into tight cylinders beside it, just waiting to be zipped back in.

"I understand. I really do. I love you. I'm so sorry it's like this. I'm really sorry," he says, lowering his head.

As I brush past him, I pat his shoulder. He puts his hand on top of mine and lets it linger.

Then I walk out.

I close the bedroom door behind me and make my way slowly down the hall that leads outside. He doesn't follow.

Ever since we were assigned to plant those flowers eight months ago, not a day has passed in which I haven't talked to Devin. Eight months of five- and six-hour-long conversations, of long-distance phone calls being my primary expense, eight months and countless emails and letters.

And after tomorrow, I won't see him again. I won't be sitting next to him in a car or lingering with him on the phone at 2 a.m. I will never know what his face would have felt like beneath my fingers. I won't know the texture of his tongue or the way his breath smells up close or what the bottom of his neck feels like against my nose. I will have to forget his favorite movies. I will have to forget which songs he loves.

When I open the door, the air outside is frigid, the windchill in the teens. Just like the heat, the cold in Mississippi is humid. It has the weight of wet laundry.

When I breathe in, my lungs reject the air, and I have to lean against a tree for support as I cough for several minutes.

Once my airway is clear, it's so quiet outside.

The lights in all the cabins are out.

The stars are crisp out here, dozens of miles from any town. I remember the counselors taking us out at night when I was an eight-year-old camper so they could tell us scary stories, and we could see what the stars looked like without any Dreamsicle urban glow to obscure them. You could map the creamy vapor of the Milky Way. The sky looked like an astronomy textbook diagram of constellations—patterns and codes you could decipher, guides you could steer by.

Thinking of myself as a not-so-long-ago camper helps me remember that there were nineteen years of me before I knew Devin. And the me that used to camp here loved those stars. She liked to hear scary stories. She liked to laugh with her friends and brothers about the stories that scared them. She didn't need to bear the weight of anyone's tortured indecision. There was no need for her to hurtle herself toward anyone in a strongman's reckless pose.

For just a few minutes, the ache in my solar plexus reaches toward a love for my own strange self.

This is a good decision.

I will be okay, and so will Devin.

There's a bed waiting for me two hundred yards down the road. Friends who love and like me no matter what are sleeping there.

I only need to walk that far.

CHAPTER 5

I hear the lake lapping at the raised edges of the walkway around it and I move my feet in the direction of that lapping water, toward rest. Wind whistles through the Scotch pines. The world is only star, lake, pine, cold, and my chunky heeled boots raking lines into gravel.

Then, a hundred yards behind me, I hear a door open, and the sound of someone else's swift footsteps in the gravel. When I wheel around to look, Devin is walking toward me. He is not smiling, as he usually does, when he sees my face. He looks like he's got a job to perform. When he gets close enough for me to hear him, he tells me to stop walking and look at him. He tells me to stand still.

If I hadn't stopped to cough. If I had just walked a little faster. If I hadn't stopped to look at the stars, this might all have gone another way.

But it doesn't. It didn't.

He stands closer to me than he ever has. I can feel his wet, warm breath against my frozen forehead. Slowly, he lifts his hands to my shoulders, and pulls me flush against his body. He puts a hand into my hair and cradles my head. He lays his other palm against my cheek.

He tilts his forehead against mine until our noses touch. Something elemental rouses itself beneath my rasping lungs. The smell of the cinnamon mints he's been sucking all night mingles with my cherry cough drops and pine resin and the scent of frozen Bed Head paste and clean skin.

"Just tell me what I should do, and I'll do it, Kelly," he says. "I wish I were easier. I know you're so tired. But just tell me what we should do."

His voice breaks as if he might cry again, but he doesn't. He's gasoline ready for a lit match. He's flushed and earnest. He keeps his forehead against mine and begins tracing a gentle line from my ears to my collarbone, over and over. In each tracing, his fingers move lower and lower down my now-protruding sternum.

I forget my need to cough, my need to sleep. I just want the heat of his fingertips to mark my skin. I want those long, piano-playing fingers to lift my shirt.

"I love this skin, you know," he says. "I have for a long time. I love this face too."

I am reeling. Minutes ago, it was over. I was out. But now here we are, Devin's palm beneath my clavicle, close enough to kiss.

"Your face is . . . okay," I joke. "I mean, you're a little ugly. I don't know if anyone's ever told you that before."

He laughs so hard he snorts, and then I am laughing too. He pulls the length of my shivering body even closer to his. His fingers draw a slow outline of the sides of my breasts and waist and then wrap themselves around the small of my back. His hips are pressed into my stomach. He pulls my head into his chest and cradles it with both hands.

"Let's figure this out, okay?" he says. I'm the only real thing he has in his life, he says.

Okay, I say.

There's a pause as I register the pressure of his pelvis against my hips.

"I don't know if you can tell, but I'm not at all disgusted by the idea of being with you," he smiles.

I'm startled by his frank physicality, and can't help but laugh again. He's the third boy I've been this close to in this particular way. And every time one of them has revealed an erection to me, it's felt like validation, like their getting hard at the thought of me means I've got currency that proves I'm desirable.

That erections themselves could be cheap currency, easily had, commonly spent, is not something that's ever truly registered. Erections are improbable. They defy gravity. They taste like salty pool water. Nearly every time I've encountered one, outside of or still in a pair of jeans, as Devin's is now, some growling, ravenous thing in me is soothed to sleep. *You matter*, it purrs as it drifts away to other dreams. *Look how much power you have to alchemize one element into another. You can beat plowshares back into swords.*

I feel his stiffness against my hip. I smell his breath, his stubbled neck. It's the first time I've touched his face in the eight months I've known him, this face I've memorized in person and in pictures.

We linger for long wordless minutes.

"Shit," he finally says. "I guess this is happening, isn't it? Things just got way more complicated."

"When have they not been?" I smile.

"Want to come see me in Oklahoma sometime soon?"

"Well, sure," I say, mimicking the way he always says, "Waalll, shuuuuurrr," as if to say *no big deal*.

"We should both get some sleep. You gotta stop coughing, sicko," he says to me, and then he pulls away and releases my hands.

I start to walk away, but when I turn around to look at him one more time he hasn't moved. He is still watching me. He smiles, then he turns and reenters his cabin.

In the years to come I will look back at this night so many

times—revisit the journal entry I forced myself to write before I finally fell asleep just before sunrise, look back over emails I sent people in the weeks following.

Mostly, in later years, I will think of what it must have felt like for him to reenter that room alone. For him to know, as he must have done, how happy I was walking away. I wonder if he was only tired and thinking of nothing at all, if he immediately fell asleep or if his thoughts spiraled while he brushed his teeth and kept him restless.

I wonder how it felt for him to know that in choosing me, he had chosen to always be alone.

Chapter 6

The first research essay I wrote in college, two years before I met Devin, was on mendacity in Tennessee Williams's play *Cat on a Hot Tin Roof*.

Mendacity, as both Williams and Webster define it, is just another word for lying. The adjectival state of being "mendacious" is being caught in a lie or being an accessory to one.

The entire play is about lying.

Big Daddy, the patriarch of the family, is dying, and everyone in the family knows but him. No one will tell him or his wife, the hysterical and hyperbolically unattractive Big Mama. When he wasn't idealizing his women characters, Williams often made them grotesque. Their eldest son, Gooper, and his wife, Mae, also known as Brother Man and Sister Woman, have come home to wrest control of Big Daddy's estate away from him—under the guise of a loving family visit. The family is rounded out by Maggie (the titular Cat) and her husband, Brick, who is Big Daddy's favorite, a former football star whose best friend, Skipper, has just committed suicide under a cloud of suspicion that the two men were in love. Having despaired of the possibility that he and Brick would be able to live together or even consummate their relationship, Skipper chooses to take his own life.

The play occurs in the aftermath of Skipper's literal death

as well as the figurative death of what Maggie coins the "Greek legend" of Brick and Skipper. Just before the action of the play begins, we are told that Brick, in his grief and nostalgia for Skipper, has returned to their high school to jump hurdles. As a result, he breaks his ankle and spends the play drunk on crutches, swigging bourbon in a bathrobe (a look Paul Newman absolutely pulled off in the film adaptation).

We see things from Maggie's perspective. No matter how ruthless she is in her ambitions, how forceful, we tend to root for her, or at least I do. She still has this naked hunger for her beautiful husband. She wants so badly to have his child, partly because she loves him and partly because her sister-in-law, Mae (whom Big Daddy dubs a "good breeder"), lords it over her that she's produced multiple children and Maggie has produced none. From the perspective of the women in the play, you can't be a real woman unless you've produced children. From an economic perspective, we are meant to understand that the inheritance of Big Daddy's vast holdings is tied, much like a Tudor monarchy, to the production of an heir.

So, Maggie's got every reason to want to sleep with her husband, but any reason he might have had to continue living at all appears to have died with Skipper. Inheritance or no inheritance, beautiful wife or no beautiful wife (Maggie was played FLAWLESSLY by Elizabeth Taylor in the film adaptation, making her white slip iconic), Brick has given up hope. He barely touches, looks at, or speaks to his wife, who, prior to Skipper's death, had slept with Skipper, either in order to make Brick jealous or to be with Brick via Skipper or to exact some kind of revenge—there are many possible takes.

But Maggie refuses to let Brick's withdrawal from her

CHAPTER 6

stand. In her words, she refuses to surrender to the "charm of the defeated." Pleading with Brick, she says to him:

> My hat is still in the ring, and I am determined to win! What is the victory of a cat on a hot tin roof? I wish I knew . . . just staying on it, I guess, as long as she can. [. . .] What were you thinking of when I caught you looking at me like that? Were you thinking of Skipper? Oh, excuse me, forgive me, but the laws of silence don't work! No, laws of silence don't work . . . laws of silence don't work. When something is festering in your memory or imagination, laws of silence don't work. It's just like shutting a door and locking it on a house on fire in hopes of forgetting that the house is burning. But not facing a fire doesn't put it out. Silence about a thing just magnifies it. It grows and festers in silence, becomes malignant.

In the end, it is Maggie's lie that she is pregnant (which, in the final scene, we are meant to understand she has either coerced or convinced a very drunk Brick into helping her manifest) that either saves or dooms the family, depending on your interpretation.

Unlike the play, in the final scene of the film adaptation we see a fully dressed Brick summon Maggie up the stairs to go to bed with him. Before she realizes his full intentions, she thanks him for not having revealed the fact that she couldn't be pregnant with his child (because they hadn't slept together in such a long time). He responds, "Maggie, we are through with lies and liars in this house. Lock the door," which she does. Credits roll as they kiss one another and Newman throws a pillow (which throughout the film has variously represented his "crutch," the physical separation between Brick and Maggie, and Maggie's power over Brick, away from him), symbolizing a few possible things, either that Maggie herself will now be his crutch or that, broken ankle or no broken ankle, he no longer needs one.

In his stage directions for the play, Williams wrote, "Some mystery should be left in the revelation of character in a play, just as a great deal of mystery is always left in the revelation of character in life, even in one's own character."

There's little doubt that Brick loved Skipper the way Maggie wanted him to love her. And yet his body is still able to betray his heart or to operate outside of it in order to sleep with her. Hands aren't the only appendages capable of magical sleights.

Or maybe, laws of silence or no, a body's as mysterious as any character in a play.

Chapter 7

After his college graduation in May 1998, Devin moves to Nashville to get a second degree in music business. For several months, he is happy there: interested in his classes, thrilled with his internship at a big international music company, excited about new friends he is making. So, I continue to request information from grad schools in Nashville.

My parents have always cautioned me against making major life decisions in order to stay tied to a boy. *Do what you want to do first*, they've always said. But I already followed my first boyfriend to college, which mostly worked out fine despite the fact that he dumped me before I ever got there. I never talk to that boy anymore, and I've still managed to make plenty of friends and learn some things and grow as a person, so I figure: How different can grad school be? Even if we break up, Nashville is a better place than Jackson to begin a new life.

English majors can do our thing just about anywhere, so why not? Devin is happy there. I could be perfectly happy there. Nashville is a proper city. We both love cities. Lots to see and do and places to eat. Trails to hike if we felt like it and mountains only a few hours away.

But slowly at first and then all of a sudden, Devin stops being happy in Nashville. He says it's too political. The people he pitches only want songs that appeal to the lowest common denominator. His friendships cool. The girls I stayed with in his first few months there, who'd eaten with him every day and who raved to me about how wonderful Devin was and how much he loved me, never hang out with him anymore.

Two semesters after entering the music business program, Devin leaves Nashville and shows up on my doorstep in Jackson, where I am ending my fall semester as a senior in college, to let me know he wants to marry me. He moves to Jackson after Christmas to be close to me. We get engaged after I graduate in the spring.

I spend that Christmas of my senior year of college with Devin and his family in Oklahoma, my first-ever Christmas away from my own family in Mississippi. His parents had decided to take us all—me, Devin, and his brother—skiing in Colorado. So, I brought borrowed gear and an excessive number of Thermasilk underthings on my flight to Tulsa. After the holiday, Devin and I drive back to Jackson together—me returning to my final semester of college and the restaurant where I am a server; him to start a new job at a bank and to live in an apartment five minutes from mine.

Before heading out to ski, Devin decides he wants to take me to see his maternal grandparents up on the Oklahoma-Arkansas border. His grandfather is slowly dying. Devin wants me to know him and his grandmother, whom he loves deeply, in much less complicated ways than he seems to love his grandfather.

Colcord, Oklahoma, straddles its own northeastern border with Arkansas and lies in a region of the Ozark foothills known as Green Country. And we are driving in it at night to see Devin's grandparents.

Lush vegetation spreads over the rolling land, interrupted only by rivers and gorges and waterfalls. Much like the Appalachian region into which it eventually flows, its stunning vistas exist in sharp relief to the widespread poverty among its mostly rural population. Devin's grandparents were respectably working-class. But paying their bills and tithing faithfully at their local church had required working ten- and twelve-hour days at local manufacturing plants as well as growing their own food and livestock.

The beauty of the scenery outside the windows is also a sharp contrast to the stiff silence inside the car. Earlier today, we'd gone to look at engagement rings at the mall, which had an unsettling effect on both of us. Looking at those diamonds sparkling under the strategically angled display lights made us feel less sure that we were ready to take this next step into permanence. Devin has barely spoken to me for the entirety of the drive. Maybe he's still reeling from our ring shopping. Maybe he's just sad that his grandfather is dying, and here we are, driving toward that death.

That's how it is with silences—without words to fill them, there are so many plausible explanations. In the car, I give myself an internal pep talk. I am spunky. I am Elizabeth Bennet. I am Anne of Green Gables. I am Meg Ryan. I can "cheer up, sleepy Jean" him out of this funk with a little levity. But every time I almost say something, I think better of it. There's something solitary in this stony silence, no invitation for me to share it with him. Something in it makes my stomach gurgle with dread because these silences of his have started to become more frequent. Is it a phase? Is it a portent of what's coming?

He has always withdrawn in silence when he is overwhelmed, but lately it seems we can't get through a week without at least one or two instances of him just shutting down entirely. He always comes back from it. He always acknowledges it. He tells me he's working on it. But it keeps happening.

When we pull up to his grandparents' door, it's dusk. We haven't passed a streetlight for miles. Constellations are already showing themselves off in plum corners of the sky, and the sight of the stars settles me. The drive hasn't prepared me for the ringing silence that greets us when we exit the car—the mechanical clicks and drips of Devin's recently shut-off engine the only audible sound for miles.

As we approach the house, we notice that the passenger side of his grandmother's maroon Buick Regal is crumpled.

We knock on the door and hear the low murmur of the nightly news blink off, then shuffling footsteps approach. When his grandmother opens the door, she gives a sly, crooked smile to Devin and winks. She grasps me by the hand and pulls me into a warm hug.

"Pearl," she says to me, by way of introduction.

"That's my grandmother's first name too!" I say and turn to Devin, playfully scolding him for not telling me our grandmothers had the same name. He shrugs and winks at me while giving his grandmother a tight hug.

I introduce myself, and then Devin asks about the dent in her car. She tells us it was a girl she knew from the bingo parlor down the street. The girl from bingo had been turned around trying to soothe her baby when she hugged the curve by Pearl's house too quickly. She'd already contacted her insurance and it was all being handled, she assured Devin in her clipped, matter-of-fact language.

CHAPTER 7

"Y'uns want to see Vernon?" she asks.

I glance quickly at Devin to see what this means. I come from the land of *y'all*, and *y'uns* is a new one on me. He winks at me, then turns to her and says yes, wrapping an arm around her shoulder and helping her walk as slowly as she needs to toward the bedroom where his grandfather is sleeping, knees curled up protectively in the direction of his chest, lying on butter-yellow sheets. Though cancer has eroded his bones, he still seems like a very big man. His limbs are long. His hands are broad and muscular. Even as they shake with tremors over the thin sheet that covers his chest, it's easy to see how powerful they would have been.

"Vernon!" Pearl shouts, much louder than I expect, as we arrange ourselves around his bed: Devin and Pearl on either side of his head, me in a chair at his feet. On a small table next to me there are at least a dozen "Get Well Soon" cards in varying shades of Easter pastels with verses and crosses and lilies on their covers. His war medals hang in a matted frame above the table.

"Vernon!" Pearl shouts again, and finally, Devin's grandfather wakes just a bit. "Devin's brought his girl for you to meet. DEVIN! IT'S DEVIN!"

"Who?" Vernon asks in a feeble whisper.

"DEVIN! HIS GIRL! DEVIN!! See here!" she shouts again, pointing at the two of us. Vernon's eyes scan the room and land on Devin. He smiles.

"Devin," he says, a self-contained and adequate declarative. "Devin."

"Hey, Granddad," he responds, his voice breaking. He takes one of his grandfather's shaking hands and brings it back to the sheet to rest. Vernon raises Devin's hand to his lips and kisses it, then holds it fondly against his cheek.

"It's Devin," he repeats.

Then something seizes him out of nowhere and he begins to shout, whether in pain or fear or both, we don't know. Pearl ushers us both out of the room and reassures us that all will be fine.

"Y'uns just go sit. I'll be right along," she says, and so we do. As we walk back toward the living room, Devin lowers the side of his head to mine and lets it rest.

"I'm really sorry I've been in such a funk today. I promise I'm so glad you are here. This is all a lot—the move and a new job and my granddad and us," he says and then he describes a circle with his fingers to indicate that it had been the entirety of things that had gotten to him. I am relieved that it hadn't been some unwitting goof on my part, and I assure him it's okay. In spite of the setting, an expansiveness blossoms in my throat and solar plexus, loosening the tentativeness I've felt around him all night.

We hear Vernon mumbling that he doesn't want to die, and Pearl reassuring him that he's not going to. We hear her telling him to hush, and after about twenty minutes, he does. Once he's sound asleep again, she shuts the door gently behind her and shuffles toward us in the living room as quickly as her inflamed hip joints will allow her to.

"He's asleep again, thank goodness," she says. And then she announces that she's got Kool-Aid and cookies in the kitchen. We follow her when she nods in that direction to get us to help carry things.

On the wood-paneled walls leading into the kitchen there are pictures of grandchildren and great-grandchildren. There are Glamour Shots of Devin's cousins taken just over the border in Siloam Springs. Their backlit blond hair haloes their

CHAPTER 7

faces, and one of them holds the flipped-up collar of a denim jacket in both hands. There are Olan Mills portraits of Devin and Chad as little boys wearing color-coordinated suits. On small end tables all over, there are tatted and crocheted cozies for teapots and Kleenex boxes, and on the walls, Bible verses adorn illustrated ceramic plates.

"I will lift up my eyes unto the hills from whence cometh my help," reads one of them. Beneath the words, there's a picture of three crosses on a hill.

On another plate, Psalm 23 is etched beside a picture of a young girl in a field carrying a shepherd's staff. Two lines I was made to memorize in my Presbyterian kindergarten jump out at me: "He leads me beside still waters / He restores my soul." And then, like the earworm melody to a song you have to sing to completion, I find myself reciting the rest of it in my head as I carry a plastic pitcher of thickly sweet cherry Kool-Aid and a bag of Oreos back to the living room: "Surely goodness and mercy will follow me all the days of my life / And I will dwell in the house of the Lord forever." Goodness and mercy. Goodness and mercy. I roll the phrase around like hard candy in my mouth.

Seated, I take a crumbly bite of Oreo and the first sip of Kool-Aid I've had in years. Consumed together, the cookie and Kool-Aid taste like Vacation Bible School, like fellowship meals after church, like the lips of all the Styrofoam cups my teeth marked like the draping folds of a necklace. Once we are married, Devin and I will buy Kool-Aid packets on special, ten for a dollar, so we will always have it in our home.

Pearl takes a seat in her floral recliner and gestures with a slanted, rheumatic finger at the back bedroom where Vernon continues to sleep.

"Welp," she intones. "That's how it's been with him these last few weeks. Off and on, you know. He comes and goes. He barely eats. I don't think it'll be too long now."

"I'm so sorry, Granny," Devin says, his voice breaking again, and though I remain silent, I nod my head in agreement.

"Welp," she says again, with exhausted resignation. "That's just what happens when folks get old. Lord knows he wasn't always easy to live with. But he's been so sweet for such a long time now. I sure will miss him," she admits, and then she pauses to collect herself.

She punctuates the silence that follows with another "So," and shrugs her shoulders to change the subject.

"Your mom tells me y'uns is going skiing up at Colorado tomorrow, yes?"

"Yes, ma'am," I say, and she giggles at my politeness. She says she likes it, even if it's not so common in Oklahoma as it is in Mississippi.

After that, conversation flows. Pearl is self-deprecating and funny and smart. She wants to hear about Music Row and the Opryland Hotel. She wonders if Devin ever drove all the way over to Dollywood from Nashville. Devin asks her about the most recent harvest and how his young cousin and her new husband are faring on their dairy farm down the road. She tells us their cows are all thriving, and they are happy and cute. She tells us how his Aunt D prayed for nearly forty-five minutes at a prayer meeting not too long ago.

"Lord, have mercy," she says, "I think she must have called Jesus the Rose of Sharon about a hundred times. I bet even Jesus gets tired of all that. But she really does pray lovely. She most certainly does."

I look around at the varnished oak table covered with Precious Moments figurines and *Reader's Digest*s and imagine that if I were to tell Pearl about the increasing number of Devin's silences, she'd teach me to worry less about them.

In the parable of the pearl of great price, Jesus says this: "The kingdom of heaven is like a merchant seeking fine pearls, and upon finding one pearl of great value, he went and sold everything that he had and bought it." And I've been trained in every way, through church, through media, every love song, every movie, every poem—as well as my own particular inclinations and proclivities—to believe that romantic love is worth it all. Sell everything and buy the field, my heart has always said. Love wins, right? The greatest of these is love. All you need is love. And I do love Devin. And Devin loves me. And we are getting married because that's what all the people around us are doing, and that's what you do when you can't imagine living without the other person. And you can't live with someone unless you are married, and you can't move to be closer to them unless your intentions are serious (which means you're getting married). In for a penny, in for a pound.

What I want most, just as I had at camp and for most of my life up to this point, is to be singular in mind, to be certain we were choosing correctly, to be certain we weren't condemning ourselves to a secondary existence, devoid of love or hope or connection.

I imagine if all that spilled out of me, Pearl would pat my arm sympathetically or pinch the back of my hips the way both my own grandmothers do. This kind woman formed and polished like the mollusk-grown gem she was named for, translucent from all those decades of turmoil she'd weathered, peaceful now, despite everything, in this still house. Pearl would hug me, knowing none of my fear of this next step was novel, knowing people had been afraid of the silences between them since speech began. And she would just say, "Welp" or

"So" or "Honey," which is what she called me the rest of the time I knew her: "Honey Girl" or "Kelly Honey." In the face of my confessions, Pearl would shrug her shoulders and pat my hand and then I would exhale, and all my dread would dissipate like so much vapor into the crisp Ozark night.

I might even become translucent and polished like her too. And maybe I could just stay with her instead of taking that long car trip to Colorado the next day. Maybe I could stay with her always. We'd drink Kool-Aid and eat cookies—just me and Pearl—we'd take all that sweetness into ourselves and keep it. She'd sit in her floral recliner, and I'd hunker down on her old tan couch. We'd flip through *Reader's Digest*s, watch the evening news, check in on the dairy cows down the road. We'd sleep soundly. On Wednesdays and Sundays, we'd go to church to hear Aunt D supplicate the Rose of Sharon.

Then no silence of her grandson could silence me.

Chapter 8

After our short ski trip to Colorado, Devin decides that before we drive back to Jackson, he needs to take me out to his favorite Chinese restaurant in Tulsa.

Devin has been promising to take me to Peking Garden since before we were even dating. A family-owned spot that had opened in the seventies, Peking Garden is kitschy in an upscale Americanized-Asian way. They'd brought Hunan and Szechuan dishes to Tulsa at a time when Chinese food mostly meant Cantonese cuisine. The well-worn take-out menu in Devin's family kitchen features pictures of the restaurant's dining room—red, gold, and green chinoiserie on the walls and booths, white tablecloths, carved dragons, and bamboo in ceramic planters next to indoor fountains.

Devin's bags are already packed for Jackson. The next night we'll have a farewell dinner at home with his parents and brother. Devin wants to take advantage of a moment when just the two of us could be alone to eat in this town where he grew up. At least a dozen times, he's repeated what he loves about the orange peel beef at Peking Garden. "They don't use orange juice concentrate," he says. "They use real orange zest and juice. They crisp the meat in the fryer, and then they toss it with the sauce, and it's SOOO good."

The thought of crisped beef dripping in a sweet, hot, garlicky glaze makes my mouth water. But I am most excited about becoming part of this old ritual that connects me to Devin's hometown past and sets the stage for a shared future.

"We always have the orange peel beef when we're back in Tulsa," I imagine us telling people in the years to come. We'll be welcomed back by the staff, who will recognize us and smile. Devin and I will drink tea out of blue and white bone cups, and laugh together, chatty and at ease.

This morning we had a late breakfast after sleeping in. The day's easy conversation revolved around the logistics of Devin's move—identifying and sorting which furniture he'll bring along now and what his parents will bring down in a few weeks—as well as my final semester of college. We've eaten only a light lunch in anticipation of the evening's orange peel beef.

I get ready for the evening in Devin's old bedroom, which is where I have stayed every time I visit his parents. Devin bunks with his brother. The walls of Devin's room are painted a dark navy blue with accents of hunter green and burgundy plaid in the bedclothes and pillows. The bedroom furniture, like the furniture in the rest of the house, is heavy and thick, made of oak or mahogany. The ceiling is low and close. Gorgeous flowers bloom brightly out front all summer long, but, especially in winter, very little sun seems to penetrate the darker rooms inside.

That evening, in the low light, I prop my round powder compact and mirror against a wooden trunk next to several pictures of Devin. It surprised me the first time I visited that all the photographs in the bedroom were portraits of Devin standing alone, posed and well lit. In my experience, people hung photographs of themselves with other people—friends, family, pets, teammates—not solo portraiture, in their own rooms.

But Devin is a popular subject for friends' photography class projects, and these photos are mostly thank-you gifts for

CHAPTER 8

his time—matted and framed tokens of appreciation. Rather than shove them in a box, he displays them, which I suppose I might have done too if anyone had ever asked that of me.

That first visit, I'd teased him about the pictures.

"Why don't you have any pictures of you with other people, weirdo?" I poked. He'd flushed with immediate embarrassment, and I immediately regretted the joke. He mumbled that he thought I'd like to see his picture and seemed surprised by my question.

I've grown accustomed to the pictures in his room, but here on the cusp of our engagement, it hurts my feelings that I haven't yet worked my way into the lineup of photos. He is ready to move across the country to be with me, and yet he has none of the fifty or so shots of us together hanging up anywhere at all. If a stranger entered the room and used these photos to form a narrative about Devin, I would be absent from the narrative.

After I pat the last bit of powder onto my nose and apply my lipstick, I glance at the clock. Too early to leave. Down the hall, I hear Devin just beginning to get into the shower. So I take my time putting on my clothes. He is as slow to dress as I am. There is no rush.

I pull the collar of my white oxford shirt over the neck of a fitted charcoal sweater and smooth my stretchy, plaid, boot-cut pants, still a size 0 that I am suppressing my hunger daily to fit into, and then walk out of the navy blue room.

In the living room, Devin's parents and brother are relaxing on the sofa watching the news.

"Don't you look cute!" Devin's mother gushes as I enter the room.

"Cute as a button," his father echoes.

"Yeah, you look alright," his brother says, smiling and winking at me.

I blush and thank them and rush to join them on the couch so I can stop being looked at.

Down the hall, we hear Devin shutting off the water in the bathroom. One of his parents, I don't remember which, informs me that before the news they'd been watching videos of old ski trips. They ask if I'd like to see a bit of those videos before Devin and I leave. I'd get a kick out of seeing little boy Devin skiing down the mountains, they say, and I agree.

What better way to pass the time before we create a ritual that bridges the story of a past I've been absent from with the story of a future we'll always share than to see videos of this kid who's been eating orange peel beef forever and skiing down mountains and playing in baseball games and attending church and Friday night movies. Somehow my having seen those videos might impose my imprimatur upon his past. Maybe it isn't the same as getting my picture hung in his room, but it could be motion in that direction.

Devin's father presses play on the VCR. We scroll past the VHS fuzz, and then moving images begin rolling. Not only does this tape have bits of old ski trips, but it also contains short plays—little skits written by Devin and Chad when they were barely adolescents. In one, both of them wearing fluorescent-spattered eighties neon and Jams, they recite well-rehearsed arguments for the existence of God. Nothing surprising in the content, except in one scene, in which we see only Devin's brother. Devin is just a voice offscreen, and the pitch of the voice and intonation surprises me.

"Is that a girl?" I ask, not at all registering the voice as familiar.

CHAPTER 8

His brother laughs, "Nope. That's Devin. His voice took some time to catch up with his body. He was probably eleven or twelve then?" When his voice goes up at the end of the interrogative, he turns to his parents, who nod their heads that yes, Devin would have been eleven or twelve at the time.

In response, I make a mortified face, embarrassed to have gotten it wrong, uncertain if Devin had heard me, suddenly wondering if the door to the room where he was dressing was open or closed. Either way, I assume he'll laugh it off. He knows so many of my embarrassing stories. In eighth grade, I slipped on a choir robe in a pair of worn-smooth Payless flats and slid down the chancel steps on my ass in front of two hundred people. I walked into a wall while talking to a boy I liked and got a bloody nose. Once, I'd been playing Hacky Sack with that same boy and, after attempting to kick it with both feet at once, nearly fractured my tailbone on the concrete floor we stood on.

And Devin has laughed and laughed and laughed at these stories and others. I am skilled at self-deprecation, and I know how to spin it so it feels to me and my chosen audience like I am telling a story about someone else—someone else's old embarrassment, nothing that still hurt me.

Even if he did hear me wonder if he was a girl, then, I feel pretty confident he'd just shove me playfully and laugh easily. "You're the worst!" I can already imagine him saying. I'll apologize. We'll laugh it off. And really, what's so very bad about sounding like a girl? Lots of little boys did, and there was nothing wrong with the voices of girls to be bothered about. And even though we'd never really had a fight we didn't eventually laugh off, I feel a new sense of dread return from the silent drive to Pearl's house, and it wafts down the hall with Devin's Banana Republic cologne as he enters the room.

We could be twins.

Like me, he wears a white oxford shirt with a collar popping out of the neck of a gray wool sweater. Instead of plaid pants like mine, though, he wears artfully frayed jeans arranged carefully to fall only on the outside of battered leather hiking boots.

Glancing over at Devin, his brother hits pause on the video, leaving his parents, several years younger, dressed in casual vacation wear at a mall in Houston, frozen on the screen.

"Dev, if you threw on some plaid pants, you two would be wearing the same clothes," Chad says.

"Shut up," Devin laughs companionably, and, shoving Chad aside, he sits in front of me on the carpet, leaning against my legs. He asks us what we are watching. When we tell him it's old ski trip videos, I feel the taut muscles of his back tense, lightening their pressure on my legs so that all that remained was the electric crinkle of static between my pants and his wool sweater.

"Hey, we can just leave now if you want to," I whisper to him, registering that shift in his weight.

His mother, having overheard me, convinces us to stay for just a few more minutes, but his brother, having also clocked the shift in Devin's energy, says helpfully, "You know? Maybe let's just fast-forward through some of this." We watch as malls, churches as big as malls, family reunions, and picnics speed past onscreen.

Devin's brother pauses only when his parents encourage him to, on a scene of the two brothers seated with their mother around a hot tub at a winter resort in Colorado, not all that different from the one we'd just left. They were all of them—as they remained—young, attractive, tanned, and even drenched in steam from the hot tub, well groomed. From behind the camera, Devin's father asks them how their day was.

"I skied a double black diamond today," Devin's brother volunteers.

"So did I," the Devin in the video responds, his voice significantly deeper than it had been but still higher and more feminine than it was in his adulthood. Whatever traces of that higher voice might have lingered, they'd long since been eliminated by the time I'd met him. He wasn't butch, but he was far from femme.

"I hate the ski pants, though," says young Devin in the video. "I swear it's the last time you'll ever catch me in bell-bottoms," he laughs, and then shoos his father away as if he were a paparazzo, immersing himself entirely in the steaming water.

"Awww! You were too cute!" I cajole, reaching past my knees to drag him back, to shake him gently, to hear him laugh at himself the way he's done before, the way he's always laughed at me—lighthearted, cathartic, cleansing. Instead of relaxing, he shifts further away.

His mother echoes my praise and says how cute both of her boys were.

Abruptly, Devin stands up and holds out a hand to help me up.

"We should go," he says. And in several quick strides, he crosses fifteen feet to the coat closet by the door.

As we mumble some hurried goodbyes, I smile apologetically behind Devin's back at his parents and brother. We all sense the way his mood has shifted, but none of us are sure what to do about it. They smile back reassuringly and wave kindly like they always do. Suddenly, part of me wishes they were coming along.

Because Devin's car is already full of boxes for his move, we borrow his parents' SUV, and the leather seats chill my legs through my thin pants.

Peking Garden is about twenty miles from Devin's parents' house, most of it interstate. Once again, here we are in a quiet car. Once again, I am left to guess what he feels. Other than monosyllabic or perfunctory answers to my direct questions, Devin barely speaks. He doesn't seem angry, necessarily, just sad. He keeps rubbing his temples like his head hurts.

Again, I cycle through my possible transgressions.

But then I recollect a thing Devin told me he appreciated about an old ex-girlfriend. He liked that instead of going silent just because he did, she'd press him to say what was going on or to shake it off if he wouldn't.

"It helped me get out of my head when she said that," he'd told me.

And while I have little problem pushing—I am the oldest child and someone's older sister, after all—so often, it felt either false or violent to probe for what he didn't volunteer.

As we pull onto Lewis, the brightly lit street Peking Garden is on, we pass churches, liquor stores, twenty-four-hour pharmacies, bars, fast food—nothing you wouldn't see anywhere else in any other city. I summon up one last shot of bravado and figure a little indirection just might shake him back to me, get him out of his head.

"You ready for the orange peel beef?" I ask, and nudge him gently with my left hand.

"What?" he asks, not unkindly, but as if he genuinely didn't hear me.

"Orange peel beef?!" I repeat. "We're finally here! Yay! You've been talking to me about this for YEARS now."

CHAPTER 8

"Yeah, no, for sure. Sorry. I'm just kind of in my head," he says quietly.

I assure him that it's okay, that I understand. I've spent huge swaths of my life staring out of windows, being summoned, after lapses of attention, with varying degrees of force back into conversations. It happens. Maybe I hadn't said something that offended him. Maybe it was the videos that have thrown him off his rhythm. Maybe I am the one overthinking it. Maybe he's just tired and zoned out. I can relate to that.

As we pull into the parking lot, he parks the car and instead of getting out asks me if we can just sit and talk for a second.

"Of course!" I say.

I don't remember how the conversation begins. I remember he tells me he was in ninth grade when the video in the ski resort hot tub had been taken, the one where he talked about how much he hated his ski pants. He says ninth grade had been the worst year of his life. Some of this I already knew, but he speaks so earnestly and sadly that I don't remind him he's told me some of this before.

He pauses for a while, and we sit in silence in the cold car.

"I know none of you meant anything wrong, and I know my voice was high, and it was dumb that I cared so much about my pants. But I'm not a joke. And nothing about that year was funny to me. It's still not funny," he says.

So, that was the landmine we'd tripped—this awful year of his we'd resurrected. I feel the bottom of my empty stomach lurch. Seventh grade had been my worst year, the only time in my life I'd felt depressed enough to barely get out of bed, a year when I cried every day after school and begged my parents not to make me go back. But if you'd shown me a picture or even a video (though my family hadn't been fancy enough for a camcorder) of myself in seventh grade, it wouldn't have sent me down this spiral that Devin was clearly going down, no matter how awkward or poorly dressed or embarrassingly clueless I might have been. *Why is it so different for him?* I wonder. *What's the big deal about a shitty year of adolescence? Don't we all have them?*

I am thinking something along those lines when Devin begins to cry, at first just a little, leaning against the steering wheel, and then almost shaking the car, weeping into the black velvet on my shoulder.

Finally, he starts to talk.

There'd been a group of boys, some older, some his age, who used to chase him down the hall, making kissing noises at him, telling him he was a girl, calling him sweetheart, mimicking his mannerisms, kicking books out of his hands, pressing him into walls in the bathroom. They lurked in corners. They waited for him after assemblies. They knew where his locker was and where he parked and what classroom his mom taught in. They were everywhere.

I know already that he'd been diagnosed around eighth or ninth grade with OCD. I knew he'd had twice-weekly trips to a Christian counselor associated with Oral Roberts University. I know he'd been hospitalized around his senior year of high school because he was having chest pains and heart palpitations after seventy-two straight hours of no sleep, fearful he would not be able to stop fixating on the feeling of his tongue against the roof of his mouth. I know that many of the tics and quirks I've observed as far back as the day I met him can be linked back to that OCD diagnosis. He can't sleep if he doesn't clear his nose and throat a specific number of times. He habitually rolls his hips if he's lying down. He spends at least a full minute rinsing toothpaste out of his mouth at least twice a day. I know all about that.

But I know nothing of the boys who followed him down halls.

Devin was twenty and popular with everyone who knew him when we met. He wasn't into sports but was coordinated and funny, and he wasn't any less conventionally masculine than most of the boys I knew. Beyond that, it took him about five minutes after shaving to grow a thick beard. Sure, he didn't whittle things out of wood or go bow hunting during deer season or grab his crotch or spit tobacco, but I barely know any boys who do those things. There are boys I know whom I could imagine being bullied for not being "manly" enough. Devin isn't one.

"The thing is," he says, after giving himself a few minutes to calm down, "I had no idea what they were talking about when they treated me like that and said those things about me. But I see it now. I see what they saw. I get why they teased me. I do look and sound like a girl in those tapes. I just didn't see it then."

Later, I will learn to be better about comparing other people's experiences with my own, but at twenty-one, hungry in that cold car, I keep assessing where the grids of our experiences overlap, where the data aligns for me and where it doesn't. Love has to be something like sameness, I think. I also had been teased for being different. Girls were mean to me about many things. It had been nothing like the severity of the bullying Devin described. But I know what it is to have one perception of yourself as passing for some version of acceptable and then to see photographic evidence that you've been foolish and wrong. I'd felt it myself the first day I met him, catching a glimpse of myself in the mirror after listening to Tori Amos, the way a body and a face can betray us and recall to us limits we can't transcend.

"Devin, I'm so, so sorry. I'm so sorry we watched the videos. I wouldn't have done it if I knew how awful that was for you. I had no idea. I'm really sorry," I say.

I reach out to touch his shoulder. I lay my hand on it and keep it there. He nuzzles his stubbled cheek into my hand and allows it to rest there.

"Of course, you didn't know, Kel. Of course. I know that. It's not your fault at all. It's not anybody's fault. I feel bad. I feel like I was an asshole to my family and to you just now. I'm really sorry. I really don't want to be like that," he says gently.

I hold his hand in silence. I notice it's almost 8:30 p.m. The restaurant will be open for only thirty more minutes. Because I wait tables, I know what a pain it is for restaurant staff to have to accommodate people this near to closing. I feel apologetic to them in advance. The easy night, the shared ritual, hasn't begun as smoothly as it could have, but maybe now, the air cleared, we can still salvage the night.

I undo my seatbelt, which I haven't even thought to do yet, and reach for my purse.

"Kelly, wait," he says. "Sorry. I just need like two more minutes to collect myself."

"Oh, of course! Sure! Take your time," I say, and mostly I mean it, but I am becoming so hungry that it's a challenge to focus on anything but food.

Just as I think he might be ready to walk in, he begins to cry again, and I become aware that there are customers leaving the restaurant who can perceive that the driver of this champagne-colored SUV is definitely crying into his hands. Embarrassment

CHAPTER 8

mingles with my hunger pangs. I shrink from the glow of the streetlight above us. Not that I know anyone in Tulsa besides Devin or that he shouldn't be able to cry or that we shouldn't be allowed to be two human beings having human feelings in any parking lot. Still, I stay hidden.

We sit in the car for fifteen more minutes.

8:45 p.m.

I want to be kind. I want to hear him. But I also want to eat. I am in no immediate danger of starvation, but at ninety-eight pounds on my 5'3" frame, hunger hits me hard. My hummingbird mind is empty of all thoughts but food. I am pure want. Pure sensation.

After the neon light outside the restaurant finally flickers off, Devin begins to talk.

"Sorry, Kelly. I'm so sorry. It's just . . . there was one of the boys who was worse than all the other boys." He proceeds to tell me how truly awful that boy was—the names he'd called him, the relentlessness and cruelty of what he'd done.

"I talked to my counselor about it. I prayed about it. I changed my schedule to avoid him. Nothing worked. I felt so hopeless about it that once I prayed for him to die."

He pauses to collect himself.

"And then he did die," he says, his voice breaking again. "He died."

There had been a car accident. The boy was being wild in the passenger seat. The driver was reckless, and there were big trucks they didn't see. That boy who'd brutalized Devin didn't survive.

Once he gets it out, all of it—and this seems like all of it—Devin seems restful and suddenly aware of our surroundings. There are only a couple of cars left in the parking lot. I assume they belong to the manager, the dishwashers, the last few waiters who will, as it turns out, never meet me or learn my usual order or recognize me and smile when I return to visit.

"Kel, I'm so sorry. Shit. We missed dinner here. Do you mind if we just drive back to my parents'? I'm not up for anything else."

Of course, I say, a little deflated, despite myself, to return to his parents, still pondering what response could gently acknowledge the gravity of what he's just shared with me.

"You know it wasn't your fault, right?" I say, not consciously trying to repeat the cathartic ending of *Good Will Hunting*, a movie we'd both loved and watched together multiple times, but nevertheless hoping, consciously or not, for a similar outcome—reprieve, a rock rolled away so the resurrected could exit the tomb, release. Ease. "Nothing you did made him treat you that way. That was him. That was all him, and of course, he didn't die because you prayed about it. You know that, right?"

"I know. I know," he says twice. He reaches over and squeezes my hand, and we don't say any more about that boy.

In the years to come, I will wonder what might have happened if he'd kept on talking. As much as I'd like to believe, twenty-five years later, that I could have been a safe person for Devin to be honest with, the truth is I don't know. I was twenty-one. I still believed—most days—in a God who loved sinners but hated sin. Part of me still believed some sins were worse than others. He could have rolled the dice of honesty. But for all it might have cost him, I'm not sure I would have told me either.

When we arrive back at his parents', the bedroom lights are all out. He enters the house first, pulling me along behind him. When the door latches behind me, Devin turns around and

CHAPTER 8

kisses me hard on the mouth. Then he pulls back and cradles my face in his hands.

"I really do love you, you know," he says. "So much. I really do."

We kiss there in the quiet dark for a long time, my peacoat still on, my hips pushed against the washing machine, where a permanent line of powdered Tide will be rubbed into my right pocket.

"I think you just might save me," he says, somewhere in the midst of the kissing.

Eventually, he remembers that his mom has a bulk-size box of Pizza Rolls in the freezer. We bake them and burn our fingers putting them onto a plate that we share on the living room floor as we watch syndicated reruns. We eat at least twenty, maybe thirty, between us, watching *Friends*, laughing, kissing until early the next morning when we sneak off to separate beds.

A day later, we wake up early, hug his family, and drive the ten hours to Jackson, Mississippi, the car full of our laughter and easy conversation all the way there.

Chapter 9

IN THE MONTHS LEADING UP TO OUR WEDDING, DEVIN AND I meet several times with our old camp director, Jack, and his wife, Susan, for premarital counseling. The most certain Devin and I ever feel about how good it would be to be married is after those sessions, not because they paint a uniformly rosy picture of marriage, but because they are honest about its challenges.

I will remember vividly the four of us seated on the patio at Copeland's, a Creole chain down the street from our favorite mall, a plate of sweet potato fries growing cold in front of us while Jack describes how surreal it sometimes feels to wake up and have four kids demanding things of you. How awful it sometimes is to have a spouse feeling out of sorts or withdrawn.

Devin and I tell them how uncertain and even unhappy we sometimes feel about all the change quickly coming our way. I am only twenty-one. He is only twenty-two. What do we know about anything? My mom and dad have voiced concerns about us getting married but have also resigned themselves to the notion that I am going to do what I want, and that they can either support me and remain in my life or refuse to support me and then become alienated from me.

Jack and Susan make us feel better about all of that.

CHAPTER 9

You love each other.
This is true.
You can't imagine life without each other.
This is true.
You won't always be attracted to each other, but the feeling always comes back.
This is true.
Marriage will never be perfect, but you can make it so good. It gets deeper and richer and easier the longer you stick around.
We hope they are right.

For our wedding, Susan, who is a potter, makes us a beautiful earthenware bowl. She almost doesn't give it to us because it cracks a bit around the top, but Jack insists, and then he uses it in a metaphor during the wedding homily he preaches for us: earthenware vessels, he calls us. Jesus uses cracked vessels to display his infinite mercy and grace and light, he says. Vessels who aren't perfect in behavior. Vessels who crack sometimes under pressure but still can hold so much.

After the wedding, we stay in an airport hotel and make it to Chicago before sunrise the next morning. Frank Lloyd Wright predicted Chicago would eventually be "the most beautiful great city left in the world." It started as a village in a swamp and grew—imperfectly, at its own pace—into a sparkling city.

It was an old place that was made new and then burned, but was made new again.

We could be new there as well.

Chapter 10

WE HONEYMOON AT THE WESTIN ON MICHIGAN AVENUE, about a block from the lake. Every night in Chicago, we walk over to the Cheesecake Factory at the base of the Hancock Building. Devin's groom's cake was a selection of assorted cheesecakes, none of which either of us had the chance to eat. So, these cheesecakes are compensatory. In fact, one night we get three slices of cheesecake: a steak dinner and cheesecake at Eli's followed by two pieces of Cheesecake Factory cheesecake later that night.

In Chicago—a place we both love—we feel fresh, hopeful. We are actually happy, unburdened by the need to perform happiness to reassure watching elders that we are ready to be married adults. It's levity without the pressure to know it as such. We go to the Field Museum and the Adler Planetarium and the Shedd Aquarium and Navy Pier, all places I remember from field trips when I lived in Chicago as a kid.

It's hot in July in Chicago, but the breeze off Lake Michigan makes it manageable, especially at night. There's little I love more than the feeling of breeze-cooled sweat on my skin, how it makes me feel embraced by something gentle and entirely pleasurable.

We don't know anyone here in downtown Chicago. It's just us. Since Devin joined me in Jackson months ago, he's been

CHAPTER 10

on my turf. We see friends from camp all the time. We live just down the street from two of them. My parents live thirty minutes away from us door-to-door, and we see them at least three times a week. My brothers come home from college to see us all at least once a month. Soon we'll live half a mile from the house where my dad and his five siblings grew up, and we'll also see that extended family often. In a month, I'll be starting a master's program at the same college my parents attended.

In Jackson—with Devin's family a ten-hour drive away—we are immersed in old narratives, and a backstory that's mostly mine.

Devin misses Tulsa's superior highway system and all its rolling, forested intermezzo between the plains of western Oklahoma and Arkansas's Ozark Mountains. He loves hiking and getting outside. He loves being able to open his windows in summer and feel a cool breeze that only altitude makes possible. No one associates "cool breeze" with summer in Jackson, Mississippi. All of these are the reasons Devin gives on the days when he withdraws from me, which still happens from time to time, but less frequently than it did when he was in Nashville. We're on a good trajectory.

One of my favorite pictures of me and Devin is of us walking down Michigan Avenue months before our honeymoon on a short weekend visit to the city with my family. We'd stayed at the Hilton & Towers and visited the Art Institute and eaten at the Blackstone, which my dad reminds us was one of Al Capone's favorite breakfast spots, and where the griddled hash browns and eggs were cooked exclusively in butter—no olive oil to be seen.

In the picture of me and Devin from that trip, a blizzard is just beginning. Our heads are turned behind us in the direction of my father, who's called our names. I'm wearing a canvas hunting jacket lined with flannel—the sort that Queen Elizabeth might wear at Balmoral. Devin is wearing a tailored brown corduroy blazer and that same gray wool sweater from our night outside Peking Garden. We are about to get into my parents' Honda Accord with my brother Craig for the twelve-hour drive back to Mississippi. On the way, we'll stop at a gas station somewhere in Missouri, where Craig will buy a chocolate milk without looking at the expiration date. He'll take his first (and only) curdled swig of it about a mile down the highway and then violently expel it onto the back of my dad's head in the driver's seat. And then all five of us—my parents, Craig, me, and Devin—will cackle and then burst into percussive fits of giggles every time we replay the scene—the projectile milk, the scream Craig let out after he spat it—for hours after. Months later, I still laugh every time I remember it.

Devin has moved away from his people and toward mine, but my people all really like him and find him easy to be around, easy to include in our regular rhythms of movie rentals and long meals and walks and debates about sitcoms and music. And he likes my people.

Devin might be new but he belongs, and that belonging began on that drive back from Chicago, driving south away from a blizzard, smiling.

One night on our honeymoon in Chicago, we eat at Bubba Gump Shrimp on Navy Pier, which feels in keeping with our already instituted weekly ritual of eating at least one night a week at Red Lobster back in Jackson. Devin loves their lemon pepper shrimp, and while I usually force myself to order grilled salmon with steamed broccoli (I've begun to allow the occasional protein alongside my vegetables), I still sneak at least one biscuit, which I dip in his ranch dressing because I order my salads dry. He offers me three or four of his fried shrimp (which is all I can ask for before he points out that I also could have ordered them if I wanted them so much).

While we eat on Navy Pier, which overlooks the inland sea of Lake Michigan, we talk about the possibility of moving to Chicago after I finish the master's program I'm about to start. Despite my occasional visits, Chicago's more or less a clean slate for us both. More than that, it pulsates with infinite variation and possibility in a way that nowhere in Oklahoma or Mississippi seems to. In Chicago, you could eat at a new restaurant every night for a year and still have thousands left untried. Heck, we could eat a different cuisine every night for a year and barely repeat ourselves: Senegalese, Nepalese, Latvian, Brazilian, Peruvian, Swedish—the list felt endless. Living in Chicago would be like living everywhere, we say. It would be like living in a movie or on TV. It would be like living where things are happening. And as we talk about this, fireworks start to explode off the edge of Navy Pier, which is what happens in movies when you are in love and looking for cinematic portents to affirm your choices.

On the third day of our honeymoon, we take a taxi up to Boystown so we can eat at Penny's Noodle Shop, where my childhood best friend, Natalie—a bridesmaid in our wedding just a few days ago—serves as a part-time hostess to put herself through grad school.

We split a pad thai and piping hot tureen of tom kha.

Afterward, we walk around with Natalie, Devin and I gawking a bit at the leather harnesses in sex shop windows and the dog collars and the taut musculature of the mostly naked men in magazines papering the shop windows. Even

Natalie, who's had plenty of time to acclimate in her third year of grad school here, raises her eyebrows once or twice. We read the plaques put up beneath phallic pylons of metal rainbow rings.

Below the rings the word NORTHALSTED is written multiple times to designate the surrounding area that comprises Boystown. Many of the apartments have gorgeous window boxes over-draped with peonies and sweet potato vines and vincas. Nearly everyone we encounter looks like an athlete—if this is indeed the City of the Big Shoulders, as in the poem I memorized in tenth grade, then Boystown is offering us no contradictions. We pass an enormous gym with spin classes taking place just behind plate glass windows.

There's a story in Natalie's family that her dad often tells: Once, when their family wandered onto Bourbon Street a few weeks before Mardi Gras, he and Nat's brother realized they had to pee. But they happened to be on the end of Bourbon Street filled with places like the Café Lafitte in Exile, where men were dancing with other men.

They had to use the bathroom so badly they ventured in anyway.

That was the whole story.

It always played for laughs I never failed to give.

I laughed then as I am laughing now at the rainbow pylons in Boystown.

I have my own New Orleans story: About a month after I began college in Jackson, my friends and I drove down to New Orleans for Labor Day weekend. We didn't realize that an annual queer festival called Southern Decadence was taking place that weekend. It was the first time I'd seen men kissing or holding hands. It was the first time I saw a pair of assless chaps or muscle daddies in cropped leather jackets over mesh hot pants.

When we passed the Café Lafitte in Exile, I told my new college friends the old story about that time my friend's dad had to go to the bathroom there. No one laughed, and I realized that maybe it wasn't that funny a story. Maybe you had to be there to hear her dad's wry delivery for it to land.

I don't know what it means to be a spectator here in Boystown. It feels to me equal parts anthropology and prurient curiosity. It's not that it turns me on. Even now at twenty-one on my honeymoon, not a virgin, I have yet to experience an actual orgasm or to understand in any practical way how to achieve one. Sex is all tangles of skin flaps and chafing hair and tiny little brain-squiggled beans.

Most of me believes sex is for men. Masturbation is for men. No one's ever come right out and said it, but most of my church leaders have strongly implied so in Bible studies and youth group sermons and church camp lectures. It's every eight seconds, they say, the flash of lust that rises involuntary.

What easy things they are, these living pocket rockets—you pull them a few times and they launch.

Such a simple mechanism.

Here we are now among so many of those mechanisms. Sex is for men. Men are for sex. And here we are in the most concentrated possible circle of it all.

And I am laughing.

And Devin is watching me.

Chapter 11

When we get back home, I make Devin go to church. Not the church I grew up in, but a white-steepled church on State Street in Jackson. My grandfather spent every childhood Sunday here. His sophisticated mother led ladies' prayer lunches under the vaulted ceilings of the Sunday school wing—homemade butter mints in glass bowls, pralines on pewter trays, a scoop of homemade mayonnaise over a canned pear served on iceberg lettuce.

I attended kindergarten at this church's adjoining school. It's an inheritance—this place like old spiritual money, some aristocratic Christian birthright I want to show that I possess. Maybe I wouldn't say it out loud, but the truth is, I am proud when I glance around the sanctuary in winter and see mink coats draped across the backs of pews, the sturdy gabardine arms of doctors and lawyers and professors snugly wrapped around the Burberry scarves and Chanel jackets of their wives.

In my favorite black tights and embroidered shantung skirt, my starched collar flipped out the way I imagine Rose Kennedy might have worn hers, and with Devin's arm draped against my shoulder, his J.Crew sweater pulled over an expertly knotted Windsor tie, his thick black-framed glasses echoing all the angles of his face, and his smartly tailored plaid pants settled over his favorite loafers, his gorgeous voice belting out familiar baritone harmonies, I think to myself, "We belong here."

CHAPTER 11

The rhythms and liturgy are all the same as the church I grew up in. I know when to stand for the Apostles' Creed. I know how to recite it without faltering, without looking at the bulletin, eyes up the whole time. I know when the enormous pipe organ will signal the beginning of the Doxology, to which I can manage a well-practiced alto part. I know the alto parts to all the familiar hymns:

Crown Him with Many Crowns.
Holy, Holy, Holy.
A Mighty Fortress Is Our God.
Praise, My Soul, the King of Heaven.

Every sermon is polished and engaging and well-constructed. There are four points to each one. There's exegesis of the Greek words in the New Testament and the Hebrew words in the Old Testament. There's application. Short, but always relevant anecdotes—never glib or silly like you see on TV. Then we get historical context of biblical texts. It all just seems to make sense. And the sense it makes—though sometimes more pedantic or conservative than my parents have taught me to be—soothes me.

Each sermon is forty-five minutes. You know what to expect going in, and no one ever runs over that limit. No one in the congregation talks or claps. There is no vocal interaction between the pastor and the congregation. We are stiffly silent, the only sound the occasional cough or the rustle of crinoline against wooden pews.

When we are first married and have the same work schedule, we rarely miss a Sunday.

On Sundays when I go alone because Devin simply can't be convinced to go, I feel less like I belong without his arm over my shoulder, no matter how well starched my collar or how lovely my embroidered skirt. When I was growing up, I always felt sorry for married women who attended church alone week after week. I projected onto their lives a sense of loneliness and disconnection.

More often than not, Devin writes notes to me in the church bulletin about how much he hates this church, though every now and then during the gentler sermons—about grace or the love of God or the fundamental acceptance of God—he tears up midway through and reaches for my hand and squeezes it or puts his hand on my knee. I know we will have sex when we get home after sermons like that, and that no matter what happens, it will be sweet and meaningful—not that it isn't at other times, but these spiritually raw and connected times somehow hit different.

The truth is, I still really believe what's being said. Even when I'm profoundly confused about how the God I've been raised to believe in can be good, I deeply believe that ignoring him, which means not attending church, is the way to have a bad life. I still believe only God can save me from the emptiness inside myself—dead in my trespasses and sins. Though I am happy, mostly, here with Devin when he wants to be here with me.

We are a oneness on those days—one flesh, one spirit—a joined kindness, my hands holding his in the pew, stroking the black hairs on the outsides of his fingers.

When Devin's work schedule changes, which it does often—no job ever feels right—I start missing church because going alone doesn't feel the same as going with him. It's like being naked. I like the story they assume about us together—the silk and the wool and the Windsor knot. I like the increased chances that we will fall into bed together if the sermon lands—spiri-

CHAPTER 11

tual aphrodisiac for a body Devin is helping me get to know in ways I haven't before. I don't like the story the congregation assumes about me alone. *She's not enough to keep him around*, I imagine them saying. *Poor, lonely woman, unequally yoked to someone who just can't hold on to his faith.*

On visits to Oklahoma, we attend the Southern Baptist church where Devin grew up. He rarely wants to go there either, but between me and his parents, we guilt him into it. It's very different than the tall-steepled Presbyterian church back in Jackson. There are praise choruses projected onto screens and people clap and the sermons are short. No structure to them really—usually just sort of a series of free associations on the theme of choice—how we can choose to be happy, how we can choose to love God, how we can choose to live righteously. How it's all about hunkering down and choosing, no matter what it is we feel. Feelings can never be trusted.

In the car afterward, Devin and I always delight in picking it all apart, which is not the case for me, at least, with our Presbyterian church back home, whose sober emphasis on God's grace and humanity's unworthiness I still see as the antidote to this brand of choice-centered, watered-down theology.

On one of those Sundays, about two years after we are married, we join Devin's paternal grandmother for lunch after church. She lives in a boxy little white house that always feels dark inside on a street of boxy white houses that, I assume, also always feel dark inside, no matter the weather.

When she greets me, she points out that I look like I've gained weight. She pats me on the hip and says, "Better hold off on dessert today. It's a shame too. Ada made her angel food cake, and I've got strawberries. You best just have the fruit."

I think of the pizza I ate at Devin's parents' last night, and

I promise myself when we get back to their house, I'll walk their neighborhood twice, which is four miles. Easy enough. That should burn off the pizza and the berries.

Later, when Devin and his brother and father are seated on chairs in the living room and Ada and I are helping his grandmother pour a sticky mustard and grape jelly glaze over a platter of sliced ham, I notice that there's a rectangular plaque hanging up behind the stove.

It reads:

> Daddy had a little boy,
> His soul was white as snow,
> He never went to Sunday School,
> Cause Daddy wouldn't go.
>
> He never heard the word of God,
> That thrills the childish mind,
> While other children went to class,
> This child was left behind.
>
> As he grew from babe to youth,
> Dad saw to his dismay,
> A soul that once was snowy white,
> Became a dingy gray.
>
> Realizing that his son was lost,
> Dad tried to win him back;
> But now the soul that once was white
> Had turned an ugly black.

CHAPTER 11

>Dad even started back to church
>And Bible study too;
>He begged the preacher, "Isn't there
>A thing that you can do?"
>
>The preacher tried, failed, and said,
>"We're just too far behind;
>I tried to tell you years ago,
>But you would pay me no mind."
>
>And so another soul was lost,
>That once was white as snow;
>Sunday School would have helped,
>But Daddy wouldn't go.

I get so distracted reading the poem that I almost drop the pot of glaze onto Ada's hand. She laughs her sunny laugh at me and says, "Hey there, daughter-in-law! You okay?"

I mumble an apology and smile back at her, and we are able to get the meal out to the table.

Later that week, Devin's grandmother comes over to his parents' house for dinner, and while I am slicing cucumbers and tomatoes to be served with ranch dressing, she asks me, "Well, are you and Devin still going to a good church?"

I know she doesn't approve of the fact that I'm a Presbyterian, but I try not to let that bother me too much.

"Well, we try to get to church most Sundays. It's hard since Devin started working brunch shifts at the new restaurant, and it's harder to get there all by myself."

"I can see that. I can see that," she says. "You know? I've always found that it's the women's job to get the menfolk to go to church. They just don't like going the same way we do, but that's alright. Because it's just important to get there. How long you two been married now?" she asks me.

"Two years next month."

"He's not trying to impress you anymore, then. This is when it gets tough to keep going to church. Don't you think so, Ada? Don't you think women have to get the men to go to church?"

"Yes, I think that's probably so," Ada ponders. "It used to be a lot harder to get all my boys to church."

I think of Bill, Devin's dad, and his easy kindness, and how organized and ritualized and thoughtful their house and their lives are, and it's hard for me to imagine him ever having to be talked into any kind of weekly ritual. Devin's distaste for church doesn't seem to be shared by his father.

Bill washes the dishes every night and vacuums the floor every day. His alarm always goes off at the same time, whether weekend or weekday. He hands the nightly dishwater to Ada, who pours it into the soil around the plump blue and pink hydrangeas outside the front windows. He goes to work at the same time. He goes to bed at the same time. He always flosses his teeth. His garage is immaculately ordered. There aren't even oil stains on the concrete below the cars. Their business is profitable and stable. All their books—particularly the Focus on the Family collection they keep on the dining room shelf, all the books about raising boys—are alphabetized and nothing is out of place on either of their desks.

Talking Bill into regular church attendance doesn't seem like it would have been much of an uphill battle, but I remind myself I didn't know him when he was younger.

CHAPTER 11

It's the same with my parents. No one has to tell my dad to go to church. He goes happily. Neither of my parents resists it or seems to put up anything like a struggle to get them there.

Like the pizza I can't keep myself from craving, my failure to get both Devin and myself there every Sunday without drama, to create a life in which we can be untroubled in the way our parents seem, looms large before me.

If we could just get there and want to be there.

In the pews, we are one. I don't know what we are outside them.

Chapter 12

For our wedding, Devin's grandmother buys us a yellow gingham couch, and in our first apartment, we burn bright yellow candles that smell like lime and sea salt. We buy an unfinished, solid white oak coffee table, which Devin strips and refinishes every three or four months, never quite happy with the stain.

I fluctuate between 97 and 104 pounds, depending on the day. I can still wear the size 0 chinos my mother bought me two years earlier. I'm on birth control pills, which produce stabbing pains in my Achilles tendon like blood clots, so I get off the pills. Doesn't matter. I get a period every three months if I'm lucky, and Devin's taken to wearing condoms when we sleep together anyway.

At night, after we snuggle on the couch to watch a rented movie, Devin and I laugh at the pink-haired lady on TBN and Benny Hinn blowing the Spirit into a microphone and Carman theatrically fighting the devil. Other nights, late, after waiting tables or studying, we watch the Real Estate Network, endless photos of houses for sale in the Jackson metro. Sometimes we watch the loop through twice, never because we want to purchase a house, but because we like laughing at other people's choices, the infinite series of mistakes you could make if you didn't know better.

CHAPTER 12

In my graduate studies I am learning new methods of discovering information, new means of categorizing that information, and new ways to interpret any information I might need.

My first graduate class is a Bibliography and Research seminar with Dr. Miller, simultaneously the hardest and most popular professor in my program. Our first night, we take a learning inventory to gauge the ways we learn best, and we discuss literary theory in its broadest sense and how we can use that theory as a lens for the translation of the academic into the personal. We also discuss the biblical parable of the lost coin, a tiny domestic drama.

In the Gospel of Luke, Jesus says: "Suppose a woman has ten silver coins and loses one. Doesn't she light a lamp, sweep the house and search carefully until she finds it? And when she finds it, she calls her friends and neighbors together and says, 'Rejoice with me; I have found my lost coin.' In the same way, I tell you, there is rejoicing in the presence of the angels of God over one sinner who repents" (NIV).

Dr. Miller summarizes the parable for us and then asks who around the seminar table has heard sermons dedicated to the parable of the prodigal son.

Everyone raises their hand.

He asks how many of us have heard about the parable of the lost sheep.

Everyone raises their hand.

Then, he asks how many of us have heard a single sermon dedicated to this parable of the lost coin.

No one raises their hand.

Dr. Miller notes that in the first two parables, God can be likened to a human man. He asks us if we think it's possible no one's preached about the lost coin because so many Christians find it harder to imagine God the Good Housewife than God the Grizzled Good Shepherd or God the Successful Patriarch and Landowner.

We're at a small liberal arts school nominally affiliated with the Southern Baptist Convention. But few of the English faculty actually attend Southern Baptist churches. Some don't attend church at all. Those who are churchgoers attend progressive churches, the ones my grandmother has been afraid for me to attend my entire life—churches where there are women pastors, for instance, which she believes signals the end of all things. When Dr. Miller asks us about the parables we've heard, he correctly assumes that we've all spent our lives listening to sermons.

Among today's class reading is an excerpt from a book called *Women's Ways of Knowing*. The passage we are assigned introduces the concept of connected knowing, which the authors posit as a kind of feminine antidote to the binary, patriarchal, categorical absolutes of what they call separate knowing.

Connected knowing consists of a collaborative, cooperative kind of knowledge, foregrounded by relationships to things, an intuitive knowledge based in personal experience, not necessarily in external authority.

Dr. Miller praises the concept of connected knowing and encourages us to consider it as a different, more holistic way of examining and absorbing our studies over the next two years. This feels revolutionary to me.

My mother is brilliant and intellectually rigorous, and my father is nurturing and empathetic. His job is to help people better process their emotions. Her job is to dissect the ways in which people fail to learn to read. She balances their

CHAPTER 12

checkbook, makes sure bills are paid on time. He vacuums and makes breakfast and cleans toilets and folds clothes. It's a joke in our family that when the dryer buzzer goes off, you better get out of Dad's way because he'll plow you over so his undershirts don't get wrinkled. My brothers and I know if we linger long enough over the dinner table, he will have washed all the dishes, even on the nights when it's technically our turn to do so, because Dad can't stand for there to be unwashed dishes just sitting around. My parents didn't pay any mind to gender roles in our home.

And yet, at every church my family attended while growing up, women weren't allowed to read Scripture or to pray in the big service. Only men could become church elders or deacons, though women were allowed to teach Sunday school or lead a youth group service. I never knew what to do with the cognitive dissonance between my home life and how the church explicitly taught and implicitly reinforced the primacy of men.

Likewise, at school I'd been tasked repeatedly with "debating" male classmates and teachers about whether the writing of Emily Dickinson and Jane Austen and Zora Neale Hurston and Sylvia Plath and so many other women was as "important and serious" as the stories and poems written by men. I entered most literature classes in a defensive hunch: my counterclaims, rebuttals, and qualifiers all locked and loaded.

Dr. Miller's invitation to not just loosen my shoulders in class, but to value connected knowing alongside separate knowing, sends a jolt of electricity through my body. That it takes a man in authority to help me see the value in a "woman's way" of knowing will not register for me for a very long time. But when I leave class that first night, I have to walk around campus three times before I've burned off enough adrenaline to feel safe to drive, and even then, my hands are still shaking.

Devin and I still dream of getting to Chicago eventually—any city, really. Cities are where no one has to sit in dark houses, suffocating for lack of light. But driving away from that first grad school class with Dr. Miller, I didn't need to be anywhere else. Not since my junior year of high school when another literature teacher recited a poem that felt like it could have come from the inside of my skin have I felt so sure of my place in the world. For now, I will be happy to stay put.

Chapter 13

I have never been a diligent student, but I've always done well in subjects that interested me. And the subject that's interested me most has always been literature, which is why I'm in grad school only three months after college graduation. I coasted through high school and college with the aid of mostly competent sentence structure and the occasional fresh insight, often rendered in response to texts I only skimmed. I'm good at remembering what teachers say in class and good at giving back to teachers what they've said to me.

But Dr. Miller and my other teachers here don't care if I repeat what they say back to them. They want me to have something to say. They want to hear from me.

And so often, it's just blank in there when I'm asked my thoughts in class.

I don't know what I have to say, and they think the phrases I was able to parrot back to professors in my more conservative Christian undergraduate program—phrases like "being versus becoming" or "absolute truth" or "Christian worldview"—are meaningless. When I submit an essay in my graduate teaching assistant practicum in response to a Mina Shaughnessy essay about grammar, and I include a thought about God's capital T "Truth," my supervising professor etches a series of red question marks in the margin alongside this: "What does this have to do with anything????"

My friend Kathleen, who will become my closest friend during this time, the one who will help me get through grad school, sits next to me in Bib and Research class, and when she decides to write her twenty-five-page research paper about domesticity in Marilynne Robinson's *Housekeeping*, I think to myself that this sounds like a thing I could be interested in too. Since I'm currently studying women Christian mystics in my medieval lit class, I figure why not kill two rhetorical birds with one stone? So I decide to write about Julian of Norwich, the woman who bricked herself into the side of a church for life, who writes about God the Mother, which is as controversial a topic as I can possibly imagine, as rebellious against the kind of capital *T* Truth worldview (written exclusively by men, preached exclusively by men) I've spent the last four years being inundated in.

When Dr. Miller assigns us an annotated bibliography asking us to critically examine and analyze twenty-five sources for our essays, I barely get it done on time. It is the second time I stay up all night writing a school assignment, and it earns me my first and only C in graduate school. "How can research be painstaking?" Dr. Miller writes. "This is irrelevant," he writes in another spot. "You need to push harder here. Say more. Be clearer and more succinct."

I want to do all of these things.

I don't really know how.

Devin is working hard—extra shifts at the restaurant—so that I can mostly just be in graduate school. I only join him there a couple of nights a week. But when he's on a lunch shift, and I don't have class, and it's just me home alone with our desktop computer and dial-up internet and my books, I mostly just want to watch television. Every day from 11 to 2 p.m., TLC shows a series of narrative reality TV: *A Makeover Story*, *A Wedding Story*, and *A Baby Story*. I tell myself I'll watch just a little of one of them, but more days than not, I watch all three hours.

When the time comes to buckle down and submit bibliographies or research proposals or early pages of my essay about Julian, I turn frantic. And Devin sees it, and sometimes he'll sit with me while I write, which makes it easier for me to do it. On nights when he's home, he'll marinate chicken tenderloins in Italian dressing and sauté them with portobello mushrooms. He'll open a can of Le Sueur peas and heat them with a healthy pat of butter. He'll bring it over to me while I comb through the writings of women theologians on the domestic in Julian of Norwich's Mother God theology.

Every once in a while, I forget to eat the food in front of me because I am so absorbed in the reading. Maybe the one thing I am becoming now is a scholar, not just a Christian, not just a wife, not just pretty or not, not just chubby or thin. I get absorbed. I fixate. I draft and draft and draft. I do my best to stay on topic. Julian was so single-minded she required only a single room. Talk about fixation. She lived, we think, from 1343 to 1416. Her *Revelations of Divine Love* captures two mystical visions she claims to have received from an angel of God.

She was the first woman to publish a book in English, and she did so at roughly the same time Chaucer was writing *The Canterbury Tales*. I've known about Julian of Norwich for only a few years, and I know of her only because a male poet I was studying (T. S. Eliot) used her as a literary allusion I had to memorize for a test question.

But ironically, even though she was a woman, she was perhaps most famous for the fact that she'd indeed had "a room of her own," unlike so many women, that anchor-hold at the church in Norwich. That room of her own had brought her a niche following even during her life. There are tales of other female mystics, like Margery Kempe, making a kind of pilgrimage to Julian's church and asking her advice. But Julian never received the same broad renown as the men who were her literary contemporaries.

My favorite passage of hers, which I've scribbled on a 3 × 5 index card and taped to the refrigerator at the duplex Devin and I live in first, comes from the eighty-sixth and final chapter of her long text. She sums up all her writing thus: "And from the time that it was revealed, I desired many times to know in what was our Lord's meaning. And fifteen years after and more, I was answered in spiritual understanding, and it was said: What, do you wish to know your Lord's meaning in this thing? Know it well, love was his meaning. Who reveals it to you? Love. What did he reveal to you? Love. Why does he reveal it to you? For love. Remain in this, and you will know more of the same. But you will never know different, world without end."

Love, in Julian's iteration of it, is not only connected knowing; it is the only knowing. The only thing that needs to be known by any of us in her estimation is that reconciling Mother God of love.

Of her impact on the Christian theology of the time, historian Janina Ramirez writes:

> At a time when the Last Judgment loomed heavy over church doorways, Julian argued that a loving God could

not condemn those he loves to damnation for sin. In the "Parable of the Lord and Servant" she describes how sin is the gateway through which a fallen person can understand what it means to be loved; to be picked up, dusted down and held close.

Julian does not frenetically encourage her readers to look to their souls in imminent belief of an End of Days. Instead, she sees a longer narrative, in which ultimately "all shall be well" for we are loved.

In one vision she sees the universe in a hazelnut, which she holds in the palm of her hand. It remains safe, and humanity continues to persevere, because it is part of a bigger scheme held together by love. This is radical stuff.

It is radical stuff to me, for sure. And I hesitate at times when I copy down quotes like these from Ramirez. For anyone to imbue God with any kind of feminine characteristics in the churches I attended growing up was borderline heresy. God was a Father. God came to earth as a man. God was a man.

In attempting to write about the mother love of God now, I feel a kind of rebellious thrill I have rarely felt. Something is shifting in me. Some willingness to break with what I was taught of wrath and judgment. For now, though, it is rebellion enough to read of Julian the radical than to contemplate myself as a radical. I channel my own nascent split through her.

As Ramirez says, Julian is perhaps most famous for her repeated line, co-opted by Eliot in "Little Gidding," which was my introduction to her, "All will be well, and all will be well, and all manner of thing will be well."

When I drive home alone from most diligent nights at the library stacks, I mutter that to myself.

All will be well.

All will be well.

The mantra isn't enough to save me from my worst procrastinations, however, and TLC wins out more days than it should. Nevertheless, with the help of Courier New font, which adds three pages, I'm able to cobble together twenty-five on Julian and her anchor-hold and a God who could be a mother or a good housewife, a God who might not hate any of us.

It's a mess, and I know it while I type it in a mania all night before it is due. Dr. Miller will give it a B and let me know where the thesis gets lost. He will be right.

Instead of being able to sleep for a few hours today after my all-nighter, I finish a ten-page essay on "The Linguistic Complexity of Black Vernacular Speech" for a History of the English Language class due the following morning, and then start research for the twelve-page essay due in two days on *Pedagogy of the Oppressed*. I observe the final class of the professor who's let me be her assistant all semester. I arrive home from school only five minutes before Devin, who, having noticed how hard I've been working, surprises me by taking me to dinner.

He drives me to Crechale's in South Jackson, our favorite steakhouse dive. We order fillets and baked potatoes and salads with comeback dressing and a side of saltines. We even get a bottle of wine.

As I take the first few bites of my salad—garlicky, creamy, crisp lettuce and salted tomato—Devin points out that I've been awake for thirty-six hours.

"I don't know how you're still upright," he says.

I'm not sure why his statement of this simple fact undoes me, but it does. My eyes well up with tears, and I can barely

CHAPTER 13

swallow my salad because of the need to sob. My face turns red. My nose swells. We're tucked away in a booth, and the restaurant is dark. I bury my head in Devin's shoulder, which embarrasses neither of us because no one can see.

"Kel, hush. It'll be okay. Hey. You got this. Just a couple more days, and you'll have the first semester out of the way. You got this," he whispers into my hair, nudging my neck.

After a few minutes, I collect myself, but only barely, and he informs our waiter that we'll be needing the rest of our food to go. Five minutes later, food in a bag, wine bottle left half-full on the table behind us, we get into our car.

I'm asleep before Devin pulls onto the highway, and all will be well.

Chapter 14

One day that first winter after Devin and I are married, in the midst of the all-nighters, I start putting cream in my coffee. Before an evening shift at the restaurant where I still work part-time to pay for grad school, I measure out a half teaspoon and watch it slowly spiral before I stir it. My standard black coffee turns a slight tan. I can feel the cool slick of dairy against the roof of my mouth long after the drink is gone. I savor it all night as I stare at the fat fillets of beef and salmon the grill chefs flip across the hot metal bars. I watch as they score grill marks onto thick triangles of seared polenta we are known for and then place them, smoking, on a red pepper coulis with a dollop of warm goat cheese. I watch as the pizza chefs spin up crawfish pizzas with a wine and shellfish velouté as the base. They top it with peppers and gouda and scallions and mushrooms. When they slide the bubbling hot pizzas out onto the wooden cutting board on the counter for us to slice, sometimes an edge of molten cheese will slip onto the cutting board, and I will have to tell myself not to snatch it up with my mouth in front of the whole restaurant.

The garde manger station plates fat slices of pound cake topped with peach ice cream and hot blackberry sauce that forms puddles of pink and purple along the sides of the plate. Red onion soup (our chef's take on French—white wine in

CHAPTER 14

place of red, red onions in place of yellow) gets a thick layer of provolone blowtorched across its top, and I can smell broth and wine and onions when I carry it to a table, balancing the soup spoon lightly with the edge of my thumb.

I watch, and I want.

And then I tell myself not eating is worth it. It's all worth it. I slide my finger easily along the inside rim of a pair of slim-fit black work pants.

I don't need pizza.

I don't need cheese on my onion soup.

I don't need to feel the frozen crunch of fresh peach with warm blackberry and the vanilla and lemon butter crumble of pound cake. I don't need it. I'm good.

Nothing tastes as good as skinny feels, I remind myself.

I can fit in these pants. My arms are toned and tight. My chin won't double itself even if I pull it all the way into my neck. My cheeks are defined and so's my jaw. My breasts don't even fill up my A-cup bra. I can wear anything I want.

And there are other things I CAN eat, I tell myself.

Baked ramen. Oranges. Tuna in water. Romaine lettuce.

But once or twice a week Mr. Broadway, the pasta chef, brings the Vitamix into the back of the house with the remnants of fresh pesto still in it and hands me a hot breadstick out of the oven to dip into the blender.

"You're getting too damn skinny, sweetheart. Eat it," he'll say, and being given that permission, and thinking to myself that basil is a vegetable and Parmesan a protein and pine nuts a protein and olive oil the good kind of fat, I will eat that pesto so fast that I will sometimes slice my fingers along the edges of the blender blades, and I won't care, because the licorice and pepper taste of basil overwhelms the trace of blood.

And I will think about that green taste all night when talking to customers, hiding from them the small Band-Aids wrapped around my fingers. Hot white bread. Garlic green paste. Oil.

When I get home to our apartment, I lie down with the small of my back pressed hard into the floor. I raise both my legs to the ceiling without using my hands. Ten times. Twenty times. Thirty. As soon as I get to one hundred, I stop. I tell myself that was enough for one breadstick and two tablespoons of pesto. But I do another fifty just to be sure.

I fear the taste of the pesto and what it will make me do. I fear the half-and-half I allowed myself in my coffee. I fear that the dam that is the size o pants and the lack of a double chin will not be enough to contain the ravenous thing in me that doesn't care if it cuts its fingers. I fear it like my grandmother's butter and cigarettes. I will corrode if I surrender control.

At first, to try to contain it, I remember to make dinner before my and Devin's shared shift at the restaurant. I make a protein smoothie for each of us. We drink them in the car on the way to work. Sometimes it's a cup full of cantaloupe and blueberries. Other times it's a cup of bananas and peanut butter sprinkled with cinnamon.

But we get to work at 4:30 p.m. and we don't finish until 11 p.m., and by the time we're done, all the food we ate at 4:30 has long since vanished with us running across the restaurant from table to table and smelling food all night—the rotisserie, grilled meat, hot chocolate ganache, bubbling cheese. And with our pockets full of cash as we walk away, we just want food.

What I want, most nights, is a burger. A burger and ice cream. A burger and ice cream with M&M's in it and whipped cream on top. A CHEESE burger with pickles and onions and mayonnaise and lettuce and soft white bread. Salty tater

CHAPTER 14

tots with chili and cheese, topped with minced white onion. M&M's broken up by an old shake machine and topped with clots of thick cream.

But what I get, whether we stop at Sonic or at O'Charley's or Waffle House or any of the three or four other places still open that late in Jackson, is grilled chicken and undressed romaine. I know how to do this now. I know how to make the crunch of the romaine mimic something I want. I know that. If the chicken is salty and warm enough, it's almost as good as a burger. I can do this, I think, watching Devin pour a mustard pack over his chili cheese tots and bite into his hot burger and offer me a bite, which I will decline, at least at first.

I won't remember which day I stop declining the bite.

Then without warning, about a year after we are married, Devin will take a job at another restaurant where he can make twice as much money. It's busier, higher-end, on the opposite side of town. Sometimes we ride together. I'll drop him off or he'll drop me off, but for the most part, we take our own cars.

Now it's just me eating alone most nights. Most nights my feet ache. I don't want to stand in my kitchen even long enough to make a salad. Sometimes I go through a drive-through. Other nights, I eat an entire frozen pizza by myself. As my restaurant grows less and less popular, I get off earlier and earlier. Devin's shift goes longer, and I learn that if I wait on him at the bar in his restaurant instead of going home alone, the bartenders will pour me big glasses of expensive wine. They think I'm funny and cute, which they always tell Devin in front of me, as if they are reminding him of a fact he's forgotten.

"Your wife's so sweet!! She's just the cutest!" they admonish him.

Sometimes he'll come over to give me a hug or a kiss on the cheek. "Of course she is!" he'll laugh. "Why do you think I married her?"

I love this attention, but I love the wine even more.

Behind the bar, there are gorgeous glass containers of infused vodkas and gins. Foot-deep cylindrical stacks of multicolored peppers for Sunday morning Bloody Marys, lemons and limes for lemon drop martinis, and all sorts of other beautiful bottles. I stare at them while I wait for him, and drink my wine.

Once I become a fixture at the bar, they realize I'm also a waiter, and they start to bring me Devin's silverware to fold. Every night, before they can check out, all the waiters have to wrap fifty individual silverware packets to be used for the following service. I wrap Devin's thinking it will get us home faster, but just as often, he joins me at the bar once his shift is over, and we both drink wine for another hour.

Sometimes the chefs will send me out something to eat. My favorite is the fried oyster salad—it's a six-inch mound of cornmeal-dusted Gulf oysters on a bed of greens drizzled with avocado cream and a citrus vinaigrette, finished with a griddled corn salsa. It's a perfect bite of food.

At first, I try to eat only a quarter of the salad, which I'm sure must come in at a thousand calories. One quarter is not so bad for a dinner. If you add the couple hundred calories for a glass of wine. Okay. Five hundred calories for two or three glasses of wine. It's a large dinner. But I've been on my feet delivering food to tables for the last few hours. All that walking burns some calories. I deserve a little something.

Other nights, the chefs will save a crème brûlée for me or a bread pudding with whiskey and chocolate sauce.

CHAPTER 14

The amount of willpower it takes not to eat all the bread pudding, with its warm chocolate and tart salt of sourdough and custard cream, is staggering. But I am ostentatiously proud of myself every time I am able to walk away.

Even though I know I've been letting myself eat more than usual, it still surprises me when my size 0 pants suddenly become too tight to zip. Then I break the side zipper on the size 2 embroidered shantung skirt I'd worn to our rehearsal dinner, just before Devin accompanies me to church, his Windsor already knotted, his shirt starched and still steaming.

For my second birthday after we are married, we buy a huge weight set, which takes up half our bedroom. We buy a workout and nutrition plan that includes drinking proprietary protein shakes three times a day. I join the campus healthplex at my grad school. I walk laps around the neighborhood or at the track on campus with friends.

But I'm tired. I'm taking three graduate classes and teaching two sections of College Writing, and I'm waiting tables ten to fifteen hours a week and staying up late sitting at the bar or waiting for Devin to come home. When I get to be home, I just want to see Devin. I don't want to take an hour of that time to go walk on the treadmill at the gym or do my crunches on the mat on the floor.

The weight returns slowly but steadily.

Size 6.

Size 8.

Size 14.

I see a double chin in a picture someone snaps of us with Pearl. When I crack a joke about getting fat, Devin thinks it's funny, but not because he disagrees with me. When I say I need to go to the gym, he encourages me to. When he starts telling me he doesn't want to kiss me because my breath smells like I have a cold or because I didn't shower that day or because he just doesn't feel like it, I don't take him at his word. I assume it's because I weigh more than he does now. Our sameness has been jeopardized.

Soaking wet, Devin weighs 140 pounds. When I go to the doctor and I weigh 153, I feel I have failed. I worked so hard to lose all the weight, and now I weigh more than I ever did. Boys are supposed to be bigger and stronger than girls. Girls are supposed to be prettier than boys. I don't know where I've picked up any of these ideas or who invented them, but I believe I'm on the wrong side of the rules regardless. When I walk into Devin's restaurant to pick him up, the chefs still send me food. The bartenders still pour me the dregs of good wine. They still hype me up, but now they talk about how smart and funny I am. No one says I'm cute anymore. Do they wonder why Devin ever liked me? I do.

But I accept the food just the same: Hammered copper baking dishes with the remnants of a potato gratin to go with a glass of last night's Ridge Petite Sirah. Or the last of the tomato tarragon soup, thick with flecks of soup skin mixed in because it had sat on the bain-marie all night.

The thing in me that is willing to risk its fingers in a blender is still afraid of so many other things, but every time a crisp, not quite burnt edge of thinly sliced, stacked potatoes in cream or even that skin of soup touches my tongue, the fear leaves me.

Around the same time I begin drinking cream in my coffee again, Devin's back starts to hurt. The pain throbs and stings and wraps its tentacles from the base of his spine all the way around his hips and groin.

CHAPTER 14

At first, we think he just needs more supportive shoes for all the restaurant work he does.

He buys the least clunky pair of Rockports he can find with the remainder of our wedding credits.

They don't help.

He spends hours and hours and hours scouring online sites for orthopedic shoes. Researching on our bed, he scrolls through site after site after site. Considering a pair, putting it in the cart, then changing his mind.

We still have dial-up internet, so when I call him to pick me up from work on nights when one of our cars is in the shop, he often doesn't answer for twenty or thirty minutes. It's just me repeatedly using the phone in the back office of the restaurant.

"Can't get through. Devin's probably looking at shoes again," I mumble to the sous chef looking through receipts next to me.

"Sure," he mumbles back skeptically.

"No, really. Honest to God, he spends hours looking for new shoes. He's bought like six pairs of shoes in the last month. Orthopedic shoes are his porn," I insist.

"Sure," the sous chef repeats.

I don't like the way he says it. I don't like the way it makes me feel, but I keep telling myself I know I'm right. *It's just shoes. It's just his back. He's just looking for shoes.*

Eventually he finds a podiatrist to make him specialty orthotics that he can slip into any shoe. They don't help. Then, for months afterward, Devin is convinced he didn't distribute his weight correctly when the orthotic was being cast. So, we get new ones. They also do nothing. Then there's a chiropractor, and that doesn't help. Then he sees a physical therapist. Then a urologist. Then a neurologist. Then a pain specialist.

He gets multiple diagnoses—fibromyalgia, immune disorder, psychosomatic manifestation of his OCD (i.e., that his fear that he would feel back pain was creating the back pain). Nothing touches the back pain—not pain pills or ibuprofen or wine or anything else he tries. The back pain remains untranslatable and thus untreatable.

Many years in the future, Devin will find a combination of yoga, meditation, and daily swimming that helps him. Slowly the pain will recede.

But for many years before that—for all the years I am with him—his back is a relentless nightmare that complicates everything—work, road trips, air travel, sleep. We still sleep together often enough, though, rarely less than twice a week, his mechanism as easy as ever to arouse, and even mine has become decipherable. His continued desire squelches any doubt for a time. *A body can't lie*, I think. *A body can't be tricked into wanting.*

So, I am—we are—trying our best not to hear otherwise.

But our bodies keep speaking anyway.

Chapter 15

One day, two years and some change into our marriage, fresh out of grad school, I am teaching "The Love Song of J. Alfred Prufrock" at a prep school in Jackson, trying and often failing to be the Mr. Keating I desire to be. Across the street in our new apartment, Devin sees the first mouse in our kitchen.

He is getting a glass of water, facing the sink that faces the high-top bar of our two-bedroom, double-balcony, open-concept apartment by the lake. Out of the corner of his left eye, a small, dark shape, bigger and slower than a cockroach, flits behind the flour canister.

He turns in that direction and initially sees nothing, but he stands still. He waits. He takes a quiet sip of water, moving his hand but not his body.

Then. Slowly.

A brown mouse pushes its whiskers out first, and next, the pink tip of its nose, nudging it just beyond the impossibly narrow enclosure between the ceramic cylinders of flour and sugar. When the black beads of its eyes finally emerge, it makes eye contact with Devin, then scurries, hell for leather, across the top of the beige oven and squeezes itself beneath the unlit electric circle of the stove's back right burner.

Devin puts the glass of water down on the counter and walks immediately across the street to the apartment manager's office, which is set on a wide cedar deck overlooking one of the complex's three saltwater pools and the fountain in the middle of the lake. The manager, a woman who's waited tables with both of us at various times, assures Devin they know about the mouse problem—that the folks below us had also had them. She tells him they are on it—traps and poison and exterminators are all headed our way. She reminds him of my debilitating fear of rodents—how one night I'd screamed and jumped a foot in the air because someone accidentally kicked a black washcloth that had skidded in my direction, and I'd assumed it was a mouse.

"Maybe don't tell Kelly about it," she encourages Devin.

"No, I know all about that. Agreed. No telling Kelly," he assures her.

But he will tell me about this, all of it, three mornings later, when I walk into the kitchen and see a six-inch tunnel chewed into the plastic bag of sliced bread I keep on the counter. He will confess to me about the exterminators and the traps and the poison in the wall. He will give a dramatic reenactment of the whole conversation between him and the manager, which makes me laugh and reassures me that everything is being handled.

The tunnel terrifies me, but it's temporary.

Lately, we see each other only in passing.

After a late-night shift at the restaurant where he still works, Devin's usually asleep when I leave for work at the prep school. He's already left for work by the time I get home. Now that I'm teaching, I'm off Saturday and Sunday. Most weekends he works both brunches and Saturday night dinners, which means I spend most Saturday nights eating chips and salsa with my youngest brother, who stays with us several nights a week. On the days Devin has off, we head to the movies and invite my parents or my brother to join us. It's rarely just the two of us alone anymore, but when it is, we still snuggle on the yellow couch, we still talk until late, we still laugh at TBN, we still rent movies at another Blockbuster.

In the car, we still listen to Tori Amos.

But more than before, even when Devin is with me, he isn't.

He's apologized for the sense of separation several times. He woke me up two months ago, crying. He told me that lately he'd felt withdrawn and depressed but he was getting better. He was going to treat me better. He would be more present. He loved me so much. But after a few days, he's gone again, emotionally if not physically. I don't know if I will see him when I come home from work, and when I do see him, I never know if I'll get a smile or silence.

Eventually, the apartment manager thinks our mice are gone for good, and she tells us so, but I jump every time the refrigerator clicks on and off. My peripheral vision never disengages when I am pouring a drink or washing dishes or folding clothes in the living room, adjacent to the kitchen. I'm always on edge for darting things—tiny, fleet streaks of brown or gray that could emerge at any moment and then disappear back into crevices I can't reach.

Tonight, I am entering my students' scores for the T. S. Eliot and Modernism exam on the desktop computer in the back bedroom. There are only two weeks left until all my classes' exams are finished, and I will be done for the semester. It's warm enough to want the windows open and still cool enough we don't have mosquitoes yet, so I've cracked the unscreened, sliding glass door to the balcony. I can hear the fountain's consistent cascade of water underneath crickets and frogs and what I always think are cicadas but might be locusts. I hear the geese that sleep at Mirror Lake across the road honking to one another.

I hear the steady hum of evening commuters returning home to their families along Lakeland Drive. I crack my toes against the thick beige plush of the carpet, then press them up and down against the thick foam layer beneath the carpet.

I've just finished entering grades for my fourth class—only two more sets of grades to go—when I decide to take a break and check my AOL account for email. I point the cursor at the multicolored circle that says "Start." I look absentmindedly at the menu that pops up, scanning for the AOL triangle, and notice beneath it a picture file I've never noticed before.

It's titled "me.jpeg."

From thumbnail size, it's hard to discern exactly what it is, but when I click the image to make it larger, I see a man who was in a class of mine three years before—my first class in graduate school. He is naked to the waist, and his jeans are rolled down far enough that I can see the taut sculpture his muscles make wrapped around each of his hips.

In the years to come, the bathroom selfie will become a pedestrian art form when phones get smart and become cameras. But in 2002, the man in this bathroom picture is holding a silver digital camera at the level of his ribs, just below one well-defined pec. The photo is pixilated, grainy, not very well lit, but I'm certain I know this person.

The back of my neck goes cold and my stomach constricts. I shift in my seat. I press pause on the *When Harry Met*

CHAPTER 15

Sally soundtrack that has become my standard listen while I enter grades.

I look at the clock. It says 8:31.

It could be at least two hours before Devin gets home.

If I call him now, he'll be busy trying to manage a few tables at once. And anyway, what would you say to someone who's talking on the phone behind a crowded bar in a restaurant, forks clinking on plates, sweaty water glasses needing refills, dessert menus waiting to be delivered?

"Hey, ummm. There's a half-naked man holding a camera in a grainy picture on our computer. Why is that?"

I try to keep entering grades, but my mind won't focus. After I enter the wrong grade for the same student twice, I give it up.

I dig in the back of the second closet, where I keep the pack of Camels I bought last time my brother came to visit. There are eight left.

Sitting on the balcony in the humid dusk, I watch the water feature play in the middle of the lake while I light my first cigarette, and then my next, and then my next. At the end of the third cigarette, I feel slightly woozy, just a little nauseous. I go inside and brush my teeth and scrub my hands and my face.

It's 9:16 p.m.

On an ordinary night, I might just to bed. I'll have to be at school by 7:15 tomorrow morning, and since I didn't get all my grades entered tonight, I'll have to be up at least by 5:30 a.m. so I can finish before classes. My students are all waiting on their averages to know whether they will be exempt from exams or not. I promised I'd tell them tomorrow.

But this isn't an ordinary night. I found a strange picture, and it bothers me. No explanation I can summon makes sense to me, and I need to hear what Devin thinks. I am afraid his explanation won't soothe anything, but I am clinging to a bit of hope there is a simple reason.

I have married girlfriends who have discovered porn on their husband's computers. Pictures of women with beach-ball breasts and landing-strip vaginas exposed. The husbands are chastened, sometimes even agreeing to accountability about their internet usage. The shirtless man on our computer feels similar but not the same. My thoughts are even more pixelated than the image. Nothing is in focus.

At 9:35, after taking out my contacts and putting on my pajamas, I decide to try to watch television. No word from Devin yet. He usually calls before he comes home.

On Lifetime, the same episode of *Designing Women* that I watched when I got home from school is playing again. It's the one where Charlene overhears one of her friends being abused by her husband, and now it's more intense than I can handle.

On E!, there's a *True Hollywood Story* about Drew Barrymore, and on Bravo, there's an *Inside the Actors Studio* with Sarah Jessica Parker.

I can't focus on anything, but I keep flipping the channels.

The History Channel is airing the second night of a four-part series on how certain drugs were made illegal—examining why some were criminalized and some weren't. This episode is about heroin. There's a *Dateline* rerun on MSNBC about a woman who slowly poisoned her husband by pouring small amounts of antifreeze into his Gatorade bottles.

None of this captures my attention, but the apartment is too quiet if I turn off the TV, so I keep watching, flipping as soon as one channel goes to commercial.

Finally, around 10:15, the phone rings. It's Devin, and he sounds chipper.

CHAPTER 15

"Hi! So good to hear your voice!" Devin says. "I missed you tonight! Want me to pick you up something from Wendy's? How about fries with barbecue sauce?"

"Sure. Sounds good. See you in a few," I say and hang up, suddenly nervous to ask the one question I know I have to ask.

It's almost eleven when he gets home.

The white oxford shirt he wears for work is untucked and unbuttoned. The chest hair that always bugs him is sticking out of the top of his fitted white undershirt. He's carrying two bags from Wendy's.

I don't know what to say to him. I fix myself against the arm of the couch like it's an anchor. I don't get up.

"Hey! How are you? You get your grades entered tonight?" he asks, setting the bags down and kissing the top of my head. "Anything good on?" he nods in the direction of the TV, pulling his shirt out of his pants and draping his tie on the back of a dining room chair.

"Not really. Same *Designing Women* as this afternoon. The one where Charlene's cousin gets abused by her husband."

"Oof. Yeah, that one's depressing," he concurs. He grabs my bag with the salty, still-hot fries and the now warm container of BBQ sauce and hands it to me. Then he goes into our bedroom to get changed. He comes back out wearing the same undershirt and a pair of loose flannel drawstring pants. He sits in the armchair next to me.

We start to eat.

I dip a few fries at a time into the smoky sauce, and something about the act of eating crisp and salty food settles me a bit.

I ask him about his shift. He responds pleasantly: One eight-top and a couple of four-tops. Not too bad. A couple of singles who came in because they were running a new special that everyone loved. Nothing too wild.

"I did okay. Like $125 or so. Not too shabby for a Tuesday," he says, his eyes on the TV, watching a prescription commercial.

I wait until he's finished his burger and Sprite, and until I've eaten as many fries as my still-unsettled stomach will allow me.

"Hey, I need to talk to you about something," I finally say.

His eyes get serious as his face falls. He wipes his hands together and rubs them across his face, and he looks at me with his mouth in a straight line.

"Let's talk. What's going on? You seem really quiet tonight. It's making me feel weird," he says.

"Well . . ." I start to say, then stop. I genuinely don't know what to say. "Well," I start again, forcing myself just to say whatever words I can identify in the blankness of my mind, "I found a picture on the computer tonight while I was entering grades. It made me feel weird."

His face is unreadable, the straight line of his mouth like the blank my mind is struggling to fill.

"What kind of picture?"

"It was a man. I'm pretty sure it's this guy who was in my first grad school class, but he's naked in the picture. Well, I mean, he's wearing jeans, but he seems naked. I don't know if that makes sense."

"Really? I wonder why that would be there. Maybe he thought you were cute, and he sent it to your email."

"But wouldn't I have to open it first? I mean, I haven't ever gotten an email from him. I'm not even sure he remembers my name."

"You know, the internet is weird like that. Sometimes stuff just floats around. I mean, I don't know. I'm not very good with that stuff either. I can take a look at it if you want."

CHAPTER 15

And I take him back to the computer to show him where the file is. Once again, "me.jpeg" expands from a thumbnail into a grainy 4 × 6 digital rectangle. The camera just below the pec. Curled blue jeans. Hip muscles.

"Huh. Yeah. I don't know where that could have come from. Kinda wild. Maybe you opened the email and forgot?"

"I mean, I don't think so?"

"Yeah, that's odd. I mean, if he did write you and he tries to write you again, just let him know you're not available."

He stares out the window while rubbing his arms. His heart wasn't in that joke.

"Do you have any fries left? I'm still hungry."

This is as far as we get on Tuesday.

We catch the tail end of *Letterman* before bed and Devin sings to himself while he brushes his teeth. He seems fine.

Once we're in bed, he kisses me on the lips before he clicks his jaw to clear his nose and shifts his hips the way he always does just before he falls asleep. Usually five or six times.

I am trying to write the picture off as an anomaly of the mysterious internet, and it kind of works.

I sleep fitfully before my alarm goes off at 5:30 a.m., and the next evening after school, I have a grading date with my friend Katie at Books-A-Million. We chat about a hundred things while we grade, and just as we are about to leave, I tell her about the picture.

"I found a picture of ____ on my computer."

"Oh yeah? Why was his picture on your computer?"

"That's my whole question. It wasn't just a picture of him with people. He was . . . naked. Or. Like. Almost naked."

"WHAT?!"

"Will you come to my house and look at it on your way home? I asked Devin about it, and he thinks I must have accidentally clicked on an email from him or something. But I honestly don't remember getting an email from him ever."

She agrees, both of us feeling freshly awake after hours of marking up comma splices and lack of specificity in student literary analyses.

Devin is at work when we get there, but he was home all day. The apartment is clean. There are fresh vacuum lines in the beige carpet. With Katie behind me in the back bedroom, I log on to the computer and now the screen is blank.

When I click on the start menu where "me.jpeg" had been yesterday, there's nothing. Just the regular list of options to choose from once again. When I open the search box to search for files, a still-open window appears with the last search flashing: "Gay."

"Huh," is all Katie says.

"Yeah. Ummm, I'm not sure what's going on," I say. "I'll see what I can find out from Devin. Maybe he was just clearing out the files or something."

Katie nods and rubs my shoulders kindly for a moment before remembering that she promised her husband to bring home dinner, so she'd better hurry back. She tells me to call if I need anything, and she loves me, and she lets herself out, while I stay seated at the computer.

There's a feeling you get when you know you are about to know something. I remember having it just before my first boyfriend, the geometry tutor I would follow to college, broke up with me. We were sitting on a swing next to a small lake, and my head was in his lap.

"I can't do this anymore," he said before he began to cry.

I had held the knowledge in my chest like a weight until he said it, and his saying it unlocked the boulder from my chest

CHAPTER 15

so that it fell in my stomach, where it rolled from side to side and jostled everything else loose.

I feel like that again, but I don't know why. I don't know why a married man, a man who has sex with his wife two or three times a week no matter what, a man who's kissed sixteen girls, and a man whose many secrets and insecurities and struggles I've heard all about for five years now, would type "gay" into a file search.

I feel wrecked. Spent. Unsettled.

I need to talk to Devin again tonight. And again, I'm going to have to wait for him to come home. I stay in the second bedroom, sitting at the computer, staring out the dark window that looks out onto the apartment pool, the underwater lights flickering pale blue.

I don't have to wait as long tonight.

Only ten minutes or so after Katie leaves, Devin calls to say it was a slow night. He might go grab a drink with Val and some of the girls from the bar.

"Actually, I really need to talk to you. I need you to come home."

He goes quiet.

"Ummm. Okay. Okay, I'll come right home."

His work is a ten-minute straight shot down Ridgewood Road, and he makes it home in nine minutes.

"What's up?" he asks nervously as soon as I come to the door.

"Can we actually sit outside?"

"Sure. You're making me nervous. Are you okay?"

"Yeah, I think so. I just need to talk to you."

"Okay, let me change. I'll meet you out there."

I wait for him on one of the folding chairs we keep on

the front balcony, a familiar soundtrack of traffic, frogs, and pool in my ears. I reach underneath the chair where I left my cigarettes and lighter last night. Devin hates it when I smoke, but I don't care tonight.

He comes back out in shorts and a clean undershirt, looking shrunken and gray.

"That bad, huh?" he says, nodding at the lit cigarette.

"I don't know," I say.

"I feel like there's more to the story of that picture than what you told me last night" is all I'm able to get out before my throat constricts.

Now it's his turn to be quiet.

He doesn't say anything for what feels like fifteen minutes but might have been only five. I don't say anything either. The silence suggests an answer but remains amorphous, hard to discern.

"Yeah, that's fair. That's fair."

Then nothing else for at least another minute.

He looks away while he is thinking and then looks at me again. He brushes my arm gently.

"Do you remember that time I told you about the boy who died? The one who teased me about being a girl?"

"Yes, of course I remember."

"Well, right around the time he died . . . no, actually a little bit before. That was when my parents first took me to see Dr. B. I was . . . I was having a hard time figuring out who I was, and I was really depressed. You know about most of that, but there's parts of it I haven't told you because I worried it might make things weird, but I don't think it has to."

He takes a breath as I light a third cigarette with the embers of my second.

CHAPTER 15

"That boy and the boys with him—they called me a girl. They said I was a girl, and I guess it just got into my head, and it made me wonder if I was gay. At the time, I didn't have that many male friends. Most of my friends were girls. I guess I just wondered. My head got all stuck on it."

"But, you're obviously not gay. I've been sleeping with you for the last four years. I think I would know. You kissed and more than kissed SO many girls."

"Yeah . . . just . . . wait. Just hear me out. I need to explain this." He motions for me to be quiet.

"Around the time that boy died, I started to have these worries that maybe I was going to have a heart attack, and then there was this whole week where I couldn't stop thinking about my tongue on the roof of my mouth. It's like, I went to school, and that's all I could think about, and finally after four or five days, my parents had to take me to the ER because my heart started racing so much, I felt like I was actually having a heart attack.

"So, I told them some of the stuff that I was thinking about—not all of it, but just some of the questions I had about myself as a man, or I guess as a boy at that point, some of my insecurities about all that, and they found out about Dr. B, and that's why I went there so much for so long."

When I first met Devin, Dr. B's name came up every couple of weeks in statements like "Dr. B says it's easy for us to forget who we are inside" or "Dr. B says it's easy to believe in false images."

Devin uses "false images," a term he learned from Dr. B, to mean beliefs we have about ourselves that aren't true. I thought I knew what all those false beliefs were until tonight. I don't know anymore.

Now that I think about it, sitting here listening to him tell this story, so many of the times he's told me about his fear of the false images he has about himself and how Dr. B used to reassure him, he's said something about how he wished his dad had been more expressive or his mom had been less emotionally needy or how he wished he had more male friends.

The edges of puzzle pieces slowly start to come into focus.

"Dr. B always said that being gay was a lie. That it was a lie I believed about myself that was planted there by some of the different things in my life. He said if I needed to remember if I was straight, I could look at pictures like that one you found last night, and remember that I wasn't gay. He said it's just part of my OCD, part of these compulsions that I have—like the thought of my tongue on the roof of my mouth."

I don't ask him how he got that specific bathroom selfie of that specific man I know. I ask him if it works.

"It actually does work. Kel, I love you so so so much. I'm so grateful and happy to be married to you. I know I've been really busy and stressed lately, but I love you so, so, so much. I'm so glad to be here. I'm so glad to be married to you. I promise I'll try to be here more. That's the one thing I know for sure. I know this is so much to hear, but thank you for listening."

He reaches out for my hand again, and for the first time since I've known him, he seems genuinely uncertain if I will take it.

I do.

I'm still uneasy, but it's late again. I'm tired. We brush our teeth together, and I try to make conversation about other things—the fact that school is almost over, that we'll be going to the beach soon with my family, that his mom called to ask about our Fourth of July plans again. He nods in response to my questions and says he'll call his mom tomorrow before he goes in to work.

It's around midnight when I finally turn off my bedside lamp after attempting to read for thirty minutes. Instead of hearing the words from the page in my head, I keep replaying our conversation from the porch.

Next to me, Devin breathes softly, sound asleep on his stomach, one hand wedged underneath the pillow, the other tucked underneath his chest to steady him.

I roll over onto my own stomach and let the weight of my body settle into the mattress. He feels me shift, and he reaches beneath the covers for the small of my back. He settles his head into the base of my neck, and we stay there until the sun peeks through the willow branches beside the window the next morning.

Chapter 16

THE FIRST OUT GAY MAN I KNEW WAS OUR TOWN LIBRARIAN. His name was John. When I was in fifth grade, he was stabbed by a boyfriend multiple times, stabbed so deep his liver was lacerated. He survived and eventually came back to work. As he often sat in the back corner by the videos and biographies and vinyl records where I spent most of my time, I would spy on him between the shelves as if he were a curiosity in a museum, as if I were an eleven-year-old Dian Fossey in the mist taking field notes: "Gay man. Their repressed masculine energy and increased feminine hysteria send them into fits of jealous rage. See sixteen stab wounds on Exhibit A."

I was born in 1977, which meant that just as I was old enough to read magazines in grocery store aisles and comprehend them, AIDS covered every page, and though a distant relative of mine would die of AIDS, and I would hear the adults around me whispering about it, the tragic skeletal face of AIDS for me at the time was mostly Rock Hudson's, whom I loved already because of movies like *Pillow Talk*. In the months leading up to his death in 1985, his face was on every magazine I remember. And because back then all I wanted to do was be in and know all about movies, I eagerly read reviews of a TV biopic titled simply *Rock Hudson* on visits to the library reserve section, usually only a table away from John.

CHAPTER 16

I thought of Rock Hudson as tragic, not only because of the way he withered, but also because his real life made me realize that the Doris Day movies I had loved were more of a lie than even the artifice of fiction suggested. For some reason that false straightness saddened me. I was most sad not that Hudson had to hide or even that Hudson had died, but that he hadn't really loved Doris Day. That one beautiful man had been lost to women from the beginning somehow registered with me as tragic, and perhaps unconsciously, I began to see gay men's lives as generally tragic. Movies like *Philadelphia*, *My Own Private Idaho*, *Wilde*, and so many of the other nineties films I saw in high school and college did little to challenge this perception.

After John's stabbing, some adults I knew in town refused to check books out from the library, afraid that physical contact with John might cause them to catch AIDS or to turn their sons gay from exposure.

But my mother, both as a woman who has always read about three or four books a week and as someone who has spent her life as a kind of bulldog defender of those in danger of being cast out, took the initial rejection of him as her cue to increase our library visits. As if she'd ever needed such inducement. We lived just down the street, and two or three times a week we walked past the Hastee Tastee drive-in, past the Triangle Cultural Center, and past the Memorial on the Square "erected to perpetuate the memory of the noble courage and self-sacrificing devotion of the women of the Confederacy" to the Ricks Memorial Library, which I did not yet realize had been a whites-only library until about ten years before I was born.

Five or six months after John's stabbing, my mom checked out Zeffirelli's *Romeo and Juliet* for me. I was only ten years old, and I don't remember why she did it. Maybe because I was obsessed with *Anne of Green Gables* and was often inadvertently quoting Shakespeare thinking I was only quoting Anne. I don't know why she brought it home that first time and she doesn't remember either, but I do know I absorbed every bit of that film as I would a punch to the stomach. I crackled like lightning for days after watching it.

After that initial viewing, I returned to check out *Romeo and Juliet* on what was basically a semimonthly rotation. I showed it to all my friends. Without the language for it, my friend Christine and I had similar feelings about the male lead, Leonard Whiting, as the ones I would later express about other crushes. "Leonard" became between us a kind of code for any boy we thought was cute. We giggled when we said it, as if the adoration of his symmetry was our secret.

The fifth or sixth time I checked out the VHS tape from the library, John said, "My, my. Does Mother know you're watching this so often?"

He had the habit, as do many folks of a certain aristocratic bent in the South, of referring to other people's mothers without the second-person possessive pronoun and also of pronouncing it in three syllables while dropping the rhotic *r* at the end.

"Does Muh-uh-thah know?"

Then he smiled at me and winked, "Ah, but tragic love. Tragic love. Who can resist?" And I remember thinking how grown-up I felt to be let in on what felt like some kind of personal admission from John. He loved tragic love too. Just like me.

Over the next few years, I saw John several times a week, often when I checked out my ritualized and repeated selections: a 1964 vinyl of Pavarotti as Rodolfo in *La bohème*; a 1955

CHAPTER 16

vinyl of Maria Callas as Violetta in *La Traviata*; a battered old green, leather-bound copy of *Anna Karenina* held together by a crumbling beige rubber band; a behind-the-scenes look at the 1939 filming of Wyler and Goldwyn's *Wuthering Heights*; and biographies of beautiful men from bygone eras of Hollywood: Marlon Brando, Montgomery Clift, Rock Hudson, and Laurence Olivier. I watched *Gone with the Wind* because of Olivier and Vivien Leigh's tragic love story, then read three Vivien Leigh biographies after the fact.

Through an interest in her, I began to read plays and watch film adaptations of Tennessee Williams—particularly *Cat on a Hot Tin Roof*, which captivated me because of the blue-eyed man at its center: Paul Newman.

Back in those middle school days with John at the library, I was also trying to write a storyboard of a film I wanted both to write and to star in about Marie Antoinette and her doomed lover, Axel von Fersen. I checked out multiple books on both of them. I ordered some as interlibrary loans because our library didn't have them, and as this fell under John's area of ownership in the library, he was often the one personally keeping track of my research interests. I think perhaps it was noteworthy to him that a middle-school girl kept returning to order more books on the eighteenth-century Swedish count Axel von Fersen, lover of a beheaded queen and eventual victim of a violent Stockholm mob, who in my movie version of this story was going to be played by Mark-Paul Gosselaar, otherwise known as Zack Morris from *Saved by the Bell*.

"Oh, it's our drama girl here again," John would joke when I showed up at his desk with my stack.

John was the first out gay man I knew, but being in acting class and theater camp introduced me to lots of boys who were either out or virtually there. And when I begin waiting tables in college, I meet T and Rick, who quickly become two of my best friends.

T called me "Kelly Cream Cheese" and rubbed my shoulders every night because he said he was the only boy who knew how to treat me right, and then we'd discuss our families back in the rural places we came from. Rick called me "Pretty Pretty Princess," and we'd share bagels from the deli next to our restaurant and talk about school and what we wanted to be when we grew up, even though both of us were already in our mid-twenties. Sometimes the three of us would talk about what we'd heard about gay people in church growing up and how hard it had been for the two of them to come out to people in Mississippi. T was Black and twenty years older than Rick, who was white, so there were significant differences in the two tales as well.

What I heard growing up in church, and what they said they heard too, was that it was all a formula. If you had a distant father and an overinvolved mother, you got a gay son. If a girl was molested or overly independent, she would probably become a lesbian. Just like it was with church sex talks, where the desire of men was always paramount, it was the gay *men* who got all the airtime. No one really talked much about lesbians. But at least once a month, I'd hear from some adult about the sin of homosexuality and the sin of Sodom and Gomorrah and how gay liberation was going to be one of the reasons Jesus returned amid trumpets and fanfare, from the sky, to judge us all.

Every preacher who'd opined on a Sunday about the dangers of leftward drift in American culture and the threat of being an affirming millstone around a misguided gay person's neck warned us of dragging them, even meaning well, all the way to a literal hell. In my mid-twenties, I still go to churches

CHAPTER 16

that sometimes say things like that. But I don't know if I believe it. There's still a nagging voice in my head some days, chiding me for not witnessing to T or Rick. By simply being their friend and not warning them about hell, am I sending all of us there?

Once when I was sixteen, I was riding home from a tennis tournament with a friend and her mother. The song "Streets of Philadelphia" came on the radio. The movie Springsteen wrote it for—*Philadelphia*, about another tragic and dying gay man of the eighties and nineties—had just come out, and the song won an Oscar. I was moved by it as it played, and I knew my friend up in the front seat also liked it. After the line "I can feel myself fading away," I muttered something sympathetic from the back seat, like, "Doesn't that sound awful? That's so sad. To feel yourself dying young like that. Can you imagine?"

Immediately after I'd said it, my friend's mother slammed on the brakes and yanked the car over into the highway shoulder.

"Kelly Foster, homosexuality is an abomination to God. I don't ever want to hear either of you girls talking that way about homosexuals again. God will spit you out of his mouth if you talk like that."

Between that and several similar incidents, I was keenly aware that even the most perfunctory and abstract empathy for a tragic fictional character could keep you off the straight road to heaven. At least according to some of the adults who were my authority figures. But as Blanche DuBois says in *A Streetcar Named Desire*, "Straight? What's straight? A line can be straight, or a street, but the human heart, oh, no, it's curved like a road through mountains!"

Chapter 17

On our third wedding anniversary, I am beginning my new job at the same college in Mississippi where I read *Women's Ways of Knowing* two years earlier, the same college where I spent the first two years of my teaching career as a graduate teaching assistant. I've now been hired as a full-time junior faculty member, and I am teaching research writing to a group of twenty students. I am teaching my students how to ask the right questions and how to form those questions into an assertive thesis.

Devin pays a local florist to send thirty white and yellow daisies to my new corner office in the English faculty wing. When my colleagues notice the flowers being delivered and congratulate me, I pretend I have forgotten it was my wedding anniversary. I affect disinterest, as if I'm so cavalier about my marriage and yet so simultaneously certain of its foundations, I couldn't possibly be bothered with its mundane details. I don't know why. Maybe it feels like a low-stakes way to punish Devin. Maybe it feels like a way to pretend he cares more about us than I do.

Just last night, I found a new chat room discussion saved to our desktop screen, lying there barely hidden. In the picture, which I clicked nervously, a shirtless white man, tanned and fit, tucked one thumb into a pair of American flag boxers just visible beneath his rolled-down blue jeans, a blue baseball cap turned backward on his head.

CHAPTER 17

"You've got a great body," Devin had written to the man in the baseball cap.

When my own research-writing class ends, I make my way across campus to the red brick building with the high windows. Dr. Miller's Lit for Teachers class is just about to start. This is a summer literary theory intensive for teachers whose lesson plans need reinvigorating. The premise of the class feels as profound to me as it is straightforward: that we need to be transparent with our students about our biases and lenses and presumptions, so that they can see both the baggage and the interpretive lenses we bring with us as teachers to any text. Thus far, we've unpacked New Criticism, Marxism, feminism, and New Historicism.

Today's theory is deconstruction, the taking apart of assumed meaning, and Derrida is its most visible proponent. His is a name I've heard in my last seven years as an English major and teacher, one of those names I am meant to know but don't actually know much about, if I am honest. I think I've even repeated a Derrida joke before to other English majors without entirely registering why or how the punch line was meant to be funny.

It's been only a few days since this class began, but on the heels of a miserable year at the prep school where I never felt I knew what I was doing, it's making me believe anew that teaching matters. Even I might be able to do it well.

Since I am now a faculty member (and I'm allowed to audit this and other classes for free as a result), Dr. Miller tells me I can call him David. I feel elated that he thinks I am mature enough to handle this shift in our relationship from student-teacher to friendly peers. I think to myself often that if I can find a way to just forget about making it to Chicago or some other place full of bigger buildings, I can be content being here as David's colleague: going to lunch with other professors and talking about books and movies and ideas for the rest of my career.

It's a sweltering day, and as I open the door to the red brick building, I can feel gummy rivulets of mascara starting to pool around my eyes. I blink hard to unstick them. In the bright second-floor classroom, David is already seated around a table with four other students when I walk in, and I take my seat at the opposite end from him. He's directly in my line of sight.

I try to slow my breathing so I look less flustered than I feel. In my nostrils, out my mouth. Diaphragm expanding on the inhale, contracting on the exhale. Expand and contract. Three slow times.

For the next three hours, nothing outside this room exists. David will talk. He will be in charge of time. I will not have to try to understand anything about Devin or what it means that—just weeks after assuring me that all his fears about his sexuality were false ones and that he would die if I left him—Devin was logging onto AOL to tell a man with a backward baseball cap that he had a good body. For three hours, I won't have to wonder why.

For now, I will only sit at this wide wooden table with room enough around me to spread my notes. I will take out a yellow legal pad and a black pen. And I will listen and write and think, but only about the words in the books, filtered through someone else's questions. That's all anyone will ask of me for three hours. It will be me and a xeroxed reading about Derrida with "SIGN / SIGNIFIER / SIGNIFIED" in big letters across the front.

The air conditioner in the ceiling vent ten feet above my head will chill the sweat on my skin and blow a small corner of face-framing layers into my right eye. The broad oak trees outside giant windows beside me will sway and make the sunlight flicker on my yellow legal pad. The shadows of the oak leaves will be so vivid that I will be able to trace their fluid curves with roller-ball ink in the margins of my notes.

As I settle myself into my seat, my new acquaintance, Beth, a high school English teacher, smiles at me kindly. She's twenty years my senior. She's got three kids. This weekend, she'll be throwing a party for twenty people at her house just down the street from the one where my grandfather was born, and I will hear about the party on Monday after I've spent the weekend packing up our apartment at Reflection Pointe for the move to Whitworth Street just a few blocks away from her. After class today, we'll chat about the party—about whether or not she'll serve cheese straws, which neither of us really likes, but what's a party in Mississippi without them, we'll laugh.

And then she'll go home where there'll be life: kids with homework, a big snuggly retriever dog, a funny husband with a cocktail clinking in a mint julep cup telling her about his day. And I'll go home to no one, Devin being at work or at a bar after work or at a club after the bar. This happens more and more, and he makes me feel like a drag when I tell him I want him to come home. But I don't have to think about that now.

The adjectival form of Derrida is Derridean, and I catch the alliterative music in the way David says it as he opens class. It's the way a choir director who's beginning practice might say it—eyes up, hands drawn out into the air, his speech somehow both flowing and clipped and well projected.

When he's not teaching or grading or reading in his corner office next to my new one in Jennings Hall, David sings in the choir and reads the liturgy at two progressive local churches and teaches aerobics at the campus healthplex. He does cardio training for the basketball teams. He's a classically trained pianist who grew up on a small farm in New York state. Despite the heat, his short-sleeved button-up and khakis have been meticulously steamed and pressed in a way I will come to tease him about as I get to know him better in the next few months.

His wide-set eyes focus on each of us in turn as he addresses a few "housekeeping" issues, reminding us about upcoming deadlines and homework over the weekend. There's something hard to peg about him—a performative energy, a projected theatrical authority in his voice—that makes him impossible to ignore when he's speaking. As soon as he begins, all five sets of eyes turn to him.

He's the nucleus in this bright room's cell. We are his electrons.

"Well, this will be an interesting day," David smiles as he speaks. "Deconstruction is one of the hardest theories to comprehend—the terminology alone can make your head hurt quickly. But I hope we can consider the possibility that, as a lens, it might also be a liberating one. So let's talk about it."

After calling us to attention thus, David asks us to consider the concept of defamiliarization, of making something common unfamiliar to us so as to understand it anew. He says defamiliarization means to slow down and look twice at something, to interrogate it as if it were unknown.

"Think of a chair," he says. "A chair is a chair. But how do you *know* a chair is a chair?"

He then uses road signs to illustrate. "Only Seeing-Eye Dogs Allowed" could just as easily mean that dogs alone are welcome in that establishment, no humans. "Slow Children"

CHAPTER 17

could mean, among other things, that the children living on the street move particularly slowly.

Signs have meaning, David says, but those meanings are not necessarily set, and that lack of definition often frightens us, which is why so many people, particularly religious fundamentalists—more or less like the ones I was raised among—fear deconstruction. But we all want meanings to be exact and permanent and easily interpreted.

David tells us to take a minute to think of something we know for sure. Anything. It could be that a chair is a chair is a chair. It could be a memory. If could be a feeling. What is something we just know? He gives us a few silent minutes to freewrite about it.

I look at the doodles I've been making on my yellow legal pad.

I consider.

I know my name is Kelly.
I know I was born in Mississippi.
I know I am a girl.

Every year at my high school, ninth graders were required to complete a set of twenty-five biology drawings. I cheated and copied mine. Most people did.

I got the drawings I copied from a friend of mine named Catherine, who was two years older. She got hers from a girl named Saili, two years older than her.

When David asks me what I know for sure and I think to myself, *I am a girl*, this is the memory that comes to me: a

Christian woman on a cassette tape telling me what girls are while I copy someone else's biology drawings.

I am fourteen years old.

Between my legs, there's a glass-topped end table with a lamp on the bottom shelf. The lamp makes it possible for me to trace the outlines of Catherine's biology drawings more easily. I am tracing pseudopods around the purple edges of an amoeba. This is my first biology drawing. I have twenty-four left to go.

Under a microscope, amoebas move along like droplets of water in oil. They shift by retracting their false feet into themselves and then pushing them out again. They roil on glass slides in our biology lab, where, regardless of what we are doing, all I can ever smell is formaldehyde and fetal pig.

"Facts of the body are also facts of the spirit," says a famous Christian woman on the cassette tape playing next to my feet. A woman is a woman. A man is a man. It's not just penises and vaginas, she says. It's not just smaller bodies and bigger ones. It's also about what we need and where we thrive. It's about how God made us. We can't be happy unless we are living in his will, working in the way he made us to work. These are all immutable, incontestable, incontrovertible facts. Bodies and spirits.

Men feel happier when women submit to them, when they are leading women in the way Christ taught them to lead. Women feel happier when they submit to the godly leadership of men.

An amoeba is a fact, though it shifts, and its feet are false ones. So what is the fact of a girl, then? I've never really felt all that attached to most of the things a girl is meant to want, except boys. And I have wanted them so very much. So, other than that, what does "girl" even mean to me now? And what, for that matter, is a man?

CHAPTER 17

Weeks earlier, in my exit interview from that awful prep school job, the chair of my department told me that men need women to shape them so they can become the good leaders God intended them to be. Based on the four times she'd met my husband, she told me my marriage seemed out of balance. I was too aggressive. He was too withdrawn and restless. She told me if I was gentler, less assertive, my husband would have space to assert himself more definitively in our life together. A woman is a woman. A man is a man. What they need is as immutable and defined as every word in the immutable word of God.

I hated what she said and hated her for saying it.

I also mostly believed she was right.

When my thoughts return to the present moment in David's classroom, I realize I've been sketching squiggles in the margins of my yellow legal pad that mimic those old biology drawings: ciliated ovals inside the rounded tracings of oak leaf silhouettes. I'm an adult thinking about Derrida, and I've got a list of declarative bullet points on the yellow legal pad in front of me. It's time for us to share aloud the thing we just wrote about.

It's been three years since my first class with David, three years since he'd helped expose the cracks in those beliefs I'd inherited from church about what it means to be a man or a woman or a person, for that matter. He was the first person to tell me there's a difference between sexuality and gender. He was the first person to teach me the phrase "socially constructed." He was one of the first three people I knew who employed the term "feminist" with a positive connotation. He even proudly wears a T-shirt that proclaims, "This is what a feminist looks like."

David was the first person to make me interrogate my facts and my claims and my beliefs, about anything and everything, again and again and again, so that I will eventually arrive not at "God's truth" but at my own. And now I'm five feet away from him, and he's asked me to consider a fact, any fact that I hold with certainty.

The only fact that arises is that I'm a girl. But I don't even feel all that attached to that. What if even that can be interrogated? What if "girl" and all that I hold when I hear it is as mutable as an amoeba's edges? Calling the class to attention, David asks us how many of the facts were purely autobiographical. All five of us, all women, raise our hands. As it happens, two other women have written the same fact I wrote.

I wonder how they hold that idea of girlness in their bodies or spirits, wherever it resides in them—whatever it is that "girlness" even means.

"Autobiography's interesting, isn't it?" David observes. And what he says next, I write down in my yellow legal pad. He says, "Biography and autobiography are always open to interpretation, aren't they? Two biographies of the same person can come to radically different conclusions based on the same documentary evidence. Even autobiographies are always undulating. Surfaces shift. Viewpoints change. Different personas will be presented."

I don't understand why, but something inside me lightens at these words. Some internal vista broadens. Even my breath comes easier.

CHAPTER 17

Whatever a girl is, whether or not I am the right kind of girl, the *I* beneath gender is deeper. I am a fact, just like an amoeba. I exist. I'm here. I'm in this room. Just like this yellow piece of paper. Just like David, who is looking at me for just a moment as if I am the only person in the room who understands him, as if he knows what I must be thinking.

David continues. He asks us again to consider symbols. Even common ones: stop signs, the American flag, a skirt on a faceless silhouette.

"Breaking these symbols down is critical," he says. "We have to teach students metaphorical thinking. We have to move them from literal to metaphorical thinking. There's more than a one-to-one correspondence between signs and signifiers. It's all so much more complex than that. WE are all so much more complex than that, right?

"RIGHT?!" he repeats louder, smiling, when none of us assent vigorously enough to his previous question.

It's hard to explain why something hits you the way that it does in the moment it does. So much of what he is saying will eventually become the framework of my entire way of thinking. Even now, hearing these thoughts for the first time, they land like things I've known all along. Like truths I've been waiting for someone to preach to me.

I've been waiting for someone to tell me my knowing was right.

"It's even in the Bible," David says. "What is the exit from the garden of Eden if not Eve being taught to think metaphorically? 'If we eat from the fruit of this tree, we will die,' she tells the serpent. And he says back, 'No, ye shall not die.' And the serpent is right! She does not literally die. She is taught that death is so much more than the cessation of breath. It is hours of despair. It is watching sadness engulf those around you. It is waiting for someone to come home who never does. It is hopelessness. It is fear. Death is so many things. 'Ye shall not die, but ye *shall* die.' That's how Eve learns metaphor."

David pauses, lets that analogy settle, then speaks again.

"Deconstruction makes us nervous because we want so badly for things to be definite, and yet things remain so maddeningly hard to define. What's the difference between a dog and a cat? We know these things intuitively, but the more you try to pin them down, the more the differences collapse. Everything has an interpretation. Interpretations differ."

He pauses again.

"Consider the simple sentence 'I love you,'" David says.

I write it down on my yellow legal pad. The clip of a dash. And three words.

I love you.

Underneath each word, I draw an arrow. Beneath "I," I write "subject." Beneath "love," I write "verb." Beneath "you," I write "object."

"'I love you' is much harder to define than it may seem," David says. "Who is 'I'? What is 'I'? How many different things am 'I'? What is 'love'? What kind of 'love'? What are the ranges of meaning within meanings we're using to contextualize that? What are 'you'? Who are 'you'? What does that mean? Is that always static or does it shift? Can 'I love you' ever mean the same thing twice if we are always changing? Deconstruction requires us to ask."

He pauses again.

"'Ye shall die.' 'Ye shall not die.' 'I love you.' None of these things ever means just one thing."

CHAPTER 17

Devin is already gone when I get home around 4 p.m. He'll be at work until midnight. He'll probably head to Martin's after. The daisies were the extent of our anniversary.

I spend an hour trying to avoid another forensic search of our computer history, but eventually, I log on and search for new images again. Even though my hands are shaking while I hold the mouse, my stomach eases when I see the desktop looks the same. No new images. Maybe Devin's just gotten better at scrubbing the search history, and even in the moment, I know that's possible, but the notion that maybe nothing new has happened—no new conversations with men in backward baseball caps—reassures me.

I return to the living room, drink a little wine to still the shaking of my hands, and continue packing boxes for our upcoming move to our third home in three years in Mississippi.

I'm alone on my third wedding anniversary. But Devin and I are moving to a new house, a bright yellow shotgun house with big windows, in a neighborhood I've always wanted to live in. It's funky, well heeled, cool—the same neighborhood where my grandfather grew up down the street from Eudora Welty and where the lawns are broad and the trees are tall and at night, people seem happy when you walk past the windows of their warmly lit Craftsman bungalows. The same neighborhood with the white church we no longer attend because we no longer really go to church at all.

I have a new job, and soon, so will Devin. He won't be waiting tables anymore. He'll be working a nine-to-five in accounts payable for the restaurant management company he's been working with for years.

Maybe we can still move forward.

Maybe we can still start over.

I checked out an audiobook of Amy Tan's *The Bonesetter's Daughter* from the library to listen to while I pack.

When I press play on the stereo, the book opens with this line: "These are the things I know are true."

Chapter 18

As a faculty member at the college, I can audit as many classes as I want. Which is why tonight I'm in a seminar room on top of Jennings Hall prepped to discuss early selections of "Song of Myself" in David's class on Whitman and Dickinson.

On the way up, I stopped by the international food potluck hosted by the global studies department in the building's courtyard. I nibble on a slim triangle of spanakopita with a feta and grapefruit sauce, shrimp chips, ceviche, and a cold sesame noodle salad with black sesame seeds while David goes over his preliminary "housekeeping" notes.

I'm self-conscious about people seeing the sesame seeds in my teeth if I talk, so I'm quieter than usual, which suits me just fine. I don't have the words to say what I want to say about these particular passages on this particular Tuesday night in winter.

We begin with the first few stanzas of "Song of Myself." David maintains that for Whitman, the grass, just like the truth, is manifold. There is no one message from the grass, just as there is no one truth. Here we are again, back at Derrida.

In the margins of my book next to section 6, the famous one that begins, "A child said *What is the grass?* fetching it to me with full hands," I scribble, "Truth is 'manifold.' Grass can be interpreted as many things. There's never just one correct response. There are many." So, in section 6, grass is "the handkerchief of the Lord" as much as it is also "the flag of my disposition, out of hopeful green stuff woven" as much as it is also "a child, the produced babe of the vegetation."

All my motion is arrested, though, as we end section 6 and shift to section 7. Whitman writes:

> All goes onward and outward, nothing collapses,
> And to die is different from what anyone
> supposed, and luckier.
>
> Has any one supposed it lucky to be born?
> I hasten to inform him or her it is just as lucky to
> die, and I know it.
>
> I pass death with the dying and birth with the
> new-wash'd babe, and am not contain'd
> between my hat and boots,
> And peruse manifold objects, no two alike and
> every one good,
> The earth good and the stars good, and their
> adjuncts all good.
>
> I am not an earth nor an adjunct of the earth,
> I am the mate and companion of people, all just
> as immortal and fathomless as myself,
> (They do not know how immortal, but I know.)
>
> Every kind for itself and its own, for me mine
> male and female,

CHAPTER 18

> For me those that have been boys and that
>   love women,
> For me the man that is proud and feels how it
>   stings to be slighted,
> For me the sweet-heart and the old maid, for me
>   mothers and the mothers of mothers,
> For me lips that have smiled, eyes that have
>   shed tears,
> For me children and the begetters of children.
>
> Undrape! you are not guilty to me, nor stale nor
>   discarded,
> I see through the broadcloth and gingham
>   whether or no,
> And am around, tenacious, acquisitive, tireless,
>   and cannot be shaken away.

I've read all these lines before. I bought a small peach copy of "Song of Myself" when I was sixteen, and in that old copy, I had underlined twice, "All goes onward and outward, nothing collapses."

But tonight, it is the last stanza of section 7 that catches my breath—"Undrape! you are not guilty to me, nor stale nor discarded"—falling at the end of an earlier list, a list that, in my mind, includes me as much as it includes Devin, who now increasingly spends his time looking at things on the computer he later confesses to me. Just a month ago, he told me he'd been forced into a sexual encounter at an adult bookstore near our first apartment. We drove two towns away where no one would know us to get tested for STDs because we are still sleeping together and he doesn't always use condoms, and for the first time ever, I got an irregular Pap smear. After we found out we were clear of anything scary, he sobbed in the living room, his head in my lap, when he told me about the bookstore, assured me it was a mistake that he'd been there at all. Assured me he didn't want any of what happened with the other man. Assured me the moment he came home and saw me, he knew I was all he wanted.

In the margins next to the heavily underlined stanza, I write it out for emphasis and personalize it.

"I am not stale nor discarded."

It feels like a promise across time from Walt Whitman directly to me. I carry it home with me and as I have a habit of doing, recite it to myself as I reenter my empty house after class: You are not stale nor discarded. You are not stale nor discarded.

Whitman has catalogs, and there's a place for me in his catalogs. I belong in Whitman's world. And I can still be saved. And so can Devin.

Three weeks later, we return to "Song of Myself" on an almost-spring Tuesday night. The windows in the classroom are open. Along the base of the beautiful old brick buildings on campus, azaleas have formed tight fuchsia buds that will burst and then petal the entire campus in pink underfoot. Crepe myrtles will burst into equally colorful bloom. The entirety of Jackson will be pink.

In David's class, we have returned to our discussion of section 11, the "twenty-ninth bather" section.

Whitman writes:

> Twenty-eight young men bathe by the shore,
> Twenty-eight young men and all so friendly;

CHAPTER 18

Twenty-eight years of womanly life and all so
 lonesome.

She owns the fine house by the rise of the bank,
She hides handsome and richly drest aft the blinds
 of the window.

Which of the young men does she like the best?
Ah the homeliest of them is beautiful to her.

Where are you off to, lady? for I see you,
You splash in the water there, yet stay stock still
 in your room.

Dancing and laughing along the beach came the
 twenty-ninth bather,
The rest did not see her, but she saw them and
 loved them.

The beards of the young men glisten'd with wet,
 it ran from their long hair,
Little streams pass'd all over their bodies.

An unseen hand also pass'd over their bodies,
It descended tremblingly from their temples
 and ribs.
The young men float on their backs, their white
 bellies bulge to the sun, they do not ask who
 seizes fast to them,
They do not know who puffs and declines with
 pendant and bending arch,
They do not think whom they souse with spray.

To aid tonight's discussion, we are using an essay by Michael Moon titled "The Twenty-Ninth Bather: Identity, Fluidity, Gender, and Sexuality in Section 11 of 'Song of Myself.'" I am scribbling in the margins and underlining as fast as I can. Just like the promise from sections 6 and 7, this essay feels like it was written for me.

After describing the poem and its place within the complex and often difficult-to-decipher 1855 edition of *Leaves of Grass*, Moon writes, "The indeterminacies of the 1855 Leaves of Grass also serve the purpose of rendering the text and the dispositions of the body which it represents fluid. . . . Section 11 is perhaps most obviously consonant with the terms that I have argued are paradigmatic ones . . . the 'fluidity,' substitutability, and indeterminacy of masculine identity and sexuality."

Every time I encounter the word "fluidity," I underline it, sometimes twice. In my head I perform its watery vowel sound repeatedly: fluid, fluid, fluid. It becomes almost onomatopoetic, a dripping-faucet word, and it sloshes around in my mind, overwhelming conscious thought.

Just last week, Devin and I watched some reality TV show about a person who goes to a spa and gets an "underwater" massage. He lies in a pool of water and two massage therapists work on him while simultaneously holding him up in the water. He was weightless because both water and hands support him. That image comes to my mind when I think of the word "fluid" now.

I think of water parks and wave pools. I think of lazy rivers and tubing at camp, the lake water splattering me in the face as I'm being pulled behind a speedboat. I think of coming in after a whole day in the Gulf of Mexico with my family, the way I could still feel the waves tossing me around when I fell asleep, the way Devin and I feel at peace, one again, when we return there.

The creation story I've been told my whole life begins with darkness on the surface of the deep, and a God who calls forth order from that primordial roil and froth. But what if all I've been missing is some return to the formlessness of water still beneath those categorical binaries? God is God. Man is God's. Man is man. Woman is woman. One man, one woman. But what would it feel like to embrace Whitman's lists of welcome instead? What would it feel like to know myself fresh and belonging, not stale, not discarded? What would it feel like to play in the water myself? To be one of the pink-house boys collecting beer bottles out west? To be dancing on the bar at Café Lafitte in Exile?

I'd written an entire thesis about Robert Herrick's "Corinna's Going a-Maying"—his own invitation to reject binaries and embrace play.

Fluid. Fluid. Fluid.

Later in his essay, Moon writes of section 11, "The action of the passage serves to bring the excluded figure through the window and incorporate her into the 'fluid' circle."

I think back to our class on Derrida, on deconstruction, this past summer.

I think back to how the first thing I'd thought of as an absolute identity marker was the fact that I was a girl, but what did that mean really? I had so little true attachment to it. David has stressed so many times that gender and sex are different—that gender is socially constructed and sex is assigned, and even that sex markers have radically altered throughout the centuries, depending on what version of patriarchy is ascendant. If "girl" is socially constructed, could I play no role, then, in defining it the way I understand it? Because it means so little of the things I was taught it means when I was growing up.

I don't want to stay at home and do laundry and cook meals. I don't want to wait for Devin to make up his mind about what he wants from life—despite a promising start, accounts payable, the sixth job he's held in three years, has already lost its luster for him—before I get to make up my own mind about what I want.

I want to research Walt Whitman in the basement of a university library. I want to ride a city bus downtown alone and walk for hours along the river. I want to write poems and publish them. I want to present at conferences and see my name on a list of names of people who are thinking about things that matter to me.

But I've been taught, if not by my immediate family, then by church, that women don't choose these things. Women follow. Men lead. If that's what being a girl is, then I'm not that kind of girl. And Devin's not that kind of boy.

But if the categories could be broken, perhaps I could find a way to say what kind of girl I am, and I could feel good about being her. Maybe the same could be true for Devin.

I want to be brought into the circle of play with all the beautiful boys in the water, to shed the weight of condemnation and my own need to condemn, to break all the categories.

I'm sure it's also what Devin wants.

It remains to be seen if we can both want the same thing and stay together. I can't spend two more weeks waiting for the results of follow-up Pap smears because of what happens in a bookstore I never choose to visit. I can't keep choosing to stay because he tells me he'll die if I don't. I need him back. I need the boy who brought me plates of buttered peas back.

CHAPTER 18

I need the boy who asked me to ride in his car at camp back. I need the boy who recorded himself singing all my favorite love songs for Valentine's Day.

In the margins of my notes on Moon's essay, I write, "Does the woman have to hide? What if she really did get out there in the water?" And I guess what I am really saying is, Is it possible for me to stay with Devin and stay afloat? If we can't both stay afloat, then which of us is going to sink first? Is there any other way this can end but in drowning?

When I drive home that night after class to the yellow shotgun house on Whitworth Street, the boys at what we've come to call "the punk rock house" across the street shout their jovial hellos.

I wave back and carry my books inside.

For the moment, I am jovial too.

Devin is drinking what smells like a gin and tonic when he kisses me at the door. I want to tell him about Whitman, the breaking of binaries. I want to be the swim coach of some liberatory fluidity in which we'd both get to live and stay together. I want to push him into the deep end of insight he never sought from me. I've done it before. I will do it again. But tonight, I don't. Tonight, it is enough that we snuggle again, like we used to, on the couch. TBN is on, and Benny Hinn blows a spirit at us, and we laugh it away.

Chapter 19

IF WE WERE EVER TO BECOME THE MAIN CHARACTERS WE'D always wanted to be, we'd have to get to a city, because that's where the main characters live. So, when I apply to English PhD programs and manage to get a doctoral teaching fellowship at Loyola University in Chicago, we jump at the opportunity for a fresh start in the city where we had honeymooned.

Devin goes up early to scout out apartments. And he succeeds: he signs the lease on a beautiful apartment right off the Red Line's Belmont stop, right on the edge of Boystown.

Loyola's Rogers Park campus is also on the Red Line, just three miles north.

I meet Nick the second time I step foot on campus for a graduate student orientation. Nick is friends with another student named Ann, who'd actually given me and Devin a tour of the campus just a few months earlier when we'd come up for a visit.

During that tour, Ann and I had talked about what I planned to study, and when I'd answered that I wanted to write about Walt Whitman, she'd said, "Oh! You should meet Nick! He's a big American lit guy."

When Ann sees me arrive at the orientation this fall, sweaty and still nursing the dregs of a purple yam bubble tea on a ninety-eight-degree day, she brings me right over to Nick.

CHAPTER 19

We end up sitting together and talking quietly for three hours through the entire orientation.

Here are some of the things I find out within those first hours of our acquaintance: Nick loves the Flaming Lips. Nick doesn't love hugs. Nick is a big supporter of Howard Dean. Nick is from Milwaukee. Nick had attended Jesuit schools for most of his educational career. He went to Marquette for high school and then straight into Loyola, whose undergraduate program he just completed. His degree is in English with a focus in queer theory. Nick is four years younger than I am. Nick works at the Camper shoe store on Oak Street. Nick has a boyfriend named Matt who is a flight attendant. Nick and Matt had met at a gym not far from my new apartment on Barry Avenue. Nick lives with a roommate named Sarah but is thinking about moving in with Matt sometime in the next year. Nick's parents know about Matt, and he's been out to them for a few years. It is still weird sometimes, but they are mostly great. He is an only child, and he jokes multiple times, even within that first conversation, that his parents had spoiled him. Nick plans on specializing in American literature and cultural studies just like I am.

I tell him all my similar facts—how many siblings I have, who my husband is, why we moved here, what I am studying.

After the meeting is over, he introduces me to Chris, the campus Whitman specialist who will become my dissertation adviser. As the conversation with Chris begins to stall, Nick whispers to me, "I'm hungry. Do you want to go split a footlong at Subway?"

And we do.

We talk for two more hours at Subway, mostly about the TV shows, movies, and music we both like. Then we walk outside and are still talking on the sidewalk when Ann comes to find us. She says a bunch of graduate students had planned to meet at a bar in Rogers Park later that night, and asks if we'd like to come.

We both say yes.

So, I go home, convince Devin to come out with me, and meet Ann and Nick and Matt and a whole slew of other grad students at Cunneen's around 6 p.m.

The four of us—me, Nick, Devin, and Matt—split pitchers of beer and keep talking for hours before leaving around midnight. And so on this first day Nick and I have met, we've talked nearly nonstop for about ten hours, and from that day until I leave Chicago, we'll pretty much keep that up.

We meet for dinner before class. We meet for lunch. We meet for brunch, sometimes even breakfast. We go to the movies. We grocery-shop together. We sit next to each other in class. We study at the campus libraries, both North Shore and Downtown. I come to his workplace to hang out.

Except on Sundays, when Devin and I sometimes go to church, which we are still trying to do and mostly failing at consistency just as we had in Jackson.

Nick is an atheist and can't understand how I can be as smart as I seem and still attend any kind of church. But he likes me, so he mostly ignores it, and I mostly never talk about God with him.

The appeal of the GBF, or Gay Best Friend, as a trope is so immediately apparent that there are idiomatic terms for women who constantly seek such friendships (hag, fruit fly, etc.), but there are not so many commonly used idioms for being that woman's friend. Neither is her appeal quite so easy to market. There is no *Straight Girl for the Queer Guy*, after all.

CHAPTER 19

But Nick doesn't see it like that at all. He loves me easily from the start, whether I deserve it or not.

And that?

That's why I love Nick, the particular person.

Because Nick does things like that.

Alongside New York City's Chelsea, San Francisco's Castro, and Boston's South End, Boystown is one of the oldest gay neighborhoods in the United States. It isn't for everyone, and it isn't for all boys. The city has recently adopted the more inclusive Northalsted moniker for the area. But my brother, who is gay and has lived in Chicago for over twenty years, says Boystown is just for pretty boys: "I barely know any real queer people who live there. It's a little like Gay Disneyworld."

Like many now openly queer communities, Boystown came to be not long after NYC's Stonewall Uprising in 1969. The surrounding areas of Belmont Harbor and Lakeview had long been places where scattered groups of LGBTQIA+ folks would live or meet up, but it wasn't until the late seventies that a "gayborhood" would coalesce around the area just east of Wrigley Field.

In 1997, the year I met Devin, two years before we visited Boystown on our honeymoon, Mayor Richard Daley officially recognized Boystown, making it the first gay neighborhood of any US city to have that administrative designation and protection.

The neighborhood has long been anchored by Roscoe's, Sidetrack, and Berlin (RIP), gay bars and dance clubs that, like most gay bars of the seventies and eighties, sported impenetrable, blacked-out windows. It wouldn't occur to me until after I'd left Boystown that the visibility inherent in the open windows of the early aughts gay bars I frequented was a recent innovation.

Because homosexuality was still criminal in most US states, the mafia ran gay bars as a profitable side hustle up through the 1970s. They were frequently raided by the police, and after the raids, newspapers would publish the names of all the people who'd been arrested, outing them not only to spouses and family members but also to employers, often ruining their lives with a single article.

Queer resistance to that chronic diminishment and harassment was what helped spark the revolt at Stonewall.

Among the things I did not know when I moved to Boystown in 2003: the extent to which the neighborhood had been decimated by AIDS, and the indifference of a public health system that failed to save them. At that point, nearly 28,000 folks in Chicago were living with HIV, and 12,000 Chicago residents, many of them men in Boystown, had died of AIDS since 1981.

I moved into a history I did not understand. In the time I was there, I was introduced to one of my grad school professors' Foucaultian visions of Boystown as a queer "heterotopia of deviation," which Foucault defines as spaces where "individuals whose behavior is deviant in relation to the required mean or norm are placed." My professor reconjugated the final verb in that sentence, shifting it from a passive construction to an active one. Boystown, he argued, was a heterotopia of deviation in which those whose behavior was deviant in relation to the required mean or norm *placed themselves*. Strength in numbers. Strength in public pride. Strength in solidarity and

CHAPTER 19

visibility. Strength in some shared sense of profound heterodoxy and difference across all sexualities and identities.

Queerness as hope.

Queerness as utopia.

Queerness as teaching the rest of us how to embrace what made us other rather than to hide it.

Queerness as teacher.

Queertopia, we sometimes called it.

I can see now how it all could sound just as imaginary and elusive and even sentimental as the maps of Narnia and Middle Earth that papered my childhood home. As farcical as Disneyworld, perhaps. But for all that, it was a vision of the world that would permanently alter my own.

After a lifetime of fearing my body, it was a revelation to come into a place where no one seemed to fear theirs. And for reasons I couldn't yet fully discern, it was a relief to live in a space where no one was hiding. I was inspired by the bravery of the people who'd made a home there by owning the thing about them that, in so many cases, had exiled them from their friends and family and the places they'd come from. It felt like a resilient place, a joyful place.

Inside those ten blocks lined with rainbowed pylons and banners, all that endangered, isolated, and wounded me in the world outside was suddenly a mark of pride, something to be celebrated.

At least that's what Boystown felt like to me in 2003. Like the freest, safest place I'd ever been. Even if I was only borrowing it.

Chapter 20

I LOVE BOYSTOWN IMMEDIATELY.

And yet, neither Devin nor I am quite ready to let go of the God we've known all our lives, and that God would not have smiled on Boystown.

So, every Sunday morning we can manage the early waking, Devin and I attend an "emergent" Presbyterian church that meets in a theater off the Blue Line. Our fellow parishioners are hip and successful. Students at the University of Chicago and Northwestern and DePaul. Lawyers. Bankers. Med students. The pastor wears blue jeans and quotes Wilco and Johnny Cash in his sermons. Women are allowed to read Bible verses from the pulpit that is really just a podium propped against the stage set of whatever play is being performed there at night.

The theology underneath the chunky glasses and fashionable clothes is almost indistinguishable from the conservative evangelicalism Devin and I grew up with. And sometimes one or both of us go begrudgingly. But usually we are glad to have gone. It feels good, when your life is one constant question, to have someone tell you they have answers. And once again, the answers, the discussions of grace, serve as connection for us. We hold hands. I lay my head on his shoulder. Like before, we fall into our old bed on Sunday afternoons in our new apartment.

CHAPTER 20

I hardly ever discuss the fact that we go to church with Nick. I'm embarrassed to say it. I know how badly his Catholic youth scarred him, and I don't know yet how to reconcile my care for him with my desire for continuity—an ongoing connection to home and the God I grew up with.

The longer Devin and I attend the church in the theater, the more the dissonance between my theology and my increasingly queer community unsettles me. Three or four months in, rather than take the Blue Line to the theater, we walk a few blocks to Lakeview Presbyterian, an affirming and inclusive church draped in Pride flags blocks from us. I'm open to it, kinda. Things have changed for me. Keep changing. I've read Julian and Whitman and Derrida. But there are times I still hear voices from Jackson echoing inside, warning against the so-called heresies of inclusion.

Devin reacts even more strongly against the inclusive churches: "I just don't trust it. You can't just say being gay is okay. I'm just not sure what I think about any of that." So, we mostly stick to the emergent church in the theater that marries progressive aesthetics with conservative theology. And unlike the boy in the poem on his grandmother's wall, Devin is the one getting us there most Sundays.

We fear careening. We cling to guardrails.

Chapter 21

In Chris's doctoral research class, we begin by reading *The Scarlet Letter* and *Dracula*, both books about men who hide truths and women who pay the price for that hiding. Both books about learning to read the signs that are etched into people's skin.

We begin with Hawthorne.

In response to a prompt about our feelings about *The Scarlet Letter*, I write a defense of Roland Jaffe's 1995 film adaptation of the book starring Demi Moore, Gary Oldman, and Robert Duvall. It's not that it achieves any kind of high art or that it is even particularly true to the spirit of the book, but I pin my defense on this premise: "Who doesn't want to fuck Gary Oldman as Dimmesdale?" Because despite the fact that my own undergraduate professor had done little else in our American Literature Survey besides complain about how maudlin Jaffe's film had been, I had seen it at the local dollar theater about six times, because . . . well, I wanted to fuck Gary Oldman in that movie.

It's only the third week of class, but already I've spent hours in Chris's office talking about Whitman and my project and bodies, especially men's bodies as they appear all over Whitman's work. I feel freer to talk about sex than I've ever felt. Our first homework reading was a piece Chris had published about his own masturbatory sexual awakening after eyeing a John Travolta poster in his adolescent bedroom.

At least some small part of me feels like, "Well, since we're discussing sexual awakenings, can I introduce you to Reverend Dimmesdale and the Meadowbrook dollar theater in Jackson, Mississippi, and one very confused and sexually frustrated college freshman named Kelly?"

Nevertheless, I hedge as I'm typing my assignment. Should I really type something so brazen and even cartoonish? Will it make me look completely inappropriate? I wonder how Chris will interpret my little joke, me winking and nudging at him as if we were girlfriends sharing coffee, as if we were Damon Wayans and David Alan Grier giving *The Scarlet Letter* two snaps and a circle on *In Living Color*. Within a few hours of having submitted the assignment, I decide that this is possibly the most self-defeating thing any new doctoral student has ever done. I am mortified at my own presumption of intimacy, certain Chris will not only refuse to speak to me in class, but also decide that he doesn't want to direct my dissertation on Whitman's "Bowery masculinity" after all, thank you very much.

Nick does an actual spit take over drinks that evening when I tell him what I wrote in my *Scarlet Letter* response.

"You wrote WHAT?!"

"I know! I know! It's terrible. I'm an idiot. I am SO embarrassed. I think I just felt suddenly bold because he laughed at that thing I said last week in class about Todd Haynes. And I had a drink before I started typing. And AGHHH! Do you think he's going to hate me? I just thought it would make me seem memorable. Like the funny straight girl who says funny things. Maybe?"

"Oh well," he laughs while still trying to clear his throat, and takes a sip of his martini. "Yes, I think you will have achieved *memorable*," he says while rolling his eyes at me and shoving my shoulder gently. Then he throws his hands up in a resigned way and makes a sort of motion as if to say, "Well, what's done is done. What can you do?"

"I mean," he says, "who knows how Chris will take it? He can be a hard one to read. Maybe he'll think it's funny? I think?" The question mark that punctuates that interrogative is clear in the way he raises his voice.

And it's the question mark that stays with me until I walk into Chris's class the following Wednesday and get his response to my response. I try to remain cool and nonchalant as I glance at it, despite the fact that my stomach is making so much noise that Nick has already commented on it twice.

"Dear, are you sure you don't need to 'use the facilities' quickly before class?" he says.

"Just nerves," I respond. "I'm worried I've already pissed off the one teacher who's remembered my name so far," as my only other professor has insisted on calling me "Lisa" every time he's seen me on campus.

But as I flip to the back of my short essay after everyone else has done so, including Nick, I see that not only has Chris underlined my comment about Gary Oldman, but he has also drawn a smiley face next to a heart in the margins with a note that reads, "I laughed out loud when I read this. And I think the answer to your question is nobody, as in there is nobody who doesn't want to fuck Gary Oldman in that movie."

On another Wednesday night in Chris's class, Nick sets down his student newspaper with an irritated sigh.

"God, another straight girl who's talking out of her ass about something she knows nothing about."

CHAPTER 21

I look up from my notes at this: "Are you talking about me again, sir?"

"She's writing about how *Will & Grace* is reductive to the gay community."

"Isn't it?"

"I mean, of course. It's a sitcom. Who's ever felt that any sitcom accurately represents reality? But it also celebrates gay culture, which is more than what 98 percent of other shows do. I mean, she's writing about us like only if you show us as angels or victims are you allowed to talk about gays. Like gay people can't be shallow. Like Karen is a moral failure as a representative of bisexuals because she's an alcoholic. Like gay characters can't be shallow? Or alcoholics? Do you know how many shallow gay alcoholics I know?"

"There's you, for starters," I joke.

He grins.

"You know, you seem awfully feisty tonight for a girl carrying a laptop wrapped in a bath towel in what is probably the ugliest backpack I've ever seen. What's the color palette you were aiming for with that? Shades of diarrhea?"

"Oh, stop being such a shallow, gay alcoholic."

"Nice quip. Maybe the folks at *Will & Grace* can hire you to be on their C team."

"Think I can march these gams all the way to Tinseltown? Mr. Mutchnick, I'm ready for my close-up," I say in my best Norma Desmond.

"Oh my god. Make all the words stop coming out of your mouth right now. You have a diarrhea mouth to match your diarrhea backpack."

"Shut up. You love it."

As silly and real-life *Will & Grace* as this whole interaction is, that night I transcribe the conversation in my journal because I am so grateful for the levity of it. Nick was funny and aglow with warmth, and he thought I was funny and aglow with warmth, and it had been a long time since I'd felt aglow.

It's ironic that literary theory is so hard to read. And unlike reading the Bible, there are no Councils of Nicaea agreeing on what comprises the singular sacred text. There is no capital *T* Truth to land on. Truths are manifold, and much like reading theology, wars are fought over which of the manifold readings is most definitively true.

As a subset of literary theory, queer theory is hard to read on purpose. As Judith Butler writes in her 1999 second-edition introduction to her groundbreaking 1990 volume *Gender Trouble*,

> Both critics and friends of Gender Trouble have drawn attention to the difficulty of its style. It is no doubt strange, and maddening to some, to find a book that is not easily consumed to be "popular" according to academic standards. The surprise over this is perhaps attributable to the way we underestimate the reading public, its capacity and desire for reading complicated or challenging texts, when the complication is not gratuitous, when the challenge is in the service of calling taken-for-granted truths into question, when the taken for grantedness of those truths is, indeed, oppressive. . . . Neither grammar nor

style are politically neutral. Learning the rules that govern intelligible speech is an inculcation into normalized language, where the price of not conforming is intelligibility itself.... Who devises the protocols of "clarity" and whose interests do they serve? What is foreclosed by the insistence on parochial standards of transparency as requisite for all communication? What does "transparency" keep obscure?

In other words, if queer theory is hard for anyone to read, it's because we've been instructed in what Paulo Freire calls the obscuring pedagogy of oppressors.

In my doctoral program, I read hundreds of pages of queer and literary theory every week. I'm so obsessed with what I'm reading that not even TLC can tempt me. And anyway, most of the time now, I'm studying with Nick at the library or on the benches by Belmont Harbor—either way, we are facing Lake Michigan. Just like at camp. Just like at the beach with my family. My feet in sand when we walk beside the water. Water all the way past the horizon line. Fluid and free. Too deep to even begin to comprehend, which is how literary theory often feels.

From Eve Kosofsky Sedgwick's introduction to *Touching Feeling*: "No deconstruction or dismantlement could really vitiate or even challenge the self-evidence of their exemplary force—these sentences are what Austin's work installs in the mind as performativity tout court, even while rendering nominally unusable the concept of performativity tout court." Along with Butler and bell hooks, I love Sedgwick more than any of the other scholars I am reading.

From Butler's "Desire": "According to this fantastic logic, women are the token of a despiritualized materiality excluded from this higher function of desire, but a materiality that persists as the unspoken and perhaps unspeakable condition of its possibility."

From Jacques Lacan's *Mirror Stage*: "Human knowledge is more independent than animal knowledge from the force field of desire because of the social dialectic that structures human knowledge as paranoiac; but what limits it is the 'scant reality' surrealistic unsatisfaction denounces therein."

Despite the challenge, I learn to use "liminal" and "praxis" and "hegemonic" and "delimit" and "ratiocinate" and "correlative" and "cathect" and all sorts of words that had previously felt cryptic to me. For the most part, I use them correctly.

Eventually, like staring at one of those hidden-image posters you'd find at the mall in the early nineties, meanings emerge.

On the density and comprehensibility of literary theory, scholar Thomas McLaughlin writes, "Theory isn't difficult out of spite. It is difficult because it has proceeded on the premise that language itself ought to be its focus of attention; that ordinary language is an embodiment of an extremely powerful and usually unquestioned system of values and beliefs; and that using ordinary language catches you up in that system."

In other words, it's supposed to be difficult to read theory. That's the point.

―――

Weeks after I copy this line of *The Scarlet Letter* into a notebook, "No man for any considerable period can wear one face to himself, and another to the multitude, without finally getting bewildered as to which may be the true," we begin reading Bram Stoker's *Dracula*.

CHAPTER 21

Chris introduces the novel to us by telling us the entire thing is about being in the closet (coffin) and navigating how to get out. He also tells us that the dates in the epistolary novel (a series of letters from Jonathan Harker to his fiancée, Mina) correspond with the significant dates in Oscar Wilde's 1895 sodomy trial in Great Britain (Wilde was imprisoned from 1895 to 1897 on twenty-five counts of having slept with men). Stoker, himself a closeted gay man, had married the former almost-fiancée of Oscar Wilde.

They shared the same beard.

I think of her sometimes. Florence Balcombe was her name. She was once known as the most beautiful woman in Dublin. She led several literary salons and helped Stoker, whom she survived by twenty-five years, promote the theater he managed for most of his career. They had one child together. Despite her own accomplishments, Balcombe is most remembered for her copyright infringement lawsuit against the makers of 1922's *Nosferatu*, an unauthorized German horror film based on her husband's novel.

Chris said that perhaps this choice on Stoker's part (organizing *Dracula* using dates from Wilde's trial) was not only a kind of fuck-you to Wilde, with whom Stoker had actually been friends for nearly twenty years, but also a kind of talismanic warding off of the evil that had beset Wilde. Stoker would, over the course of his twenty-year on-again, off-again friendship with Wilde, move from semipublic (if anxious) identification with Wilde's sexuality to publicly advocating for the arrest of all homosexuals. And many scholars feel that Wilde's trial and subsequent arrest served as the catalyst for this shift.

But it's not just Wilde with whom Stoker interacted. Chris, who is primarily a Whitman scholar, informs us that Whitman and Stoker had also carried on a correspondence for many years before the publication of *Dracula*.

Stoker had been the first to write to Whitman after reading and loving *Leaves of Grass*. He wrote Whitman a general letter of praise that hinted at later being able to say to Whitman in person all that Stoker "[could] not write," but enclosed within that letter was the following, written on a small slip of paper:

> Be assured of this, Walt Whitman—that a man of less than half your own age, reared a conservative in a conservative country, and who has always heard your name cried down by the great mass of people who mention it, here felt his heart leap towards you across the Atlantic and his soul swelling at the words or rather the thoughts. It is vain for me to quote any instances of what thoughts of yours I like best—for I like them all and you must feel you are reading the true words of one who feels with you. You see, I have called you by your name. I have been more candid with you—have said more about myself to you than I have said to anyone before. You will not be angry with me if you have read so far. You will not laugh at me for writing this to you. It was no small effort that I began to write and I feel reluctant to stop, but I must not tire you any more. If you would ever care to have more you can imagine, for you have a great heart, how much pleasure it would be to me to write more to you. How sweet a thing it is for a strong healthy man with a woman's eyes and a child's wishes to feel that he can speak so to a man who can be if he wishes father, and brother and wife to his soul. I don't think you will laugh, Walt Whitman, nor despise me, but at all events I thank you for all the love and sympathy you have given me in common with my kind.

CHAPTER 21

Multiple interpretations exist of what Stoker meant by "wife" and what he meant by his "kind." Sedgwick points out that public expressions of adoration for Whitman "functioned as badges of homosexual recognition" in Stoker's England. Still, when I read this letter as I was researching *Dracula*, it pierced my heart too. I too felt the same about Whitman, that he'd seen me. That he'd really seen me, reared conservative in my conservative country as well.

You are not stale nor discarded had become a kind of mantra to me, and I felt the truth of it most when I was ensconced with Nick in the comforting stillness of our campus library, reading *The Scarlet Letter* and *Dracula*, trying to parse the sometimes unparseable tongue of literary theory.

Gary Oldman also starred in Francis Ford Coppola's 1992 *Dracula* as the titular character. Perhaps the most memorable scene is one in which Oldman as the withered count—with what appears to be a giant butt on his head—helps shave Jonathan Harker, played by Keanu Reeves. Oldman approaches Reeves after the latter has just nicked himself shaving, then takes the straight razor and uses it to collect blood from Reeves's cut. Turning away from Reeves, he then licks the blood off the knife with a sound not dissimilar to the one Anthony Hopkins makes in *The Silence of the Lambs* after describing the fava beans and the nice Chianti.

By the time I am writing about Gary Oldman, Devin's temporary job at an advertising agency has become a permanent job. On one of the rare nights I am not studying with Nick or he is not out for drinks with coworkers, Devin and I walk down to the giant Blockbuster on Clark Street. I convince him to watch both *The Scarlet Letter* and *Dracula* with me. I'm struggling to write an extended essay about the two films, and I convince him he'll be doing me a huge favor to watch along with me, to sit with me while I research just like he did when I was writing about Julian.

Older movies are not in high demand, and we have no problem finding both films on the shelves. We pick up brats and cheese fries from Clark Street Dog and eat the fries from the paper bag on the way home, wiping cheese and salt off our chins as we enter our apartment on Barry Avenue. Every now and then, we eat out better than that, but I make a paltry stipend. Permanent job or no, Devin doesn't make much more, and neither of us has access to a huge restaurant employee discount anymore. Clark Dog is what we can afford now.

We stay up until after midnight, watching those two movies about hiding and secrets and the ways our identities can get seared onto skin. But I will never finish my essay about them.

Chapter 22

We're watching the 2003 Cubs playoff game, the one where Steve Bartman catches the ball, at Cooper and Brian's apartment when I floated the idea of the Liza look for Halloween. We are only about two blocks from Wrigley Field, and when Bartman catches the ball, we can hear chaos erupt. The apartment shakes. Because of the lag time of the broadcast, we know from the noise that something bad must have happened just before we watch it happen on television.

When the broadcast interrupts itself for a commercial, I turn to Nick and ask him if he thinks I can pull off Liza Minnelli for Halloween. While there would likely be many Lizas in Boystown, I'd likely be one of the few assigned female at birth. "I mean," I say, somewhat apologetically, "sure, it's done A LOT, I know. Liza with her gaggle of gay men. But still, I've got my big brown wide-set eyes. Even my nose looks like hers."

I know Nick not to have too much of a personal attachment to Liza Minnelli, if for no other reason than he is twenty-two years old and not forty-five. But we'd just watched a student film Todd Haynes made once about Karen Carpenter, and Chris had asked us afterward what made a gay icon or an icon at all, for that matter. Liza's name had come up. She was fresh on our minds.

Nick and Devin think I can pull it off, and so I try to.

On Halloween night, while my Liza Minnelli eyelashes dry, I make a seven-layer bean dip to bring to my friends. Even though I don't cook as much as I used to, it sounded good. The Halloween on Halsted parade begins in a couple hours, and I want us all to eat at least a little something hearty before we drink all night.

This layer dip is the kind I have eaten at church fellowship meals and Super Bowl parties and family reunions since I was a child—seasoned refried beans underneath a layer of guacamole underneath a layer of lime sour cream underneath shredded Colby cheese. On top I have thrown salted and drained tomatoes, scallions, and black olives. You serve it in a clear Pyrex so all the layers are visible. When I'm done, it's almost pretty enough to eat, as my Mississippi grandmother might have said, winking.

I wrap the Pyrex dish in clear plastic and stick it in the refrigerator for an hour or so to chill.

The clock on the wall says it's 4:45 p.m. We won't walk up to Cornelia Avenue to our friend Cooper's apartment until 6:30. At least two hours remain before the parade. Plenty of time left to get ready.

I can hear Devin watching TV in the living room. But in the kitchen, the radio plays the news from WBEZ. *All Things Considered.* The weather report says it will be unseasonably warm tonight for October 31.

High of sixty-nine degrees.

"Oh, good Lord," I think, and I wonder which of my friends will be the first to say that it's always sixty-nine degrees in Boystown. I practice how Liza might react to such a joke. She might simply raise an eyebrow or maybe just laugh a little in her dusky whisper.

CHAPTER 22

I walk from the kitchen to the bathroom to check on the sixteen or so individual false lashes I had applied to my lids with tweezers and glue. Although I had lost about six of the lashes from the package in the process of trying to apply them—mangled and crumpled them up past redemption—they are fuller still than I could have hoped for, spidery across my upper and lower lids.

Just like Liza's.

It all started with the lashes for Liza too.

Once when she was asked how she prepared herself to play Sally Bowles for the 1972 film adaptation of *Cabaret*, Liza Minnelli told Dick Cavett, "I was driving down La Cienega, and I saw this eyelash shop. I went in and said, 'Hi there. Whaddya got? I'm making this character, and I want her to be extraordinary!' And she made those big eyelashes."

In another interview, she said of her character, "Sally doesn't want to be beautiful. She wants to be special. And it's the pair of long eyelashes that does it."

While the dip sets, I begin getting ready in earnest. I want to be special too. It may take the entire two hours that remain to get ready, and I know it will matter if I'm not convincing. I bat the eyelashes once. Then again. I move my face quickly back and forth, left to right and right to left. None of the glued lashes fall out.

It was her hair and face as much as her acting ability that some felt free to criticize, even after she won an Oscar for her performance. It was as if they were all Michael York from the movie. As he cuttingly remarks to her as Sally Bowles, "Behaving like some ludicrous little underage femme fatale. You're about as fatale as an after-dinner mint."

I can see why she wanted the eyelashes.

In order to match my Liza, Devin had agreed to dress up like David Gest, and while I prep the dip and turn my attention toward making myself look as much like Liza as possible, he is already wearing his costume—a disheveled tuxedo, open at the collar. And he has already made himself up. The stubble on his square jaw whitened by my ivory foundation. The rest of his olive complexion made whiter too. He had used my violet eyeshadow to blacken one eye and a large black brow pencil to exaggerate his already thick eyebrows.

He walks into the kitchen to pour himself a second vodka with sliced lemons by the time I begin my makeup in the bathroom.

Contours are the key as much as the eyelashes.

It is how you layer things that matters. That is what I took away from the makeup artist my mom had sent me to back in college as well as all the years I'd spent doing stage makeup in plays, and also from conversations I was beginning to have with drag queens around Boystown.

First, I whiten my eyebrows with ivory foundation dabbed on a small sponge. Then I use a cream foundation in toffee to accentuate the lines of Liza's cheeks. I then use a brush to add a thin line of toffee along the sides and the tip of my nose. I blend it all with powder and use a third foundation in "True Medium" to blend them all together. A beauty mark with liquid eyeliner.

CHAPTER 22

Then I line my eyes first with liquid kohl, then with pencil, then with shadow. I add a highlighting base shade along my brow bone in pearl, and accent the deep crease below the brow bone in slate. It is working. All it needs is scarlet lips, rouge, and powder.

Liza Minnelli, gay icon and daughter of a gay icon, was also a beard and a daughter of a beard who was the daughter of a beard.

One biography of Vincent Minnelli, director of *Meet Me in St. Louis*, Judy's second husband, and Liza's father, suggests that the first time Judy Garland attempted suicide, it was after she'd caught Vincent in bed with another man.

"Oh, it was a lavender marriage for sure. I mean, come on, look at him," Chris had said when we'd brought up Liza and David that night in class, the night we were talking about icons.

One definition of "lavender marriage" that I looked up after that night's class suggested it had a particular usage in Hollywood when there was an arranged marriage between a man and a woman, often a celebrity, to conceal the fact that one or both members of the couple were not primarily heterosexual.

If the rumors are true that David Gest was gay, then Liza had at least two lavender marriages.

And so had Judy.

And so had Judy's mother, Ethel Milne. It is why her family moved to Hollywood in the first place. Judy's father had slept with too many young men in small-town Minnesota. They got run out on a rail.

Many sources have pointed out the three-generational proclivity of Ethel, Judy, and Liza to be drawn toward gay men. One of those sources is Judy's daughter Lorna Luft, who discussed how her mother would tease her about her own boyfriend's being gay. However, that wasn't the only quality shared by these three women. All had, at various times, been ostracized or critiqued for their nonconformity to conventional beauty standards.

In a famously acerbic review of Liza's Oscar-winning performance as Sally Bowles in 1972's *Cabaret*, notorious critic John Simon wrote of her, "Plain, ludicrously rather than pathetically plain, is what Miss Minnelli is. That turnipy nose overhanging a forward-gaping mouth and hastily retreating chin, that bulbous cranium with eyes as big (and as inexpressive) as saucers. . . . And given a matching figure—desperately uplifted breasts, waist indistinguishable from hips—you cannot play Sally Bowles. Especially if you have no talent."

I think of my own turnipy nose as I contour and shape it with makeup beside my own saucer-sized eyes.

Once, when asked by Larry King why she seemed to have had such consistently bad taste in men, Liza responded, "I don't know. I guess it's where I grew up. See? I grew up in a land of dreams."

I had never felt more connected to her.

I'd done the same thing in Mississippi, a land of romanticized lost causes and white nostalgia for simpler bygone days as imagined gentry in hoop skirts and bow ties. I'd also grown up somewhere between posters of Narnia and Middle Earth. And for a time, I'd wanted to be onstage and in front of a camera as much as anyone had—including Liza.

On that Halloween, there at the edge of Boystown, the Liza that is me sprays her teased wig one last time. She applies a

CHAPTER 22

final coat of scarlet lipstick. She clicks the garters into place on legs that might be more dimpled than they once were—but still a runner's legs, for all that—and steps into her six-inch heels. She looks down the deep V of her cleavage and wonders suddenly if Liza would call them tits or knockers. Knockers, she thinks. Definitely knockers. Though maybe tits if she was drunk.

Before she calls Devin to come into the bathroom from the living room, she pauses to listen to what he's watching. It's *American Justice*. Or is it *Cold Case Files*?

Either way, it's Bill Kurtis on A&E. They love these shows. They watch them in two- or three-hour jags at night, still snuggled together on the couch—him behind her, one leg draped over hers, one arm across her hip and one wrapped underneath her head and over her shoulder. A wrap sandwich. It's the only time they talk easily anymore, the only time she never questions if he is happy or (harder somehow to answer) if she is—when they are on a couch and there's a show on TV. What they do at home is watch TV, and the shared couch is maybe the only place that for either of them feels most like home.

When she registers the show he's watching, she experiences a sudden moment of doubt. She thinks to herself, What if they just stayed in? What if she just removed the eyelashes? She could wash off all the makeup. She could remove the garters and tights. She could throw the damn heels into her closet for next year. Or for never. It wouldn't matter. They could eat all the dip themselves. The whole bag of Fritos. They could run up the street to Dominick's in their pajamas for frozen pizzas after if they wanted.

Her shoulders unclench at the thought of it.

She takes one deep breath and then another.

He is holding his vodka with lemon slices and tonic lightly, letting the ice hit one side of the glass and then drift slowly back. Aimlessly. Mindlessly. His eyes are on the TV, but his head is leaned into the back of the couch. She can't judge yet if he is tired or sad or merely the kind of empty he becomes when he is watching something.

When he sees her head peer around the corner, he turns to her and smiles.

Sad, she thinks. It is a sad smile, but there is kindness in it.

She forgets that they must leave. Her body forgets, at any rate, and it anticipates a familiar motion toward him—her hips incline in that direction, carrying her toward the couch, heavy with the urge to just recline, to settle into the sturdiness of his body behind hers. But he extends no invitation.

"You ready, Liza?" he asks simply.

And she thinks she is.

Chapter 23

Six or seven hours after I take the bean dip to Cooper's, I'm seated at Roscoe's on a red settee tenderly placing Band-Aids on my blistered feet. From that perch all I see is men in costumes—fifty of them at least—pulsing under strobe lights to a song I don't know. Nick, who has come over to check on me, is dressed as a high school cheerleader in green and gold polyester, his hairy legs exposed. Matt, his boyfriend, is dressed in his old high school band uniform. Matt is dancing with our friend Brian, who is dressed like a 6'3" baby and uses his giant pacifier as a prop, helicoptering it in concentric circles around his head.

Brian and Matt wave and blow kisses in my direction. They've been doing that all night. One of them checking on me while the other waves. I enjoy it but don't understand it.

It's not that their affection comes as a surprise. I know they like and maybe even love me as much as Nick does, but it is this continual coddling, this rubbing of my shoulders, this kissing of my forehead and cheeks and squeezing of my sides, that seems a bit unusual. Short of this set of blister-bled feet I am now sporting, I don't feel especially feeble. And I've had a much better time tonight than I expected. I danced to "Sweet Dreams (Are Made of This)" at three of the five clubs we've made it to, as well as to dozens of other songs I don't know.

But my friends are still watching me as if I'm unhappy, no matter how fervently I reassure them.

Devin dances alone at the edge of a small circle of our friends, his black bow tie now loose and his top buttons undone. His eye makeup and pale foundation have now sweated into cadaverous wedges, more Alice Cooper than Liza Minnelli's recent ex. Cooper is at a high-top bar table talking to Miss Foozie, the drag hostess of Boystown. Just a few hours ago, Miss Foozie was driven down Halsted Street on the back of a small white convertible, throwing candy and shouting "Hello, pineapples!" to the fifteen thousand people who, like us, had come out for her parade.

Cooper and Miss Foozie laugh over our fifth or sixth pitcher of watery cosmopolitans, and when I glance in their direction, both of them wave at me and smile. Cooper leans in and whispers something to Miss Foozie, who looks momentarily serious. Then they walk over to join us.

Nick, who is stroking my jet-black Liza Minnelli wig absentmindedly as if I'm his pet, nods at them and announces, "Kelly's feet are bleeding." He then points, grimacing, to the crumpled pile of waxy wrappers next to me.

"Ugggghhh!" Cooper groans. "That looks awful."

"Poor little pineapple. Hang in there," Miss Foozie coos at me. She pats me on the back, hugs Cooper and Nick, and walks off to continue greeting the rest of her fans. It's 2 a.m., but Halloween on Halsted comes only once a year, and this has been a busy one for her.

Cooper and Nick consult each other in serious tones as if I can't hear them. "Kelly needs to go home. Should I go tell Devin he needs to walk her or should you? Which one of us will he be most likely to listen to?"

CHAPTER 23

"No, no. Don't get Devin yet. I'll be okay," I protest. "I can wait a little longer. Look, I haven't even gotten all my Band-Aids on yet," I say, pointing to my half-bandaged feet.

They look at me doubtfully and then look at each other.

I know what will happen if they tell Devin I'm ready to go home. He'll roll his eyes and say something like, "Of course," and I will feel more like a party pooper than I already do, sitting here with my sad little bag of Band-Aids. But things do seem to be winding down. Matt is yawning. Nick looks tired.

There's a record scratch, and the song shifts, and now it's another remix of "Sweet Dreams." Brian and Matt wave Nick and Cooper back out onto the dance floor, and all the energy that seemed to be draining from the room has returned. Nick shouts at me, "I'll just dance to this one more song, then we'll figure you out. Okay?"

"Have fun! Go dance!" I shout and wave them away from me, smiling.

Now that I'm left alone again, I imagine what it will be like to walk the seven or so blocks home to our apartment on Barry Avenue. I picture the easy give of my couch cushions. I consider shedding the layers of Liza it took me so many hours to put on. I imagine myself turning on the TV, watching whatever syndicated sitcoms or infomercials are on at 3 a.m. while I remove each of the individual lashes I applied tonight. I picture putting thick, soft socks over my brutalized feet.

I'm ready to ditch my push-up bra and the curved wires that have been digging into the sides of my breasts for hours. To place a fleece-lined sweatshirt over my head. To drink several glasses of water and heat up a frozen pizza—something bland with a crunchy bottom. And then, when my mind has sufficiently stilled, to climb into bed and not be aware of anything again until roughly lunchtime tomorrow. Or. Today. *It's Saturday, already,* I remind myself. *It's after 2 a.m.*

I look up at Devin as "Sweet Dreams" ends and some other song—some generic club song I don't know—begins to play, its synth-pop beat heavy and persistent. The lights go white and flash and the steam returns.

Devin and I have been married for four and a half years. I know, after all this time, how hard it is to get him to leave places he isn't ready to leave. Increasingly, it seems the places he never wants to leave are places where pitchers of cocktails flow freely. I watch as Devin walks toward the bar table where our next pitcher of cocktails has just materialized. I try to remember if it's our credit card or someone else's who opened this particular tab.

When Devin gets to the table, he slides around it, though I don't think on purpose, so that his back is facing me. He pours himself another drink and dispatches it quickly. Then he goes down the hall to the bathroom, and he doesn't look back at me.

Matt walks over and smiles a little drunkenly. "Hebiddy," he says.

"Hey, buddy," I smile back. "How are you?"

"Oh, me? I'm fine. It's Halloween!" he giggles.

"Yes, it is," I giggle back.

"You're cute," he says, and he pinches my cheek.

"Awww, you're cute," I laugh, amused at Matt's big grin, patting his hand with my own.

"Nick says those Ragstock shoes Devin and I picked out for you were shitty," he says, sobering up a bit, though still smiling. "Sorry about that."

"Well, I think my feet just weren't used to them."

CHAPTER 23

"Well, listen. If Devin isn't quite ready to walk you home, then I will. Just wave, and I'll come right over. I can sit with you now if you want company?" he says, but he's begun to look back out on the dance floor at lights that are now blinking purple.

"No, I'm not going to ruin your night. Go dance. I'll wave if I need you."

Ordinarily, I'd walk myself home. I'm twenty-six years old. People are always out all night. Running. Walking dogs. Stepping out to one of the three or four all-night diners in our neighborhood. Ordinarily, Boystown is one of the safest places to walk home at any hour. But the last few weeks have not been ordinary. In that time, there has been a series of 2 a.m. rapes of women walking alone in our neighborhood. One rape occurred just a week ago on the street where Devin and I live.

The other obstacle to a quick walk home is the fact of my bleeding feet. Who knows how many bottles have been broken and scattered across our sidewalk over the course of this long night? I don't think it will be possible to walk back in my shoes, but walking home barefoot feels equally impossible.

While I ponder my exit, Matt returns to the dance floor. Devin does too, though he's still not dancing with any of our friends, and now that I'm watching them, I notice he's not looking at them, and they're not looking at him. Noticing this unsettles me much as the solicitude of these friends.

As I'm watching all my boys dance, wondering what they are thinking, out of nowhere, a man in a red Rita Hayworth dress comes to join me on the red settee. Rita's wearing a wig with a cascade of auburn pin curls that frame her face. Her dress is bright red, and there's a heart-shaped dip where her breasts, if she had them, might be. The dress is just loose enough that, through the slightest gap between skin and fabric, I can discern the foam edges of falsies stuffed beneath each risen heart. She sits with legs uncrossed beside me. She appears as over Halloween as I feel and just as ready to be home.

Rita grins at me and nudges my leg with what looks, at first glance, like a small, oddly shaped picket sign. "Well, hello, Liza," she smiles.

After the four hours it took me to get ready, and the six hours I've now spent hopping from one bar to another along Halsted Street, I feel gratified every time it's immediately apparent that I'm dressed as Liza Minnelli. It feels almost as good as getting a callback to an audition. It feels like I've hit my marks.

I've rotated responses to shouts of "LIZA! HEY, GIRL!" all night—acknowledging the shouts by doing jazz hands and an improvised version of the Charleston. Or I've danced while singing a few bars of "Cabaret," usually falling back on the chorus itself ("What good is sitting alone in your room? / Come hear the music play!"), which is all I really remember. But it's late. I don't want to do jazz hands. I don't want to sing.

"Hello . . . Rita Hayworth?" I say simply, not quite sure.

"Almost," Rita laughs, flipping the sign over so I can see the front of it. "Lovely Rita, Meter Maid. Get it?"

I can see now that the picket sign is meant to look like a parking meter. I laugh hard. "That's genius," I say. "My dad had an old vinyl of *Sgt. Pepper*. I used to listen to it all the time."

"Me too! Well, thank you, Liza. I must say, though, I am done with this damn dress, and I'm ready for all my stupid boys to take me home so I can get some sleep."

"Me too!" I say, almost too loudly even over the loud music.

Rita laughs. "Boys are stupid."

"Yes. Yes, they are. Very stupid."

CHAPTER 23

"Which stupid boys are your stupid boys?" Rita asks me.

And one by one, I point out all five of them: Nick, then Matt, then Cooper, then Brian, and finally Devin, now leaned alone against the side of the high-top table, squeezing an extra lime into another highball of diluted cosmopolitan.

"That one's my husband. The one with the square jaw and the pretty eyes," I say, batting my own eyelashes and smirking in the comfortably flirtatious style I've adopted these last months in Boystown.

"Oh, okay, I see," Rita laughs. Then she stops laughing, and looks serious for a second, seeming to wake a bit. She leans forward and turns all the way to face me. "Wait," Rita says. "Your husband or Liza's husband?"

"My husband," I say. "We just moved here six months ago from Mississippi. That's where I'm from. He's from Oklahoma, actually. But we lived in Mississippi for the first few years after we got married. He works downtown in advertising. I'm studying English at Loyola. I'm getting my PhD. I'm getting my PhD in boys, actually."

I don't know why I'm volunteering all this information or why what I'm volunteering is spilling out of me so quickly, but Rita still looks confused, as if I'm suddenly speaking all this in another language, and I guess if I keep giving information, what I'm saying will start to make more sense.

"I'm getting a PhD in boys," I repeat, and I hiccup, two hours after my last drink—the hiccup is the onomatopoeia of a drunken cartoon mouse. It sounds like *hiccup*. I laugh at myself.

"Wait. Circle back," laughs Rita. "That's a thing? A PhD in boys? What the hell is that?"

My dissertation has the working title *Bowery Masculinity: Sexuality and Class in Thomas Wentworth Higginson's Cri-*

tique of Walt Whitman. Because my master's program back in Mississippi required nearly triple the amount of coursework as Loyola's, I'm already ahead of some third-year PhD students. I began nearly ABD (all but dissertation). Despite that, when it comes to writing, I'm still just scribbling out endless research notecards, holed up with Nick. And I've got time to change the dissertation's title if I want to. To save time lately I've just been joking that I've decided to get a PhD in boys. It's quicker.

"Well, hmmm. That sounds like a lot of reading," says Rita, in what feels like a diplomatic tone. "I'm a doctor of putting people to sleep."

"You are?"

"I'm an anesthesiologist. I'm on call all day Sunday, but I'm hoping to spend all of tomorrow sleeping and watching movies. Do you live close?"

"Yeah, not too far—just in a walk-up over on Barry Avenue," I say. "How about you? You live close? I forgot to ask which stupid boys are your stupid boys."

"I live just down Cornelia, and my stupid boys are all dancing right next to your stupid boys. I'm going to go tell them I'm ready to walk home. You better go tell your husband over there to walk your pitiful little Band-Aids back home . . . He's very cute. You're right. Well, nice to meet you, Dr. Liza, PhD. Lucky, lucky Liza. Good night."

In the elliptical space between the "home" and the "he" where, if she were Southern, Rita might have inserted a "bless your heart," she scans Devin's face over at the table, and then she scans me, not intentionally, but I watch her eyes. What I read in that scanning is what I always read when people look at us: that I am lucky to have landed him. If we are cardinals in winter, he is red and I am brown. I know this is the way of

CHAPTER 23

all cardinals—boys are red and girls are brown—but I feel it more than usual tonight. I can be pretty enough when painted. But despite the faded makeup running down his face, Devin is always beautiful. There's no getting around it.

What I can't quite place is the gravity in the way Rita has called me "lucky." It feels heavy, full of pity. But who's pitiful? Maybe we don't exactly match, but surely neither of us deserves pity.

I don't have time to keep puzzling it out. Devin is walking over to check on me. He's clearly very drunk, but he isn't silly and smiling like he usually is when he's drunk. "Nick said your feet look awful" is all he says, and he stares at a space on the wall above me, waiting for me to respond.

"I used up all my Band-Aids," I say, in the same coy voice I'd used with Rita. After all, Devin's the one man in this room I know can be counted on for sex. It makes infinitely more sense for me to be flirting with him than with anyone else. But he's not having it.

"I'm not ready to go home and stay there, but if you're ready, I'll walk you."

"What? So you'll just come back out? Isn't it already like 2 a.m.? Do I just have to wait up for you?"

"God, Kelly. You can go to sleep alone. You're an adult. Besides, you're the one who has to grade papers tomorrow. I've got nothing to do. I can sleep as late as I want."

It isn't the first time lately he's attempted to sway me with this logic. I was grading, so he was going out. I was reading at the kitchen table, so he was going out. I was on the phone with my parents in Mississippi, so he was going out. I'm tired of feeling like I have to fight him to stay home, so I shrug my shoulders.

"Okay, guess I'll just heat up a pizza by myself, then," I say, one last Hail Mary pass, thinking maybe I can sway him by appealing to the comforts of our apartment.

"Yeah, I'll just come back out. You'll be fine," he says brusquely. But for the first time since he walked over, he flashes a smile that feels real at me and pats me on the back. It's the first time he's touched me since we got to Roscoe's. I can feel the warmth of his fingers on my skin after he takes his hand away.

Devin grabs our coats, and opting at last for bare feet, I tuck my shoes and tights into the soft purse I'd brought with me, grabbing my waxy Band-Aid wrappers to throw away in the garbage can just by the door. I blow kisses to my stupid boys.

"Be careful! Love you! Call you tomorrow!" Nick shouts after me.

"Love you too!" I shout back, while Devin helps me get my coat on.

He wraps one arm around my waist and carries my bag with his free hand.

"Alright, my Liza, let's get you home to bed," he mumbles solicitously, suddenly kind. I can't piece out the shift in his tone, but I'm so tired that I only feel grateful.

"Yes, please. Thanks," I murmur, tucking my head into the soft skin beneath his neck, which smells, even sweaty, like soap. Like home.

Chapter 24

IF I HADN'T MADE THE BEAN DIP, WE MIGHT NEVER HAVE GONE back to Cooper's the night after Halloween. We might never have gone over to pick up the clean Pyrex dish at the same time Matt and Nick had also happened to come over to pick up their jeans and T-shirts. We might never have agreed to head over to Cocktail for a quick drink before everyone retired to their respective homes for a more relaxed post-Halloween evening in.

After grabbing the Pyrex, Devin and I are only planning on bratwurst and cheese fries from Clark Dog and a rewatch of *The Sopranos*, season 2. But when Matt and Nick ask us to come out for a quick pitcher of drinks at Cocktail, we both say sure. Why not.

Cocktail isn't crowded for a Saturday night, so we easily snag our favorite high top, the one with four soft swivel chairs. Pouring myself a cranberry-colored martini out of the clear plastic pitcher, I chalk up the lack of people to last night's collective debauch. Everyone is doing what I am about to be doing: staying home and eating something fried and salty. I'm still exhausted and mildly hungover. I'd graded all afternoon while Devin did laundry and picked up the house and bought groceries.

Much as I love both Matt and Nick, this outing feels like one more hurdle to get over before I can just hunker down at home again and be left alone. I'm trying to be polite, but I'm clear that I intend to be home and on my couch after one round of drinks. Only one round.

That's all I'm thinking, when the moment arrives. A moment that might not have ever arrived if we'd never gone out or if we'd sat at a different table or if we'd lingered just a few minutes longer at Cooper's apartment collecting our things.

If the bar table is a parallelogram with one corner facing the stage, I am seated to the left of the vertex that faces the door. Devin is seated to my right. Matt next to him, and then Nick to Matt's right and my left.

From my peripheral vision, I notice two things at once.

First: To my left, I notice that Nick sets down his glass abruptly and shakes his head at Matt. He seems panicked by something.

Second: To my right, I see a brunette man in a camel-hair coat approaching Devin. I won't put together any details of his face at all—if he had a beard or didn't, what age he seemed to be, what kind of haircut he had. All I remember is brown on brown. Brown hair. Brown coat.

I won't remember, in part, because as soon as Nick sees him coming, he puts his hands on each of my knees beneath the Pyrex dish and turns my swivel chair to face him. I have to grab the dish to keep it from falling and shattering at my feet.

"Have you finished your response essay for Chris?" he asks me, loudly, I think, in a way he doesn't have to, because it's not that crowded.

To my right, I am trying to hear the conversation taking place between Devin and the man in the camel-hair coat. All that I can piece together is the man saying, "I saw you at Clarke's a couple weeks ago at breakfast," and then Devin responding in a way that sounded defensive that I was his wife,

CHAPTER 24

which seemed a weird response to what sounded like a fairly innocuous statement.

I attempt to turn to my right to acknowledge the conversation taking place about me, but once again, Nick turns my chair, this time hard, toward him. I'm confused.

"Hey! You know what? I'm getting tired. I don't know if I feel like a drink anymore. Do you think we should all just walk home? I'll be happy to walk you if Devin isn't ready."

"No, that sounds good," says Devin, the man in the camel-hair coat already walking away. "I just . . . ummm . . . I just have to go to the bathroom real quick."

When Devin returns from the bathroom, he is gray. He looks leeched.

"Do you mind if we go now?" he asks me solicitously. "I'm not feeling great."

Matt and Nick are already gathering their coats.

None of us have even half-finished our martinis.

Matt offers the pitcher to the table beside us on the way out, and he makes our excuses to the bartender for us.

"One of them got sick," he says. "Long Halloween!"

The bartender waves back knowingly.

We say goodbye to Nick and Matt, and I walk Devin home in silence.

I know something just happened.

I don't know *what* happened.

But I know something just happened.

Did Devin throw up in the bathroom?

Why?

He was feeling fine when we left home.

As we walk up Orchard toward the back entrance of our apartment building, I ask him what just happened.

He tells me that the man who came up to talk to him had told him a few weeks back that he liked Devin's leather jacket—the one with the smooth leather that looked like a blazer—the one his parents had given him last Christmas when we were in Oklahoma.

"He was telling me he remembered seeing me at breakfast a few weeks ago at Clarke's, but obviously, he just had me mixed up. We haven't even eaten at Clarke's yet."

"Oh," I say, feeling for what feels like the fortieth time since I saw the man with the rolled-down jeans on our computer that this is not the entire explanation, but feeling equally that I have no way of locating a better one.

"That's all?" I ask, pressing him a bit further. "You're sure?"

"Yeah, that's all. Absolutely," he says, and he looks at me to underline his certainty. "That's all. Just a mistake."

About the time we get to the door outside our apartment, I remember that we forgot to rent a DVD or get dinner in all the confusion. Devin bought groceries today, but there's nothing quick to make, and nothing that sounds good to me right now. I ask Devin if he wants anything, and tell him I'm just going to run up the street to Clark Street Dog and get us some bratwursts and cheese fries and pick up *The Sopranos*.

He says his stomach still feels unsettled, and maybe he has a virus.

I tell him I'll be twenty minutes, and he settles himself on the couch, but he doesn't take off his jacket.

When I get back, I find a note taped to the front door. It's from Devin. It says, "One of my friends from work called, and he needs to talk. I'll be back in a couple hours. Love you."

I set down the warm bag of food on the coffee table, take off my shoes, and go into the kitchen to pour myself a glass of

CHAPTER 24

water. I change into my pajamas and decide, after eating the first bratwurst, to eat the second one too. Over the course of the second episode of *The Sopranos*, I also polish off the large cheese fries, and even though it's later than I usually let myself have caffeine, I pour myself a cold Cherry Coke from the fridge.

By the time the third episode of the first DVD has ended, it's 10:30. Despite having slept until noon, I'm utterly exhausted, and all my best attempts at avoidance aside, I keep mulling:

What happened tonight?

Why would he leave to talk to a coworker? He's barely mentioned any of his coworkers since we moved here, other than to repeat a few jokes here and there. They all sound nice enough, but it surprises me that he would get a call from one of them on a Saturday night asking him to lend an ear. I don't understand it.

I want to sleep.

I want things to just feel normal.

I want to know why Devin isn't home yet.

Eventually, I brush my teeth, and try to read myself to sleep, but my eyes won't stay focused on the words. They blur and blend. At some point, I fall asleep with the lamp on. I wake with a jolt at 2 a.m. and look around. Devin still isn't home.

I try but can't fall back asleep. When I call Devin's cell, no one answers. I call three times, each time feeling myself become, for the first time in ages, angry. Really angry.

At 3 a.m., I get out of bed and turn on the TV. I wrap myself in a blanket and hunker down on the couch with the remote control. I'm pulsating with anger, and the motion of it inside me keeps me awake. I turn the channels, but nothing's on—just infomercials: weight loss, skin care, a better vacuum, a waffle maker that you can make cupcakes with.

At 5 a.m., Devin finally stumbles through the door, barely awake.

I don't know why this time is different.

I don't know why I don't care anymore if he tries to make me feel bad for wanting him to come home.

But I don't care.

In the years to come, there will be a gap in my memory between the moment he walks through the door and the moment—could be ten or fifteen minutes later, maybe less—I am seated on the bed and he is standing in the doorway to our bedroom and he begins to talk. I know I must have told him it was time for him to be honest, but I won't remember how I said it or why, finally, he was ready to take me seriously.

All I will see when I look back on the scene, as if through the roof of the building, is us from above.

My feet are tucked underneath my hips, which are on the edge of the bed—the denim Ralph Lauren comforter we chose for our wedding registry is tangled beneath me. When I break eye contact with him to look down in order to straighten it, Devin says:

"That weekend you went to visit your parents back in October, I went to Berlin . . ."

Berlin is a gay club practically underneath the platform of Belmont station. I've stood above it every day for months, but it's the one club I haven't been to yet. Unlike some of the newer clubs along Halsted, the windows are still closed and blackened—not because of any mafia history (Berlin didn't open until the early eighties), but because it makes for better light effects at night, and I'm sure it also helps with heating and cooling bills. Also: It's great for privacy.

Devin continues: "I met someone there."

A pause.

CHAPTER 24

A long pause.

He begins to cry.

What I won't know yet—because Nick turned my chair—is that the man in the camel-hair coat at Roscoe's didn't just say he saw Devin at Clarke's. He said the name of the person he saw Devin with at Clarke's. And that was the same person he'd met at Berlin, the same coworker he'd gone to meet just now.

The rest of what Devin does tell me takes three hours. I don't move from the edge of the bed from 5 a.m. until 8. The room is hot. At a certain point, Devin sits on the floor. He sobs every time I speak. When I tell him I need to go to the bathroom, he puts his head between the arches of my two feet and wraps both his arms around my legs so I won't leave even to do that.

At the end of the first conversation, I learn that the weekend I was gone, Devin went home with someone else, and that this someone else wanted to sleep with Devin, and that Devin had started to let that person sleep with him, whatever that meant, and then changed his mind and stopped it all.

That is all he tells me at first.

Then he tells me about this one time in Jackson. Actually, these two times in Jackson. Actually, no, there were more than two times in Jackson. A couple of times when he met someone off the internet. It wasn't just that time in the bookstore. He sobs so hard as he tells me these stories that I can barely understand him.

For my part, my eyes are aching. But I can't cry.

All I know now is that the confusion he's told me about all this time wasn't really confusion. How the hell had I missed it? What kind of self-deluded idiot misses the fact that her husband has been cheating on her for most of the time they've been together?

After he tells me he's cheated four or five times, maybe six times, he tells me that every time he cheated, he came home and knew he loved me, that he knew he wanted to be with me, and that it was the last time he would ever cheat.

He swears to me that he'll call a therapist that night. We'll set up an appointment for Monday.

He will.

We do.

We talk for hours and hours that Sunday afternoon. It occurs to me that now that I know he has cheated on me, it might be alright for me to leave. The thought has flitted through my mind more than once in the last couple of years, but I've always found a reason to stay. Devin is home. We have these phases of disconnection, but they are cyclical. There's always a rented movie. A drive to take while listening to music. The comfort and complications of our families to parse. But now, even though I'm not even sure I believe in the old church logic of marriage and divorce at all anymore, I think, "Biblical reason. I have biblical reason now. I could start all the way over." But I feel guilty for my flash of relief at the thought of just getting out of here, when I look at Devin on the floor sobbing, still reaching over periodically to wrap his arms against my legs.

At some point later that night, we walk to the Bagel on Broadway and split a matzo ball soup. Devin keeps looking at me warily like I might get up and run away from the table at any moment. I don't run, but I am also not there anymore. From the moment he said, "I went to Berlin," something essential in me left my body and remained outside me, watching us.

Chapter 25

COUNTERINTUITIVE AS IT MIGHT SEEM, I THINK PART OF ME wanted to move to Boystown so Devin could, around us and through me, know other men who felt attracted to men. I thought if he knew other men who'd been ostracized and bullied like him and who, I assumed, knew the profound loneliness he must often have felt, that it might settle him. I wanted him to name these fears about himself until he released them and came back to me. Essentially, I wanted this gay place to make him straight. You might not call it conversion therapy, but not even Liza could dance her way around the truth of what I expected from him.

Maybe I wanted to move to Boystown because I wanted to play detective and anthropologist the way I had back in my hometown library. Maybe it's just that I've spent a lifetime feeling drawn to gay men, even when I didn't fully clock that reality. If *Queer Eye* 1.0 and 2.0 have taught us anything, it's that so many of us want some platonic ideal of a gay best friend. Maybe I unconsciously went there looking for my own personal Fab Five.

Maybe I just wanted to force an ending of our marriage. Maybe he did too. When I look back on how rapidly things escalated after we arrived in Boystown, it doesn't seem implausible. What I do know is that every chance I get in the weeks after Halloween, I ask Nick and Matt questions about what it had been like for them to be queer kids growing up in smaller places than Chicago. They know more about me and Devin than they let on, but they are gracious enough when they are with us together not to let it show. Behind my back, they've chastised Devin for taking his time telling me all of his truths. But I don't know that yet.

So, I volunteer stories to them about Devin being bullied, hoping it'll encourage him to connect with them. He nods along good-humoredly. If he minds me speaking for him, he doesn't show it. I ask them about their own high school experiences on a night the four of us—me, Devin, Matt, and Nick—are seated at yet another high-top table back at Cocktail.

"Well, suffice it to say, we both got called bad things that rhymed with our surnames."

It takes me a second to process what those might have been. I must have showed this on my face, because Nick fills in the blanks: "Girly and F-gner."

In addition to all other possible motives I had for Boystown and my PhD in boys, I wanted Devin to stop hating himself, with the idea that perhaps if he stopped hating and berating himself, he would be able to love me, no matter what sorts of sexual attraction or confusion he felt.

Because that was the thing. He didn't want to be gay. All my life before grad school, I'd been taught that being gay was like being an alcoholic. Sure, maybe you were born with a predisposition, but you could avoid it.

I will find out later that in the arguments Devin had with Nick and Matt, they encouraged him to come out, to accept

CHAPTER 25

what he wanted and the ways he wanted to love and be loved. It's not because they didn't love me; far from it. They were making that case so that Devin would stop lying to me and give me the chance to move on. They were making the case so he no longer had to hate himself, but they were making it without the agenda I had.

They had told him it was pretty clear that he was actually gay. But he had said, "I don't want to be gay. Gay men are obsessed with sex. That's not who I want to be."

When Nick responded to him that they weren't the ones cheating on their partners, Devin had no response.

Devin never used the phrase "conversion therapy" or even "ex-gay therapy" to describe the years he spent with Dr. B. He said things like "same-sex attraction therapy" and "false images" or "exposure and response therapy" when he was discussing the ways he felt confused about what he wanted.

Having never had much personal experience with those phrases, I didn't have a means of contextualizing the things I found on the internet about sexuality and people who want not to be gay but fear they are.

In our first session of marriage counseling, Devin tells the therapist he doesn't want to be gay. When he argues that the encounters he's had with men and the fears about his desires are just obsessions like all his others, the therapist's response is veiled. I can't read it. But Devin's so miserable, so palpably sad, that I think to myself that maybe if you really, really don't want to be gay, you shouldn't have to be. He is afraid. He is afraid to tell his parents about the boys he's loved and slept with. He is simultaneously afraid to tell Nick and Matt that sex isn't simple for him—that he isn't lying to himself when he sleeps with me. He is afraid to tell the people he grew up with. He is afraid to tell the people he works with. There is nowhere he can easily belong right now. Not even Boystown, which at least then was a safer place for me than it was for him. Not because they wouldn't have welcomed him if he was out and certain, but because his uncertainty made belonging that much more unattainable.

One November night after he's gone to sleep, I sit on our brown couch beneath our framed engagement photo. I type the phrase "men who don't want to be gay" into my search engine. Up pops a site from a group called Love Won Out, and beneath that, Exodus International. They seem to be describing Devin. They seem like legitimate sources. There's the language of therapy all over it. Nothing seems overtly Christian that I can perceive, at least not from this first glance. My fingers are shaking as I keep searching. I don't know the extent of why, but despite the veneer of care, something about these sites feels deeply wrong.

They mention how no one should have to be what they don't want to be. How if a man wants to be straight, he should be allowed to be straight without being condemned. They mention how if what a person wants is a wife and a family, that should be possible. They mention how so many men who identify as gay have been bullied and shamed and judged, and how their services and groups could help those men see that their inner conflicts could all be chalked up to confusion. It felt like gracious language. It felt generous. Who wouldn't want to choose who they wanted to be if that was an option? Who wouldn't want to belong in the path of least social resistance? If he loves me, if he's desperate for me to stay, as he says he is, wouldn't he want to give this a try, maybe?

The next morning, I bring the websites up to Devin while we are walking to Intelligentsia and then to Belmont Harbor.

CHAPTER 25

"NO!" he almost shouts, just loud enough to embarrass us both.

"Sorry. Sorry. But absolutely not," he says, more quietly. "It's just . . . let's just say that's a lot of where I come from. That's the curriculum that I used when I was younger, and it sounds good at first, maybe. But no, I don't want that. I can't do that again."

I don't understand yet.

But I never bring it up again.

I loved Boystown.

I talked to Nick every day. I loved Matt and Brian and Cooper. I loved the queer classmates I was just beginning to get to know: Zach, Katrina, Joy. I loved my queer professors. I felt loved and cared for, and despite everything happening, I did my best to reciprocate that care. Every day, the assumptions I'd been taught in my youth about gay "agendas," and gay people more broadly, were being demolished over and over.

There were moments late at night when the hard-won joy that surrounded me with my friends out among the people of Boystown felt like more of a blessing than I'd ever known in a church. It felt like walking up to a Catholic priest during the Liturgy of the Eucharist, an outsider to the ritual, unable to take the host onto my tongue but able, nonetheless, to cross my arms over my chest, to bow my head in reverence at the sacrifices that made the sturdy joy around me possible, and to walk away consecrated, hallowed, made more whole.

And yet, I was also beginning to believe, that in the words of the Lady Macbeth I'd once played in high school, the secret goal of at least a portion of the men I saw out in Boystown was to unsex me. In 2003, a phrase still in common parlance today to describe straight women who spend most of their time around gay men was "f-g hag."

Some of my friends in Boystown used to play on that affectionately when they were around me. They'd say things like, "What a cute little hag you are!"

The image that came to mind when I thought of hags was the old woman that the Evil Queen (whose entire motivation for murder derives from the threatening of her sexual potency: "Who is the fairest of them all?!") in Disney's *Snow White* transforms into. That unsexed queen, that cartoon hag, had scraggly, gnarled, wiry, gray hair and bulging, droopy eyes as well as a humped back and wrinkled skin. She had a single tooth and a giant wart on her nose. Like most of the other hags I'd heard of, she certainly didn't read as fuckable in any conventional sense I knew. She was unsexed.

Every now and then, I'd feel Boystown's most judgmental eyes on me when I walked down Halsted or Broadway or Clark. Some of this might have been resentment about a probably obviously straight woman infiltrating a neighborhood that gay men had carved out for themselves. But occasionally I'd also catch a whispered pejorative about my makeup or my pants or my shoes. It certainly tracked with what I'd heard from T and Rick at the restaurant while they frequently "fixed" my face or collar or belt as soon as I walked into work. And Devin had always teased me about my lack of attention to my clothes. Once he burst out in exasperation that I'd just walk around in pajamas all the time if it were all up to me. Nick and the other boys often teased me about my bag and my shoes and my hair.

CHAPTER 25

It's the same thing that would happen to me years later when I was walking down a street with friends who lived in Provincetown, Massachusetts. "Honey, take those chinos back to Old Navy!" a stranger outside a gift shop said to me. Days later, another man commented to his friend, the two of them walking past me while I was sunbathing on the beach in a bikini, "Well, not all of us were made for bikinis, were we?"

It's the same thing that would happen to me in Slovakia, when I immediately befriended a then-closeted gay man on the leadership team of the English language classes I was hired to run. "That purse looks like fish scales," he volunteered the first time he met me. "You should throw it away." Two nights later, when we were all throwing a Frisbee around, he said that the salmon-colored athletic shorts I was wearing were "so ugly they don't even deserve to be burned."

The truth is, while my sexuality has always been clear to me—I've only ever been attracted to men, to belly hair and leg hair and penises and wide shoulders and deep voices and all of it—my gender is something to which I've never felt particularly attached. If I'm a girl, it's as squiggly a fact as that amoeba I drew once. I grew up with brothers and mostly boy cousins. I had interests that skewed masculine: sports and military history among them. I could quote all three *Godfather* films from memory by the time I was sixteen. I have watched every single Ken Burns documentary at least twenty times. I was more straightforward in my career path than any man I knew. I had bigger and more ambitious vocational dreams than most of the women I knew. For all of my first marriage, I was, if not the primary breadwinner, then at least the steadiest one.

In my thirties, I mostly gave up makeup.

In my forties, I've mostly given up dresses, though I still play with makeup and dresses when I feel like it.

I feel neither a profound dissonance with the idea of being a woman nor a profound attachment to the idea of it, and so my attachment to the trappings of womanhood as I was reared in the South to see it, has waned and was already beginning to wane in Boystown.

But the truth is that for large swaths of my marriage to Devin, if any man had ever presented himself to me, femme or not, as a viable one-night stand, I would have taken him up on it. I tried to flirt with every man I saw, straight or gay. I spent one mortifying afternoon trying without saying it out loud to proposition a straight-seeming barista at the Caribou Coffee by my apartment, who'd complimented my sweater the day before and winked at me. The truth is, despite how attached I'd always been to the idea that Devin and I could work things out, I was so hungry to be seen as attractive, so hungry to be wanted, that there were any number of times I would have cheated on him in the midst of his prolonged emotional withdrawals had the chance been offered to me.

It just never was.

If there ever was an actual gay villain in my story, then it was the man who owned one of the salons on Addison a few blocks from my apartment in Boystown.

A cluster of sex shops and queer bookstores and coffee shops and bars surrounded his salon. In the weeks after the post-Halloween revelation at Cocktail, I'd been femme-ing myself up as much as I ever have. I spent five hundred dollars on Bobbi Brown makeup. I bought unguents and lotions and exfoliants. I applied a sugar scrub to my entire body and wrapped myself in Glad wrap to heat it. I doused myself in Banana Republic Classic, my signature scent ever since the brief stint Devin had worked at Banana Republic before we were married. I wore dresses and heels and tight pants. I showed cleavage. I drew winged eyeliner on the corners of smoky eyes. I bought blood-red lipstick. I spent hundreds of dollars we didn't have on Blue Cult jeans, specially designed to make your ass look good. I bought a knock-off Chanel jacket to wear over a ballerina skirt with fishnets. It felt like the kind of thing Carrie Bradshaw might wear.

Finally, I decided to get a haircut to amp up my appeal. I don't even know how consciously I was trying to appeal to Devin particularly as much as I was just trying to remind myself that I had some potency, some agency, some viable chance at a bodily power all my own.

Meg Ryan had been my hair icon for so long, and I thought maybe if I could summon up her irreverent bedhead, her insouciance, her sassiness, the romance of her in *You've Got Mail* and *French Kiss*, then I could disregard the unsexing that surrounded me. I could speak back to the mirror that even if I wasn't the fairest of them all, at least I was fair. No matter what Devin did or said or felt. No matter what the whispering men of Boystown critiqued in me, I had sex, and I still wanted to have more.

Weekly installments of the first iteration of *Queer Eye* had led me (perhaps subconsciously) to the conclusion that gay men were singularly devoted to the actualization of the straight people around them. For each episode, the "Fab Five," a team of gay makeover experts, would take on a straight male client, revamping his wardrobe, physical appearance, and home décor. Back then, the show was even called *Queer Eye for the Straight Guy*. Most main characters in most movies I'd seen were straight people. I was finally in a city where I believed, maybe less than consciously, that I'd become a main character.

Thus, I walked into that Boystown hair salon at dusk one evening, wearing a yellow Fair Isle sweater that Devin hated, but I'd run out of clean clothes and it was all I had. I was taking my main character's head of hair to be lovingly cared for by a benevolent gay man, whose interest in me I presumed.

There I was, as desperate as I have ever been to feel worthy of love and attraction. The man who met me at the desk was as immediately hostile to me as anyone has ever been. I tried to explain to him what I wanted: Meg Ryan, bedhead, chunky, irregular layers—something I could maintain with a thermal round brush and some stiff hair paste.

He just said, "Mmm-hmmm," with lips pursed into something close to a snarl.

After he roughly cloaked my shoulders and washed my hair and scrunched it into a towel to catch the drips, he said, "No offense, but I don't think you have the cheekbones to pull off a Meg Ryan. Maybe we should go for something a little more conventional?" He could have been my adolescent acting coach.

I held back tears as I choked out "Oh, okay."

He proceeded to crop my hair close—not in a pixie cut, which could still have been funky and fun, but in a haircut that echoed Sophia's in *Golden Girls*. It was the kind of haircut my grandmother had "set" once a week. Foam curlers and hair spray and a curling iron with a teasing comb.

Two hours later, Devin arrived home to find me sobbing, seated on the floor of our entryway facing the full-length mirror on the back of our coat closet, a pair of shearing scissors in my hands. Like Samson, like the Evil Queen, I sat before

CHAPTER 25

the mirror, my power now a desiccated pile of brown curls collecting on my thighs.

I was cutting chunks and edges into the tight, matronly curls I'd walked all the way home sporting, looking like a middle-aged, brunette Annie at the age of twenty-six. I was then taking those chunks and rubbing them with my most expensive hair paste between my fingers.

"Awww, Kel. What happened?" Devin asked sympathetically.

Between sobs, I tried to explain to him about the bad haircut and the mean man and the thing he said about my cheekbones.

He put his bag on the floor, threw his coat and scarf down beside it, then took the scissors from me. He surveyed the damage, sat himself down behind me, and helped me make the best of it. For the next hour, he shaped it up—holding my hair up between his fingers, pulling it straight, snipping at the ends here and there. Once he finished, it was still too short, too symmetrical, to ever approximate the artful, sexy mess that was Meg Ryan's nineties hair, but it was better.

I wasn't crying anymore.

He kissed me on the cheek and rubbed my shoulders and assured me it looked good.

We ordered takeout orange peel beef from Mars Chinese down the road. We rented season 5 of *Sex and the City*. Afterward, we walked to Dominick's for ice cream.

It was good and easy for one more night.

Chapter 26

I hear Kevin before I ever see him.

On a Friday night two weeks after Halloween, I spend the evening at the Hilton and Towers conference room in downtown Chicago for MMLA (the Midwest Modern Language Association Convention). It's the same hotel Devin and I visited with my family before our engagement—the blizzard on the way home, the bad chocolate milk. That night in 2003, during the keynote, I am three seats away from the famous literary theorist Stanley Fish. Walking down Michigan Avenue, I call Devin from my cell to let him know I'm on my way home. I can't resist dropping in the detail about Stanley Fish, who had complimented my scarf, even though Devin has no idea who that is.

"Who's Stanley Fish?" he asks, and I can hear laughter in the background.

A man close to the phone echoes loudly, "Yeah. Who's Stanley Fish?"

Devin gets the giggles.

He sounds drunk. And now he's laughing, with someone else, at me.

I'd meant to call in a kind of fizzy way, had meant to be playful and to ask him if he wanted to pick up a movie at Blockbuster so we could stay up late and grab dinner—brats and fries?—and debrief it all. Instead, he's drunk already, and giggling at me, and my stomach feels as if it's ready to void itself. I can't imagine eating anything now, much less bratwurst.

"Who's that?" I ask sharply.

Devin clears his throat.

He's serious now.

"It's Kevin from work. We went to a sports bar," Devin says.

"Sports bar," I can hear Kevin giggling in the background. Devin doesn't giggle back.

"Umm, I'm coming home, and I just wanted you to know. Bye," I say, and I hang up the phone abruptly and go home to an empty apartment.

Devin's parents fly up from Oklahoma for Thanksgiving.

Over dinner the first night, we are seated at Devin's grandmother's old round table with a linoleum top and polished metal legs in our tiny kitchen in Chicago. Devin's brother, Chad, who's also in graduate school, and I have a conversation about queer theory, which for eight to ten hours of every day of the last four months has been all I've read.

Chad keeps the conversation going despite the fact that Devin is visibly uncomfortable.

I notice that Devin is uncomfortable, but I'm not stopping the conversation. There's a small part of me, a new meanness in me, that wants to see how close I can get to the line of telling Devin's parents exactly what is happening, of telling them that their son has been sleeping with other people—specifically, that their son, the one who spent six years in therapy trying to become straight, never was, and that he's been fucking boys in reckless ways, for years, and now we're in a whole other kind of therapy trying to decide if we can stay married at all, and now I'm trying to write a dissertation about boys who love boys and living in this neighborhood full of boys who love boys and my whole life now is boys, and I am angry at them in this moment about all of this for some reason, profoundly angry with them for never seeing what they were leading me into, for never realizing the cost of turning him against himself for all those years.

I want to shove Boystown in their faces, want to flaunt every rainbow pylon, want to talk brusquely about the dancer wearing a cock ring that I saw on Halsted Street last weekend, his big erect dick barely contained by lavender hot pants. I want to tell them about the sour schnapps boys and their suspenders and their trays of sticky tart shots they carry around from bar to bar. I want to walk them past the window display down the street, the one with leather masks, whips, and thongs. I want to tell them about butt plugs and vibrators. I want to tell them how much Devin is drinking and that even now, what looks like water in his glass isn't water, and do they really not smell it, can they really not tell what's going on here, and I'm afraid that his drinking will upset them as much as anything else, given how convinced they are that any alcohol is evil.

And I want to shout, "YOUR SON IS GAY. HE WAS ALWAYS GAY. YOU MADE HIM HATE HIMSELF. AND NOW I'M TRAPPED AND HE'S TRAPPED, AND I DON'T KNOW WHAT TO DO."

Part of me wants to flatten them so my punches land harder.

But a whole other part of me wants to appeal to the kindness and mercy I also know in them. They never meant to inflict this damage. I want to lay my head in his mother's lap.

CHAPTER 26

I want to rest my head on his father's shoulder, and I want to sob, "Tell me what to do. Tell me we'll all be okay. Tell me he won't actually die if I leave him. And if you can't say that, then tell me how to stay without dying myself. PLEASE. Not even our counselor will tell us what we should do."

I don't say any of that, however.

Instead, after Devin's father comments on my and Chad's extended conversation about Sedgwick's reparative readings of gay men by saying, "Weird, the stuff that they put in classes these days. I'm not sure I'm comfortable paying taxes for you to be learning that in a public university, Chad," I get up wordlessly and bake the lasagna I'd made the day before they arrived. It has fennel sausage and bechamel and spinach and basil and whole-milk ricotta made just down the street. The noodles are flat and fresh too, not the dry kind with curly edges. It's bubbling when it comes to the table.

Over dinner, things feel slightly more normal, if only for a little while.

We talk about menu plans for Thanksgiving and discuss what we want to see when we go downtown. They tell us stories about the business and about Bill's recent MS diagnosis and about both of Devin's grandmothers—funny things they'd said recently, what sorts of medical care they needed. They tell us about church and about friends of Devin's they'd seen around town.

It's a performance of an old normal that brings me some comfort. It's a performance of an old normal I wish I could make real.

The next day, after a nice breakfast and a walk along Belmont Harbor, the performance falls apart again when Devin slips off while I'm busy navigating my small kitchen alongside

Ada, her making turkey and cranberry sauce and sweet potatoes and me trying to finish cornbread dressing and mashed potatoes and green beans. I'm bumping into her enough to feel generally irritable. My shoulders keep clenching up to my ears.

Then I notice Devin has snuck into our bedroom with the door closed behind him to make a call. He never calls anyone. If he talks to friends at all, it's over email. He'd already talked to both his grandmothers earlier in the day. There's no one else I can imagine him calling. And I never heard his phone ring. So when I hear him talking softly in the room next to where I'm trying to negotiate enough space to finish our holiday meal, I put down my knife halfway through chopping some garlic and twist the doorknob so hard it sticks as I open the door.

"What are you doing?" I ask brusquely, not making any effort to hide my annoyance at him.

Embarrassment floods his face.

But instead of answering me, he mumbles into the phone, "I've got to go. Kelly needs my help."

He doesn't get up from the bed where he's sitting, and I close the door behind me. I know his mother heard me ask him angrily what he was doing. I don't want her listening, but I also don't want to have to wait until they've left to have this conversation.

"Who were you talking to?"

"Kevin. He had a long drive. I wanted to see if he was doing okay. He was up late last night, and he asked me to call him to be sure he didn't fall asleep on the drive home."

It would be one thing if this was customary behavior on Devin's part.

It would be one thing if he was that person for anyone in his life besides me, the person who calls to see if his friends are

CHAPTER 26

okay. He is not that person. For anyone but me. I go cold and tense. Once again, the thought of food makes me feel queasy. I can't imagine eating any of the cornbread dressing I'd spent the week prepping layer by layer—cast-iron cornbread two days stale, sautéed onions and garlic, homemade chicken stock with rosemary and sage, a real roux-based, savory white pepper custard to help thicken it instead of cream of chicken soup.

"Why did you call Kevin? He's an adult. He can get home by himself. You never call your other friends when they are driving," I spit the words out slowly, letting each one hit.

He doesn't defend himself.

He just shrugs and says, "I don't know. He just asked me to, and I wanted to know he was okay."

He even smiles a little while he's saying it.

I hate that smile more than anything I've ever seen. He looks like a little kid telling a dumb lie badly, one that even he doesn't believe, and I hate him so much in this moment, I want to find a word, a killing word, that will make it so he never smiles again.

And for just a second, I know I have no such power, have maybe never had it, might never have it, and that there is no such word.

It's been too long with the door closed already, and I know it will be awkward for both of us to reemerge, but we both know we will do it anyway.

For just a moment, underneath my anger, I can feel how much I want him just to say, "Hey. Kevin is nothing to worry about. I know that maybe seemed weird back there, especially since you know now that I've cheated on you before, but you have nothing to worry about. I love you. I'm here. We're going to work this out. It's going to be okay."

But he doesn't say anything, and I just say, "Okay. Well, I gotta go finish the food. Your mother's waiting on me."

He offers to help, but lamely, and I shut it down before he even finishes the question.

"Nope. There are already too many people in that kitchen. I'm gonna lose my mind if we add another," and I open the door.

Devin's dad and Chad are watching football on the TV in the living room. Ada is quietly basting our small turkey. She looks nervous. I summon up some semblance of happy underneath things and say, "Well, how are things looking in here? Anything burning?"

To my great relief, she plays along, summoning up her own happy, genuine or not, "Nope. It all looks delicious. I bet it'll be thirty more minutes on this turkey, then we should be good to go. Want me to set the table?"

"I'll get the placemats. You get the silverware."

After dinner, we take a train downtown to the bottom of the Hancock Building to see hundreds of toy trains and the Christmas lights of Chicago all glowed up for the first time that season. There's enough to see that it distracts from the afternoon's discomfort.

Devin's family is headed out early the next morning. I'm not sure if I feel relieved or devastated that they are leaving us alone again. Even the false or fleeting familiar, however intermittently uncomfortable, has been better than the isolation and confusion of the last month.

CHAPTER 26

I will miss them. I promise that we will come to see them at Christmas, but I will not keep that promise.

The first time I see Kevin will be weeks after he's already slept with my husband, though I won't know that for a while. He will be waiting outside my apartment beside his parked SUV, ready to pick up both me and Devin. There will be a Bob Dylan CD on the back seat. Kevin will say, "Devin tells me you're a real Bob Dylan aficionado. Thought you might like that."

I had arranged the visit myself.

I told Devin since he was spending so much time with Kevin that we should hang out. Kevin agreed. What I know of Kevin is that he is a straight person who studied film as an undergrad and who now works with Devin at the ad agency downtown.

When I'd informed Nick the day before that I was going out for dinner and a movie with Devin's straight friend from work, he'd seemed a little quiet at first but then said, "Well, hopefully he'll be nice."

What I also won't know is that later that night, Nick will run into Devin out in Boystown while I'm at home grading essays. He will tell Devin that he needs to tell me the truth before he takes me out on the town with someone he's already slept with. He will tell Devin that it's his job to tell me the truth, not Nick's job or Matt's job or Cooper's job or Brian's job. He will tell Devin that he owes me that.

Devin will refuse. He will tell Nick he just needs a few more days. He will tell Nick he doesn't want to hurt me more than he has to.

"You already have," Nick will say, and he'll tell Devin he has a few more days before he will tell me the truth if Devin won't.

So, there I am, on the last Sunday night in November, two days after Devin's parents have flown back to Oklahoma, exactly one month after Halloween and all that I learned after it, climbing into the back seat of Kevin's car. Devin has already had three drinks before we get in, which, tonight, means that he's both withdrawn and silly at the same time somehow, making lots of extra hand gestures when he talks, which isn't often, and mostly just staring out the window quietly at Chicago as it drifts past us.

First, we go to the Landmark Cinema just down the road. It's an easy walk, but Devin's back has been hurting and Kevin insisted on driving us both because of that. I don't know why it makes me angry that he has thought about Devin's back hurting, but it does.

We see *21 Grams*, the online description of which reads, "In a film that plays with the idea of straightforward storytelling, a group of troubled people find they are linked in unpredictable ways." The film stars Naomi Watts, Benicio del Toro, and Sean Penn, and I will remember very little of the plot or the visuals except that there are repeated shots of Naomi Watts's nipples, which both Kevin and I comment on over fish tacos and drinks afterward at Bar Louie.

It's the first time in months I've gone to any bar outside Boystown, and I say this out loud as we drive away from my now familiar neighborhood.

Kevin responds, "I don't mind a gay bar every now and then, but sometimes I feel more comfortable at a bar for straight people." Devin says nothing, not just then, but hardly at all over dinner either.

CHAPTER 26

I make up for it by mindlessly chattering away about class and about movies and music I like. I ask Kevin about film studies and what he likes about his job and what he wants to do and what sorts of TV shows he likes. And we share many of those likes.

He tells me he's got a female roommate he often shares a bed with, and that his family is putting pressure on them to date, and that he just doesn't know if he likes her that way yet, and I say, "Ooooh! That's fun, though! I haven't talked to a boy about a girl in a long time. It's usually just me talking to boys about boys these days."

Kevin laughs.

Devin stays silent.

When Kevin drives us back to our apartment, Devin tells me his head hurts and that's why he was quiet.

The following night when we return to therapy, at the end of the session the counselor looks at him and says, "Devin, is there anything else you need to tell Kelly? Part of being able to gain her trust back is to be honest with her." Devin says, "No. There's nothing else to say."

Two nights later, when I come home early from class, I open the door to my apartment to find Kevin and Devin sitting closely together on the couch. They look surprised to see me and very uncomfortable. I know there is a word for what I'm feeling—deep in my bones I know there must be such a word to name what's happening—but there's this disconnect between what I'm being told to believe (Kevin is straight, Devin is trying to figure out how to make this all up to me, Devin loves me, Devin wants me to stay) and what I'm seeing (Kevin seated next to Devin so close on the couch it looks as though they were kissing just before I entered the room) and what I'm feeling (this isn't right, something is not right here, someone is not telling me the truth).

I am flustered, and I fumble with the key before putting it in the pottery bowl by the kitchen door the way I usually do and laying my backpack next to the coat closet.

"How was class?" Kevin asks loudly, a little too brightly, smiling just a little too wide.

"Ummm, it was good. What are you guys up to?" I ask, not wanting at all to know the real answers.

"Nothing much," Kevin answers me again. "Just finding something to watch on TV. I was just about to head home."

Devin doesn't say anything while Kevin wraps a striped cashmere scarf around his neck, which as I watch him doing so I realize is also the way Devin has now begun to wrap his own scarf, making a kind of soft aperture first and then looping the ends through that rather than just knotting it as he used to. Devin doesn't say anything while Kevin grabs his messenger bag and coat. Devin doesn't say anything when Kevin smirks at me on his way out the door in a way that feels decidedly unfriendly.

When I ask Devin, moments after Kevin has left, why it felt like such weird energy in the room when I walked in, Devin says there was no weird energy, and that I am making it up. He says they were just watching TV, and now that I knew everything about his struggles, why was I being weird now that he was finally hanging out with a straight friend? He says that being with Kevin makes him feel like himself after all these months of hanging out with our gay friends in Boystown, and that he doesn't understand why I need to make him feel bad about that.

CHAPTER 26

And I don't know what to say to any of that.

I brush my teeth and go to bed and set my alarm to get to campus to teach my next to last regular-semester class the next morning.

But I don't sleep well at all, and I stumble bleary-eyed onto the train. My backpack feels impossibly heavy. The train car feels impossibly full. There are too many sounds: people using cell phones like walkie-talkies, people complaining about their bosses, people stamping their snowy boots into the brown grooves of the train car's floor to scrape them, people shouting, "BRRRR! SHIT! It's cold out there. DAMN. I hate winter!"

Noise.

There's always so much noise here.

Suddenly the Chicago I have spent years hustling to get to is the last place I want to be, but there's nowhere to go now and no one I can talk to who will understand how much I want to leave.

I am here.

There's nowhere else for me to go.

He hardly ever talks about Kevin, but in the weeks after Halloween, he confesses other things in the middle of the night when neither of us can sleep. Sometimes I wait for him to wake up when the thought of a person he might have slept with intrudes. Other times, I nudge him awake myself.

I say, without preamble:

"Robert from the restaurant. When he lived down the street in Jackson. That's why he'd invite you over for wine after you'd already gotten off work."

"That night you made us leave Nagoya before we'd even looked at our menus. You saw someone you'd slept with, didn't you?"

Sometimes the questions tend in a different direction: "Did you kiss them or just fuck them?"

Nearly every time, he answers as I've come to expect him to: Yes.

Chapter 27

Nick hasn't made me say anything out loud.

Not yet.

It's been five weeks since Halloween.

Now he calls at least once a day, sometimes from his job at the Camper shoe store on Oak Street when they are having a slow morning.

"I'm bored," he'll say. "Want to get falafel later at the place on Belmont? It's only a block from your apartment. You should probably get out."

I say yes. Almost always.

He knows I have trouble going out if Devin is home too. I feel antsy leaving him behind. I wonder what he's doing if I'm not there. I stare out the window absentmindedly. I take too long to answer simple questions. So sometimes Nick adds on, "Devin can come too if he's around. I'll call Matt and see if he's home yet. He could maybe meet up with us too."

I don't know what else Matt and Nick know about Devin. Or knew. But now I know about Devin seeking out people who weren't me to touch and to comfort and to be comforted by. I know about Berlin. I know about back in Oklahoma. I know about back in Jackson. I know it's been going on since before we were engaged. I know. Because I now know, I assume everyone else must too, like the knowledge is projected across my face like it's a screen.

Nick and Matt must know.

Right?

Whatever they do or don't know, as winter sets in, Matt and Nick grow colder and sharper with Devin. Maybe they have figured out that I know, and they're wondering why I'm still there. I am wondering that too.

Nick is one of three reasons I ever get out of the house. Some days he is the only reason. Otherwise, I wait alone in my apartment in my pajamas—my face unwashed, my teeth unbrushed—until Devin gets home from work. I teach on Tuesday and Thursday mornings. I take classes on Wednesday afternoons. Other than that, I could conceivably spend every other minute in my apartment. And maybe I should, given all the reading I must do.

I read one novel a week for the Nineteenth-Century American Novel seminar I'm required to take, and about two hundred pages of dense literary theory every week for that and for Chris's class. I'm compiling reams of research for my dissertation with Chris. My twenty-page final essays are each due in a week. My composition students have been waiting on grades for their process essays for the last three weeks. But I haven't begun any of the essays—not my own essays, not the essays I'm grading.

I wait. Everything waits.

My gray-and-brown, "shades of diarrhea" backpack is heavy with the weight of it all—with the weight of my clunky PC laptop still wrapped in its beige bath towel, and three hardback books I am attempting to read for my dissertation: *American Manhood*, *The Feminization of American Culture*

CHAPTER 27

(which Chris hates but wants me to read anyway), and Foucault's *History of Sexuality*. And then in the front pocket, always, I keep the large, green, annotated edition of *Leaves of Grass* from David's class next to the small, faded-peach abridged version I bought in high school. *Not stale nor discarded*, I can still hear the book saying sometimes when I ride the L home.

On the jacket of that old book, a youngish Whitman, not yet bearded as bold as Zeus, has one hand in a pocket of his loose linen pants and the other hand folded, resting against his hip as he stands at an angle. His shirt, also loose, hangs from him in folds. He looks out from the portrait directly, his country walking hat cocked to the same angle as his hip. I cling to both editions. I cling to Whitman. I cling to David, who taught me to read Whitman, over email. I email him too much—coded emails about things falling apart like the coded things I used to say in class, wondering if he could understand me. I scan my marginalia for notes to hunt for both their voices, to remember myself before Boystown.

Writing about Whitman seemed like such a good idea back in Mississippi. Back in David's class in the small conference room with the glass door overlooking the Jennings courtyard. Just down the hall from my own door, from my first office with my own third-floor window. Back on the same campus where my mother once refused to wear skirts and where my father once studied history. Two blocks from the house where my grandmother still lives with a picture of Devin, whom she adores, still on her wall. Two blocks from my Aunt Cindy and Thursday night dinners with them all.

Walt Whitman had seemed like everything. And Thomas

Wentworth Higginson, the other focus of my dissertation, had seemed like such a fascinating, underexamined figure. No dissertations had been written about him in my field. He was the editor of *The Atlantic* for years. He'd been the connection between Dickinson and Whitman—her preceptor, his detractor. He'd been a champion of abolitionism, the captain of a Union regiment of freed slaves in the Civil War. But he'd despised Whitman, had referred on more than one occasion, pejoratively, to his "Bowery masculinity," by which he had meant two things: Walt Whitman lacked breeding, and Walt Whitman slept with men.

But the more I read of them both now when it matters, now when I have to make something of it all—Higginson, Whitman—the muddier my thoughts become. The harder it is for me to sum things up or to arrive at any fresh insight in my weekly dissertation check-ins with Chris. For the thousands of notecards I have filled, all that I think can more or less be summed up in a single sentence: Thomas Wentworth Higginson, who championed the rights of women and slaves, was also a classist homophobe.

That's basically all I have.

Now that I barely sleep and often eat only because Nick reminds me to, I usually just find myself staring at a wall when I am meant to be thinking new thoughts. When anyone from back home calls, I share the barest details of my day, then I don't stop asking questions until they are ready to hang up.

"I'm reading Mark Twain."

"I went to the Melrose with Nick for cabbage soup yesterday. We split a Reuben."

"How's school?"

"How did Granny's appointment go?"

CHAPTER 27

"Did Craig come home last weekend?"

"Is Dad still raking up the cottonwood leaves from Miss Glo's yard? Are he and Miss Sue complaining about that?"

When Nick is at work at the Camper store and Devin is at the ad agency downtown and I can will myself out of the house alone, I lug my heavy, gray-and-brown bag to the Intelligentsia on Broadway. I take out the heavy books and heavy computer. I peel the blue rubber band from the fat stack of blank notecards and place them beside me.

I read. I reread. I stare out the window. I eavesdrop. The notecards remain blank.

I remain blank.

Though I listen to music on earphones attached to the heavy laptop, I can still hear the roar of steam frothing milk in copper pitchers. I can hear the conversations of people around me—saying things that make sense. Making statements that progress logically from beginning to end or connect themselves with some larger, abstract principles. Laughing. Reading books in which they are absorbed in a way that seems untroubled. Pure. At ease.

It's December 7 and Nick has called me every day for the past few days to make sure I show up tonight. His apartment. *Angels in America*. The premiere. "You can't miss it. Bring Devin. Bring that apricot toast you made last time. Bring yourself. Just come," he says. "It's hard, but it's good. You won't believe how good it is," he says.

On Friday, he had told me to bring my stuff to the Barnes & Noble on Michigan Ave. to hang out after he got off work.

I went early. I managed to take some notes. I got a tentative outline of my essay on "passing" for my American Novel intensive typed up. I even got three or four process essays graded. I stared out the window down the Magnificent Mile, festooned for Christmas. Tourists bundled and unbundled themselves as they entered and exited the front door. When Nick got off work, he brought his sleek messenger bag with him and settled in to study with me. Well after 7 p.m., he said, "Alright. Want to take the train back to Joy's? How does Thai food sound? Matt's flying tonight. He won't be back till tomorrow."

"That sounds good. Devin's gone too. Dinner with folks from work."

I stood and reached to get my bag off the chair, and Nick stopped me.

"Hand it to me," he said. "I'll carry it."

"I can do it, Nick. You hate this bag. I'll be embarrassed for you to have to carry it. It's ridiculously heavy. You have your own bag," I laughed, or tried to.

"Kelly, give me the bag. I promise I don't mind. I can handle it. Let me carry it," he said, and he wasn't smiling.

I didn't entirely know why this made me cry, but it did.

Nick, who doesn't relish public displays of emotion, gave me a gentle shove on the shoulder.

"God. You're a bit of a mess, you know," he laughed.

And I laughed too, actually, the clouds above me punctured briefly by light. And then I wiped my eyes and smiled at him.

"I know. I know. Thank you," I said.

And he carried my heavy bag.

To the train.

To Joy's.

To home.

CHAPTER 27

Before Devin and I go to Nick and Matt's for the premiere of the *Angels in America* HBO miniseries, I split three bulbs of garlic down the middle with a sharp knife. I slather them with olive oil, kosher salt, and cracked pepper. I roast them in the oven for almost an hour. Slowly, the apartment fills with the aroma. After the garlic cools, I slide each roasted clove from its layers of paper peel into a bowl already filled with softened butter. I mash them together into a paste. More salt. More oil. More pepper.

Then I slather the paste onto thin slices of baguette.

I tear rosemary needles from their stems, chop them fine, and mix them into some expensive French apricot jam I bought at the Whole Foods off the Brown Line. I spread the rosemary jam over the garlic butter on the baguettes and cover each piece with a bit of room-temperature Brie. I boil the remaining rosemary and some lemon zest in a thick simple syrup to candy some almonds, and I scatter the candied almonds over each bit of cheese.

I arrange the toasts on our prettiest pewter platter. I place a sprig of rosemary on either end. I cut two apricots, wholly out of season but hungered for, into rose-gold slices between the toasts. I eat a couple of pieces of toast and a couple of slices of apricot and let myself enjoy both, and then I rearrange the lot and cover it all in plastic wrap. It looks like enough for the ten or so guests Matt and Nick are expecting.

I call to Devin, who is drinking vodka tonics with my zested lemon slices while watching TV in the living room, and I tell him it's time to go.

"Do we have to leave now?" he asks, though he turns off the TV and gets up to leave just the same.

"Yes, we'll be late if we don't. The show starts at 7."

"It's six hours long, you know. One of the girls at work was telling me about it," he yells at me from the bathroom, where he is peeing with the door open.

"It's not the whole thing tonight! Just part 1. Just three hours. But I told Nick we can't even stay for all of that. We'll just stay as long as we can, then head back. He really wants me to see it."

We wait on the platform at Belmont for the Brown Line train to Kimball. It's early evening and already growing dark. A couple of weeks ago, the CTA powered up the heat lamps on the raised platform. Now if you press the red button, tubes of light above us begin to glow the electric orange of space heaters.

Devin taps the button with his elbow, it hums to life, and we huddle for its warmth beside two other passengers while we wait for the train. No one speaks. Devin holds our pewter platter with the apricot toasts and keeps adjusting the plastic wrap so it won't get blown loose by the biting wind.

I keep my eyes up.

I glance south in the direction of the skyline—the Hancock Building with two towers of light on its roof, right on the edge of that vast black lake, and the Sears Tower with its two taller fingers of flashing light further in. They are the highest things I can see. Beneath the buildings, all the other lights are blinking. The line of cars processing up Lake Shore Drive never ceases its motion. I have watched this now for months—these lit tracks of cars beyond me—parallel lines of light. I say to myself, as I did when we first moved in, *I am here. I am here.*

But I do it for different reasons now.

Because Berlin is just below the train platform where we now stand. There's the flashing neon logo in the dark gray-blue storefront. And if I look at it, I hear Devin's voice that morning after the morning after Halloween: "The weekend you went home, I went to Berlin alone. I met someone there. We went to his apartment . . ." I will hear it again and some thread taped to the interior spool of me will begin to loosen. I will have to tug it tighter if I look down at Berlin below me. So, I don't. I don't look at it.

Now instead of looking directly below me at anything at all, I look up and to my right. I keep my eyes fixed on the buildings I can identify. I consider what would happen if I boarded a Red Line train instead—northbound toward school perhaps. I tick through what I'd see. Graceland Cemetery off Sheridan. Little Vietnam off Argyle. The Edgewater Ann Sather's that you can't even see from the train but I know is there. There are Swedish folk paintings on the walls there. They bring you giant cinnamon rolls just for showing up. The streets are so quiet in the morning, my ears always ring when I am walking there.

Then I return my thoughts to where I am going tonight.

Just tonight.

Nothing past tonight.

I am going to Nick's. I am going to Nick's. I am going to see my friends. We are going to watch HBO. Before the show begins, there will be that crackly, static noise with the HBO logo that flashes before each episode of *The Sopranos* and *Sex and the City*. I brought the apricot toasts, just like Nick asked. Devin is carrying them. I'll take the Kimball Brown Line train past Paulina, past Southport, then I'll get off at Irving Park. Walk three blocks. I'll call Nick when I get to the gate. He'll press a button, and the gate will click open. My friends are waiting for me.

―――

Nick opens the door and takes the platter from me.

"Oh my god, this smells so good! And it looks so nice!"

"It's my prettiest platter. We give many platters for wedding gifts in the South. We are a platter-giving people," I laugh, words spilling out of me too fast after a day of no talking at home.

"Ha! Apparently! I'm not sure what we give in Milwaukee," Nick says. "Shitty beer? Crucifixes? Something ugly to hang on the dark wood paneling? God, who knows?!"

"Come on in, dear!" Matt calls to me from the kitchen. "There's room on the table for your toasts." There are three other men already here at the apartment. I don't know them, but we introduce ourselves. They say nice things about my platter too. Someone else has brought chips and guacamole, and warm pita bread in a wax-paper bag and hummus in a Styrofoam container.

I notice Matt has nice wineglasses out—Riedel glasses. There's white wine in the fridge and red on the table. Beer in a cooler with ice.

I take a wineglass and fill it with red.

We all chat briefly and load up our plates, but Devin and I have made it just in time. The show's about to start, so we ar-

CHAPTER 27

range ourselves quickly around the TV. Devin, who hasn't spoken more than two words since before we left the apartment, nods his head politely in the direction of Nick and his guests and decides to take a dining room chair that Matt had pulled behind the couch. Nick gestures at a place next to himself for me. He's in the middle of the couch, and I nestle into the arm of the sofa on one side while he sits close to me on the other.

We watch Harper Pitt, the generously depicted beard at the heart of Kushner's play, struggle to understand her husband, Joe. I see myself in her numbness and pain. At some point, I begin crying on Nick's shoulder. At some point, Devin leaves the room to sit in the kitchen until I'm ready to leave.

Afterward, we take the Brown Line back to Belmont.

We don't speak as we walk in the darkness to our apartment. For the first time in our marriage, I close the door when I go to the bathroom, when I brush my teeth and wash my face.

And for the first time in weeks, I fall asleep quickly. I fall asleep hard. I won't wake again for hours.

Three mornings before HBO at Nick's, Devin is getting ready for work.

He is trying out a new look he's been experimenting with for the last few weeks: a crisp, patterned, short-sleeved button-up shirt with a flannel tie. He wears it sometimes with a sweater vest, sometimes without. This morning, he's tried on two sweater vests and changed his mind about both. The first sweater vest worked, but it needs a different shirt, so he pulls out the one he'd just bought at Banana Republic and irons it, even though it has no apparent wrinkles. It still smells like Banana Republic.

I have watched Devin's grooming ritual often enough to accept this as well within the average range of meticulous. More than once this man has ironed his undershirts before we've walked to Blockbuster just to rent a movie.

But this morning, the ironing, the checking in the mirror, the tick of him clicking his jaw to open up his sinuses and ears while jutting out his hips to check the crease of his pants—it suddenly registers with me that none of this effort is being made on my behalf.

I sit on the bed behind him watching him dress. I am meant to be writing my dissertation and grading essays from home, so I am still in my pajamas. The bedroom is small, but we each have our own closet. On each ivory-painted closet door there is a leaded-glass mirror, secured with its original art deco pins. His closet is to the left of mine.

He is rechecking his tie in a way that seems fidgety but resigned, and suddenly, I feel an overwhelming impulse to injure him.

I want to take every pair of size 28 and 30 pants we have had altered into the exact size 29 and a quarter inch that he demands and light them on fire, then toss them, smoldering, out the bedroom window into the snow.

I want to wash all the product from his thick hair, the hair he hates because it gets fluffy no matter how furiously he tames it.

I think of the scores of times we have browsed retail outlets for hair pastes, gels, and powders cheap enough for us to afford but strong enough to shift his self-perception—each gel promising more supercharged control, more extra-firm hold. Pondering the countless times he has fixated on some aesthetic

CHAPTER 27

that inevitably failed to please, I return to thoughts of my own hair, made so recently matronly and so short by my latest haircut that it can't be tricked into any form but what it is, its tendency to curl blunting all the jagged edges we'd cut into it in the hours after I'd returned from the salon.

Devin has taken to calling this look of mine my "Hayley Mills circa *Parent Trap*" hairstyle, and though it makes me laugh when he says it and I know he means it affectionately, I absorb it as censure. How naked I feel in this blunted hair—how unable to hide. Words for nakedness, for exposure, for too many years of not being enough elude me as do the words that would signal an end to the parade of sleepless nights. So, I puff out my chest and sit erect in our bed. I coil my tongue, hold all the words in my mouth, feel them gather weight, serrate their edges.

"He has no hair, you know."

"Who has no hair?"

"Kevin."

"Why are you telling me this?"

"I'm saying he's bald. That's why he shaves his head. He's already bald, and he's not even twenty-five."

"Why are you telling me this? Who cares if Kevin has hair?"

"It seems like you do. You've tried on about eight different outfits this morning. Does Kevin know about you? Does he know that boys like you want to be more than friends with boys like him?"

I don't say the word out loud, but I am certain the impact has landed. We both know what I've just called him.

He turns around to face me, the gray of his face like a slap to mine.

He mumbles a word I can't hear.

Then, walking slowly through the kitchen and grabbing his coat from the hook by the door, he leaves without looking back. The lock clicks into place behind him. And I think to myself, *He doesn't even love me enough to slam the door.*

It's not yet 8 a.m. He will board the train downtown and will not be home until 7 p.m. at the earliest, and probably he will find a reason not to come home at all until well past midnight—a movie with friends, a coworker's birthday, a project that needs finishing. He will turn off his phone. I am alone, retracting my serrated tongue, feeling it catch and sever all the way down.

The radiator clatters on. An ambulance siren. A garbage truck. And in that silence that was never stillness, I roll over and try, without success, to make myself think about Walt Whitman.

That night after *Angels*, I have a dream in which I see my grandfather, dead seven years. He lets me touch his cheek. Then I wake up on my side facing the bedroom window, my back toward Devin. My pillow is wet. I've been crying in my sleep.

There are no garbage trucks yet. There are no sirens. The radiator appears to be resting. The steady white noise of our fan is the only thing I hear. I don't even hear Devin's breathing, which makes me aware that he is either out of bed or awake beside me.

I turn to see. He's there. He's awake. He's also been crying.

And finally, I know what I have to say, and I know that once I say it, something permanent and unfixable will be lodged between us.

CHAPTER 27

I hold the words in my mouth and taste them. I feel already the emptiness in my belly, the bile rising in my throat, my bowels twisting, because even though I will frame my statement as an interrogative, I know the answer.

"Kevin's not straight, is he?"

I hear a sob and a long pause for breath.

"No."

"Fuck. You," I spit at him.

My body surges with the kind of energy that causes children to flail their arms in retail stores, the kind of energy that makes drunks on street corners punch brick walls and fall down for missing. I throw the covers off. And I lie there wondering whether I want to hit him. I know that even hitting him, as hard as I could and for a long time, would do nothing to erase Kevin's smirk the last time he'd left our apartment.

He laughed at me, I want to say to Devin. *He laughed at me all through dinner. Before he left here, he laughed at me. In my own apartment where you brought him on purpose. And you slept with him in my bed. That man who laughed at me.*

Devin is sobbing. Only sobbing. Not saying anything. He lies crumpled underneath the comforter, holding it over his face, trying to protect himself from me or to protect me from him or to find his breath for just a few final minutes in the solitude the secrets had once carved out for him.

My eyes scan the room frantically. I've always judged people pretty harshly for throwing objects in houses. Always seen that behavior as beneath me—erratic, irrational, unhinged. But I feel like throwing something, if not at him, then at the wall or the floor or the window, at the god-awful radiator perhaps. But looking around, I see no object that doesn't matter to me. And even in that moment, I still feel aware that as a third-floor apartment in a four-story complex, there are people sleeping above, beneath, and beside us, who could be wakened.

I step as loudly as I dare across the room and snatch my keys and a pack of cigarettes from the front pocket of my gray-and-brown backpack, which I unzip in such a manic way that I rip off the already broken zipper and cause about six of my cigarettes to spill onto the floor. My hands shake as I attempt to return them to the paperboard case. A couple of cigarettes get lodged between the cellophane sheath and the paper package. I break at least two others shoving them back in, and so I leave a trail of tobacco leaves behind me as I wander into the kitchen to claim my lighter.

I keep two pairs of shoes by the door: flip-flops and winter boots. The winter boots require socks. Socks would have to be retrieved from the bedroom where Devin still lies crying audibly.

I just want to get away from that sound. I just want to go where his tears cannot argue me into staying, as they always have before.

If I was in any other place I've ever lived, I'd have gone straight for my car. I'd have cranked up the radio, ridden as far away as I could get from buildings and garbage trucks and sirens. But we sold our cars when we moved to Chicago.

I don't want to be on a bus. I don't want to be on a train. I don't want to walk down Clark or Broadway or Belmont or Halsted. Because there are always people on those streets all the time.

I need to be alone, and I need to walk, no matter who's lurking outside. Doesn't matter anymore.

I throw on the flip-flops. I grab my black commuter coat from its hook beside the door. I put my lighter and cigarettes

CHAPTER 27

into my pocket and step out into the hall. The moment I close the door I feel, if not better, at least safer. The door between me and Devin does for me what the covers seem to be doing for him.

―⁓◯―

This is where my memory will always grow hazy.

I know I go outside in an undershirt and flip-flops, with only my jacket for warmth. I know there is snow on the ground. I know it is dark when I go outside and light when I come back in. I know I smoke three-fourths of the remaining cigarettes before dawn. I know I walk only the back roads and alleys in an attempt to avoid human contact.

I know I smoke the last cigarette sitting on the back stoop of our building, watching the lights come slowly on in the houses on Orchard Place, the dead-end street between Barry and Briar.

Feet away from me, an ivy-covered lantern still lights up the back of the Unitarian church next door. In the small yard to my right lies a child's bicycle and a small primary-colored playhouse with a blue plastic slide. Both are dusted with fresh snow. I realize I am also covered in snow.

I sweep the snow from my hair with ungloved hands. I become aware that, after what has to have been at least one hour, maybe two, my feet in their flip-flops are aching with cold and are shifting in color from red to violet. I pull my knee-length coat as tight as I can over my bare legs. I recall a story a man had told me once about getting frostbite after crossing a street, fully clothed, in December in Chicago.

I am thinking about that, in fact, when the door hits me in the back of the head.

It is a woman from an apartment on the first floor. She is carrying a purple yoga mat in a knit bag over her shoulder.

"So sorry!" she apologizes vigorously. "I didn't see you there! You should get back inside. It's cold out!"

"Absolutely. You're right," I say, trying to smile casually.

There's a brief pause.

"Well . . . have a good day," she eventually says, and she walks down the street without looking back.

As I watch her walk away from me, I imagine her opening the door of the yoga studio down the road. I imagine the first warm gust of heated air hitting her in the face as her hands pull on the curved steel door handle. I imagine she is meeting friends—her regular Monday morning Vinyasa Flow friends, perhaps. They'll drink herbal tea, heavy on cloves. The room will smell like lemon and lavender and pine. Someone will make a joke about how early it is. Someone else will say, "Sure is cold out!" or "Sure feels like a Monday!"

Then a light comes on in that yard to my right, and through the uncurtained kitchen window, I can see a woman in a bathrobe filling two lunch boxes with apples and sandwiches. Today is still happening for everyone else on this street, I think. They'll still go to work. Drop off kids. Eat breakfast. Laugh with friends about a movie they just saw.

To my east, I see the faint haze of sunrise beginning over Lake Michigan. I become aware that the L has been clattering for quite a while. And I hear faintly (or imagine I hear) the automated voice on the train saying, "Doors open on the right at Belmont." And then, "Doors closing." The garbage trucks that hadn't been beeping when I came out are now doing so in the alley behind me. Orchard Place is waking up. And I am still outside in my underwear in December in Chicago.

Suddenly I feel hungry. I smell the cigarettes on my hands,

CHAPTER 27

and I want to wash them off. I want to get in a warm bath and feel the weight of the water on my skin. I want to smell lavender and lemon and pine.

I want to sleep.

I imagine walking upstairs. I wonder what I will say. I know I have to leave. I have to go home and see my brothers. I want to drive around for hours with them in Craig's green Civic, smoking and laughing and watching white tufts of egrets lift off from the broken knees of swamp cedar and cypress.

I want to see my grandmother. I want to sit beside her on the couch where I'd held my grandfather's hand for the last time before he died.

And I want to see my parents. I want to hear Miss Sue commiserate with my dad about Miss Glo's cottonwood tree always shedding into their yards. I want Miss Joan to share with me a bag of candy and give me a hug. "You always did love a sweet taste," she might say, as she usually did. I want to watch *Masterpiece Theatre* on Sunday nights with my mom. I want my dad to brew a cup of watery coffee for me and to make me the same spinach and canned mushroom omelet he's made me a thousand times.

I want to go home.

Chicago isn't home. Boystown isn't home.

And I wonder to myself how I have landed here on this doorstep in a neighborhood full of ghosts who'd faded away in the same space where I was sitting only five, ten, fifteen years after they'd passed on, all those men whose loves had cost them blood money I would never be asked to pay.

I picture Devin upstairs. Did he go back to sleep? Did he worry about me? Did he notice I walked outside without proper shoes or even pants?

Suddenly I become aware of a thought that has been ringing in my ears like tinnitus for years, just under the level of my awareness. The thought is "if." And the "if" is legion.

If only I was thinner. If only I was less jealous. If only I wasn't smothering him. If only I worked out every day. If only I ate smaller portions. If only Devin could like his job. If only he would talk to me again. If only he could relax. If only he could find some peace. If only his back didn't always hurt. If only he didn't drink so much.

Each "if" is constant and the noise of each is frantic, grounded in this dogged belief that if I could just stretch far enough, I could capture and keep some stillness that had always seemed to elude us both.

And I think, far from the first time, that if only Devin had been stronger, if only he'd been tougher, if only he'd tried harder, it wouldn't have been like this.

Then something happens that I will never know how to explain, but all that I ever know of future good will be rooted in it.

I hear a voice in my head. It sounds like my own voice, but it could be God's or a god's or the universe's or my grandfather's or perhaps the ghosts of the boys who'd sat on that same doorstep before me, steeling themselves for their own revelations.

"He tried" is all it says.

He tried.

He'd been trying his whole life. He tried so hard he landed himself in the ER with chest pains three times before he even graduated high school. He tried so hard he'd gone to therapy

CHAPTER 27

for most of his adolescence. He tried so hard his entire abdomen had been filled with stress-induced shingles by the age of twenty-four.

He tried.

He tried.

He tried.

He'd prayed the prayers. He'd walked the aisles. He'd asked again and again and again to be changed, to be healed, to be redeemed. He'd written songs about God's love for everyone, hoping to make those songs true about him too. He'd asked to be different, newer, better, kinder, more faithful. He'd beaten his body into submission countless times. He'd flagellated his heart with a thousand whips of the mind.

And now, on the step, I know absolutely, more than I know my own name, more than the fact of my cold feet, that more than his fear of hell or God or exile, what Devin had feared more than anything else in the midst of all that trying, since that frozen night at camp when we almost kissed, was ever wounding me.

He had wounded me anyway, of course, but it was his fear of wounding me, just as it was his fear of what it would mean about him if he ever told me the truth, that kept the lies going.

It is an impossible thing to say, no matter how many times I say it later—the way I try to explain what I learn in this moment, how you can know yourself to be a kind of killing softness you never meant to be. I know that I am that killing softness now, and I know I will not be anymore. I don't want either of us to die. There is no need. I cannot care anymore about hell. He is already in it. I have been watching him burn in it all this time, and now we are both there.

He has to stop trying, I think. *I have to tell him I know about his trying. I have to tell him I want him to be okay. I have to tell him I don't hate him.*

And suddenly I can't get back upstairs fast enough. I turn the lock in the back door. It takes me three tries because my hands are shaking from all the nicotine and snow. I bolt up the blue-carpeted flights of stairs two at a time.

When I walk into our apartment, Devin is sitting up.

He is on the phone in our armchair.

He turns around to acknowledge my presence and holds up his hand as if to ask me to wait for him to finish before walking back to the bedroom.

I don't move. I don't sit. I stand next to the hall closet. I take off my coat. I slip out of the flip-flops. I rub my hands together and roll my numb toes against the braided rug in our entryway.

He says, "Thank you. We'll see you tonight at 6:30. Thanks for making time for us. Sorry for the early morning call."

He hangs up.

"That was Sam. I told him my marriage is falling apart and I have to do something. He says he'll schedule an emergency therapy session with us at 6:30."

And then I walk toward him. I still don't sit. I don't touch him. But I stand close.

"I needed to walk for a while. I've been thinking a lot about what to do. But something happened just now outside," I say.

"What happened?!" he asks, jumping up as if he needed to race out the door to defend me, worried I meant that I'd just been assaulted.

"No, no. Listen. Sit. Nothing like that. I realized something

CHAPTER 27

I never realized until just now, and I'm so sorry I haven't ever seen it. I'm so, so sorry I haven't seen it. You've got to stop trying. You're going to die if you keep trying. I'm going to die if we keep trying. And I don't want to die. I don't want you to die. I don't ever want you to die," I say, and my voice catches from tears or lack of sleep or too many cigarettes, but I feel like I repeat the words several times.

When I stop talking, it's as though the slow-killing poison in any oxygen we've shared for the last few years has finally drained all the way out of the room.

The air is clean.

It could be camp again, the drive through the woods in the breeze, the smell of resin, stars visible in the sky.

He doesn't speak. He drops his head into his hands, and I can see the sharp blades of his shoulders convulsing. He weeps for a long time, but these tears seem cathartic. I feel no compulsion to soothe them or to try to make them go away. He doesn't reach for my hand. He doesn't beckon me to sit down.

I do not cry.

I walk into the bedroom and put on socks and pants.

I go to the bathroom.

I wash my hands and arms thoroughly and slather them up to the elbows in the cranberry lotion my mother sent me last week.

I make myself toast with the last of the apricot jam with rosemary and lemon zest and brew some coffee. He gets up from the armchair and walks toward me in the kitchen. He puts his hands on my cheeks, tilts his forehead to mine, and then kisses me. We stand like that for a long time there between the chipped white galley counters in the kitchen.

"I don't know what to say. I need some time to think, but I'm so tired. I already called in to work," he says. "Do you want to go back to bed? Do you think you can sleep some more?"

"Yes," I say. "But I'm going to finish my toast first. I'll see you in there."

Light is now streaming in from the east-facing kitchen window. It's a sunny winter morning. Cloudless. I stand by the round kitchen table in the light. I leave my plate with pumpernickel crumbs and jam on the drainage board by the sink to wash later.

Finally, I walk into the bedroom and pull the comforter around me. Devin turns to me and asks if he can hug me. I let him. He wraps one arm around my side and another underneath my head. He drapes one leg over mine and nuzzles his foot into mine.

"I'm so sorry. I'm so sorry. I'm so sorry," he breathes into my hair.

"I know," I say. "Me too."

Then there is stillness: the sound of the fan, the crisp smell of new snow and cold daylight from the slightly open window, radiator warmth.

Our arms and legs entwined, we fall asleep together in our bed for the last time.

Chapter 28

It is my last night in Chicago.

A Thursday.

December 11.

On Monday after I woke, I sent an email to the graduate director at Loyola. I told him there were issues in my marriage, and that I needed to go home to consider what I was going to do next. He said he was sorry to hear that. I responded that since there would now be some leftover money that would not go to my stipend, perhaps they could give Nick the class that I was planning to teach? He wrote back that it didn't work that way. I was so embarrassed by my naivete and bravado, I didn't respond.

I wrote Chris, and told him I needed to take a semester off. I told him there was no way my brain would slow down long enough to finish my final essay before I left. Could I get an extension? An incomplete? He said sure, but he asked me to come by his office and chat before I made anything permanent.

"Are you certain about this?" he asked when I came by on Tuesday.

"I don't know how much Nick has filled you in on my situation, but . . ." I began to say. And he interrupted, graciously, to save me from having to say out loud again what I'd already had to say out loud so many times that day to the department secretary, to the faculty chair of the teaching assistants, to our landlord. Nick had told him the basic story. There was nothing to be done about Devin, unfortunately; it's just the way those things are sometimes, he said. It takes some people a while to figure out who they are, he said. They don't always do that well.

"I understand," I offered. "It's a lot to figure out."

He nodded, but waved his hand as I was talking as if I was missing the point of this conversation.

"Look. He fucked up. Maybe you did too. But don't let him wreck your momentum," he cautioned. "What do *you* want? Don't let him dictate that for you. Do you want to stay? Why can't he leave? Why can't he move back to wherever he comes from?" And perhaps realizing he had asked me all these questions without pausing for answers, he stopped and just looked at me, waiting for some response.

"I don't know what I want. Honestly, Chris. I don't know. I can't think when I sit down to write my essays. I feel like I'm playing a game with words where the answer is always 'hegemony.' I can't concentrate. I can't focus. I can't read. I can barely teach my class. I just can't imagine having to start it all over in January. I don't know how I would pay for my apartment by myself. Or how I would eat even if I could pay the rent. I just can't see it," I said.

And that was mostly the truth.

The other truth, of course, was that my parents' home was the only place I could imagine myself being in two weeks. Beyond that, I could see nothing.

I had called my parents Monday night.

I had been crying before I called them, and I did not stop crying until hours after I hung up the phone.

My dad had been the one at home.

CHAPTER 28

My mom had been across the street taking dinner to Mrs. Jackson.

"Kel, are you okay?" my dad asked when I had taken too long to respond to the simple question, "How are you?"

"Things are bad here. I need to come home. I can't talk about it right now. Can you get Mom to call me when she comes in?" I managed to stammer out, taking long pauses to inhale, to try to catch and control my breath.

"I'm so sorry," was all he said. "Of course. Do you need us to buy you a plane ticket?"

"Yes. Please get Mom to call when she comes back in," I said. "I need to go, Dad. Please get Mom to call."

And then about twenty minutes later, she did call.

She didn't bring up my marriage or even ask me how I was doing. She wasn't crying. She didn't coo over me or ask me any questions related to my feelings at all. She just said, "Dad told me you need to come home. When is your last class? Can you leave on Friday?" After I responded, she said, "Alright, we've got some Southwest miles. I'll get it all taken care of. You get some rest. I'll let you know when I've got the ticket."

After we hung up the phone, she called my brother Craig and told him I was coming home and that he should be with them to meet me at the airport. Maybe he and I could go to the movies after they picked me up. They made a plan for him to take his last exam early so he could be there the Friday I arrived. Colin still had exams he couldn't get out of, but he would drive over from Birmingham the following Monday.

The arrangements, then, were all made. My mom had the Southwest counter at Midway hold my tickets for me. Matt talked to Cooper, who worked for Southwest, and they made sure it would all go smoothly.

I said my goodbyes to the classmates I was able to catch, but didn't go out of my way. No one knew what to say. Many of them still barely knew me. I kept my explanations to a minimum. I thought they maybe saw me as noncommittal. Or that I hadn't given my marriage a fair shake. Or that I was neither a serious nor a capable academic. I attended my last classes. I met with my own class to collect their final portfolios, and it took me all of an hour in the fishbowl teaching assistant offices to give each of those packets a peremptory glance and then walk my final grades over to Academic Services.

Today I took the train home a little after noon.

In the white plastic laundry basket we'd packed tightly with our wedding china on the way up from Mississippi, I carried my dirty clothes to the basement laundry room. I used one of the dining room chairs we'd gotten from Devin's grandmother to dig my black rolling suitcase out of the top of my bedroom closet. I laid it, open, on the bed. I dumped my clean clothes next to the suitcase in the place where Devin slept. Somehow, I lost my favorite black sweater in the chaos. It got tucked between the edge of the mattress and the headboard. Devin would find it after I'd been gone for a day. Later he told me that for months after I left, the only way he could sleep was while holding that sweater. It still smelled like me.

It's just after five now on Thursday, our last night in Chicago, our last night married and in the same home, and Devin walks in the door.

He is already crying.

Every night this week, he has slept at Matt and Nick's so I could have some space. Nick has insisted on this. He is putting

CHAPTER 28

distance between me and Devin that I don't have the will or the foresight to create. Matt insists on meeting me in the morning to carry my bags to Midway.

"Forget it. No way we're letting you go there alone," he'd said. And Nick had backed him up. One of them has called me every day for the last two weeks to ask if I've been sleeping. If I need anything. If I've been eating.

I have not been able to eat.

Neither has Devin.

Our refrigerator is packed with leftovers from restaurants all over Boystown that neither of us thinks about after we've put them in there—sweet potato gnocchi from Ann Sather's, orange peel beef from Mars Chinese, pad see ew from Joy's, a pastrami sandwich from The Bagel, a small container of cabbage soup and half an eggs Florentine from the Melrose Diner.

I want none of it.

Devin is crying when he walks in the door, and suddenly I am crying too. From the mindlessness that has been an afternoon of laundry and lists of toiletries I don't want to forget, I am suddenly returned to clock time.

It is 5:15 p.m.

Devin has told Nick he will be at their apartment no later than 8 p.m.

That leaves us less than three hours to say goodbye to each other. Nick will call. He will berate Devin for prolonging things. He will tell me to make him go. "Don't kiss him. He doesn't deserve it," Nick will say. I will kiss him anyway. Because no matter what, I've been kissing him every day for five years. But I can feel the pulse of the second hand ticking him irrevocably away.

We decide to eat dinner at a Thai place just across the street. We don't want to spend most of our three hours walking to Joy's. We order as soon as we get there. Pad see ew again. Wide, flat caramelized noodles. Seared broccoli almost burnt. Paper-thin chicken. Bits of sweet scrambled egg. I take three bites and then give it up as a lost cause. I can't swallow anymore. When the waitress comes to box up my food, it is still hot. Devin has no more success with his pad thai, a three on a spice scale from one to five. It gets boxed up along with mine and thrown in a white plastic bag with "Thank You" in red cursive written on the side.

When we walk in the door of our apartment together for the last time, he goes to the bathroom.

I carry the bag into the kitchen and place the leftovers in the refrigerator, rearranging things so they will fit.

I place the plastic bag under the sink with the other plastic bags I keep there.

This act feels so normal that I am almost able to forget what is about to happen. It is 7:15 p.m. now. To make it to Nick and Matt's before 8 p.m., Devin will have to walk to the train soon. When he walks into the kitchen, I say, "Well, you'll have enough food for at least a week here. That'll be nice, right?"

He nods.

He's barely been able to talk without crying all night. Then, out of nowhere:

"How do you make your mashed potatoes?"

The question makes me laugh for the first time in days.

And I proceed to show him. I never use a recipe, so I show him about how much butter. How much milk or cream. How much salt and pepper. What kind of potatoes I use depending on my mood. Which varieties I peel and which I don't. I tell him that sometimes I even mix a little horseradish into some mayonnaise and throw that into the mix.

CHAPTER 28

He makes a disgusted face at that.

Like most naturally skinny people I know, he hates mayonnaise, whereas I always lick the mayonnaise knife clean before setting it in the sink.

I tell him I often put Tony Chachere's seasoning in the water, especially for red potatoes. I show him where those spices are hiding in the cabinet. I show him the russet potatoes I bought two weeks ago underneath the counter. I stop just short of boiling the water, as I have done hundreds of times in the last five years to get some mashed potatoes started.

And then there's nothing else to say.

I will go back to Jackson tomorrow.

Devin will not be with me.

He will never visit my parents with me ever again. We will never go to the movies again. Or make a late-night Waffle House run. Or eat a Totino's pizza while laughing at the Real Estate Network at 1 a.m. We will never go to Blockbuster again. The list is infinite. We will never. We will never. We will never.

We both cry.

We say things I will not recall afterward other than I love you. I am sorry. I already miss you. We agree to check in with each other by phone on Sunday. We promise to keep it light when we talk. Let the dust settle before deciding what will come next—what a separation that we both know will actually be a divorce would soon look like.

He puts on his scarf and coat and hat.

It is cold outside, and he needs them.

The last thing he says as he closes the door behind him is "Get some sleep, okay?"

And he touches my cheek one last time, crosses the threshold again to kiss me. I close the door after he walks briskly down the hall, and that is it. I lie down, right there on the entrance hall floor. I lie down and curl up into a ball. I can see my wretched self in the hallway mirror, the same mirror where just a few weeks ago, Devin took the scissors from my hand and gently shaped my hair into something I didn't hate. I let myself sob and sob and sob until I can't anymore. And then I just lie there, spent. I can hear the clock in the kitchen. I can smell that the people next door are cooking with cumin and garlic. I can hear the people upstairs watching basketball—I can hear the broadcasted squeak of basketball shoes on a televised floor.

I remember that I have one last load of clothes still waiting for me downstairs in the basement. I dump the previous load of clean clothes onto the bed and take the empty basket downstairs myself. In all the months we've lived in this apartment, I've never done laundry at night. I've never wandered down to the basement in the dark alone to retrieve our clothes. It feels strange. It feels like one of so many million things I am about to do differently. But it isn't as scary as I imagined. I turn on the light. No one else comes downstairs. No one else is in the halls. For the first time since I can remember, I feel alone in this complex.

I carry the last load upstairs, and instead of taking it back to the bedroom where the suitcases sit ready and waiting, I carry it to the couch in the living room.

Suddenly, I am ravenous—hungry for the first time in weeks. I dig around the refrigerator through the leftovers. I decide on the noodles from tonight. I realize they're still lukewarm as I dish them onto a plate and into the microwave. I take out a tumbler from the glass cabinet, get some ice from the freezer, pour a little vodka with some grapefruit juice, and suddenly I've got a 9 p.m. cocktail and dinner all to myself.

CHAPTER 28

I sit on the couch, put the plate on my lap, and turn on the TV long enough to catch the opening credits of *Primetime Live* with Diane Sawyer. It's a special hour-long episode, she says. Devoted to documenting the strange history of pop singer Björk's stalker. Crime writer Patricia Cornwell will be joining her to examine the details of the case and to provide insight into stalking behavior particularly, as well as the criminal mind generally.

I have not, up until this point, listened to Björk much. My brother Colin is a fan, but all I know is that she once wore a swan dress to the Oscars and that she was in a movie even my brother admitted was depressing. I have a vague belief that she is from Iceland, but I think suddenly, perhaps is it Denmark? Is she from Denmark? Is it Norway?

These are the first questions I have asked myself in weeks that have nothing to do with divorce or moving or sexuality or fidelity or betrayal or grief. Where is Björk from? I think again to myself, and it feels like my brain is dancing a little bit. Where is Björk from? I let myself think again. And I don't even bother with the answer. I just keep asking the question. I'm pretty sure it's Iceland, but who cares?

The commercials end. And Diane Sawyer begins to speak. "Reykjavík, Iceland," she begins as the camera pans over a green volcanic landscape, mountains and cliffs and wild gray oceans, steaming hot springs and black lava rocks. "Aha!" I think. "It IS Iceland. Björk is from Iceland. I was right. I was right." I raise my tumbler to toast myself and laugh out loud. I take my first bite of the crisp-tender, briny broccoli in its sweet soy sauce. It is SO good. SO good. I take another bite of noodle, fork some egg and chicken. *So good. So good*, I think to myself. *Björk is from Iceland. Noodles taste good.*

I finish the whole plate and heat up the other container of Devin's leftovers. Hell, he owes me this pad thai. I'm not even full when I finish eating his leftovers, but I decide not to eat anything else. I finish my grapefruit juice and vodka and then make myself some herbal tea. I fold socks.

And for the first time in so long, I feel something like ease.

Epilogue

Ever since she could remember things and repeat them back to me, I have told my daughter about you. She knows I was married before I met her dad. She knows I loved you then and love you still. She knows you will always be important to me.

Now that half my immediate family lives in Texas and I live in Minnesota, we often drive through Oklahoma. I still smile when I pass a Braum's or we fill up at a QT, the same chain you used to visit every day after school for fountain sodas with your friend Christy. When we pass Reba McEntire's restaurant in Atoka, I tell my daughter about the line in the video Reba made with Huey Lewis. You know, where she goes back to school and her daughter accidentally spills coffee on her essay and she says, "What have you done? I don't need any more accidents in my life!" I tell her how you and I used to howl at that and repeat it back to each other anytime one of us dropped something.

I tell my daughter that *Steel Magnolias* is a comedy, but then, both of us sobbing by the end of it, I remember I found it funny only because we used to recite most of it together and cackle. "Yeah, exercises are good for her," we used to say when we'd go for a walk. Or "I'm pleasant! I saw Drum Eatenton at the Piggly Wiggly, and I smiled at the son of a bitch!" when responding to a critique about our moods.

These days, there are periods when you and I text or email regularly. Sometimes months and even years pass without any messages at all. You write to tell me you've seen the pictures from my second wedding. You tell me you find the look in my eyes promising because you know it means I'm happy, and you are grateful for that. You text me on a random Thursday to ask if I like Taylor Swift. It's important to you to know that I do, you say. And I do.

I have a recurring dream that I killed you and buried you beneath a bank somewhere in Mississippi. I always forget that I did it, but then they find you—a hairy knee in good jeans protruding from the asphalt. I remember what I did. I know I will be caught. I wake up before I'm arrested. Sometimes the reason I text you is I had that dream, and I want to know you are still okay.

I use Yukon Golds when I make mashed potatoes now. I peel the potatoes before I steam them. I leave out the mayonnaise slurry and use three sticks of butter and Diamond Crystal salt in place of Tony's. I use a ricer like the one you and I were given for our wedding but never used. The potatoes are feathery these days, airy where they used to be dense.

Light.

My daughter eats two helpings.

Twenty years after that last night we were married, it's still the dish I'm asked to make for every Thanksgiving, the first food I ever learned to make without a recipe.

I wish I could bring some of that lightness back in time to you.

I don't care anymore if I'm beige or not. Not just because someone I love loves me back. Not because I have nothing to prove to him. But because I love myself now in ways I didn't when I knew you. I could do worse than to end up a Sophia on *Golden Girls*. I could certainly do worse than to still look like Judy Garland.

I am the age Judy Garland was when she died, and barring something unforeseen, I will outlive her. I have joked for years that she is my patron saint, but now I'm beginning to believe it. Like Judy and Liza might have done if they were still together, my daughter has accompanied me to Pride as long as she can remember. The first time, I pushed her in a stroller behind the banner of the state school system I now work for. When her many adopted queer uncles and aunties asked her how she liked the parade, she shrugged her young shoulders as if it were not really all that memorable.

"There were men in shorts there. I threw them pencils," she said.

Now she keeps a book on her shelf called *God Did TOO Make Adam and Steve*. At the church we now attend, she reads the call to worship many Sunday mornings. All the pastors she's ever known there, the ones who drape her small shoulders with stoles to let her know she is holy, possessed of authority, have been woman.

Our first Sunday at that church, a kind man in his eighties, a retired physics teacher, joined us for coffee after the service. It had been years since I'd been in a church at all, and I was nervous. But my daughter had wanted to see what it was like, and so we went. The kind man who sat next to us asked about my religious background. I told him it was all black-and-white—full of capital *T* Truths. He nodded his head as if he knew all about it. He said I wasn't the only one coming from a faith tradition like that.

"I like to think of this place as a sanctuary for people who are refugees from certainty," he smiled as he told us.

I knew then I'd found a place where I could feel at home, a place where my daughter could feel at home.

If I was ever your camouflage, I know now that you were mine too—my bright display of plumage, my only Monty Clift. Your Windsor knot and wool beside me in a pew. Your stubbled face in all my pictures. Your platinum and diamond on my ring finger. Your soapy scent all over me. All of them shorthand signals of my enough-ness.

Every time I see some new law has passed to harm you, I wish I was actually like Bella in *Twilight* and could astral-project some bubble of safety. I can't, and anyway, you are strong and don't require it. More than that, any safety my presence ever offered you was illusory.

Still.

May you always have cover.

May there be no more need of it.

Acknowledgments

It took me twenty years to write this book, and I signed the publishing contract on the twentieth anniversary of my divorce. I've attempted many different iterations of *Beard* over the years, and therefore, there are many different groups of people to thank along the way. For this current iteration of *Beard*, there would have been no start without Vanessa Ramos. Thank you to her and to WAG: Morgan, Bronson, Catherine, and Katherine.

For earlier versions, I am so grateful for the huge team of folks at the SPU MFA—program administrators and instructors and cohort—Ann, Nancy, Jessica, Chad, Matt, Becky, Amie, Mary, Meg, George, Brian, Karin, Mark—genuinely too many other folks to name here—but I'd like to particularly thank Robert Clark for sticking with me long after the program ended.

I am grateful likewise for everything that *Image* journal, past and present, has been to me. For Greg, Mary, Anna, Julie, Beth, Grace, Taylor, Tyler, Dyana, and so many others, especially Caroline Langston Jarboe. Thank you to Milton Fellows, behind and before. Thank you to the Glen Workshop, especially Harrison Scott Key's 2017 memoir workshop—you know who you are. Thank you as well to my 2021 *Kenyon Review* Writers Workshop group, and to Jamie Quatro and

Lisa Ann Cockrel for leading it. Thank you to *Last Syllable Lit* and *Whale Road Review* and Ellen Ann Fentress at *The Academy Stories*.

Thank you to Chris Stedman, without whose enthusiasm and particular genius for grace I would never have finished this.

Thank you to the Central Minnesota Arts Board and my *Catapult* workshop crew. Thank you to Anna Qu. Thank you to Kate Hopper. Thank you to the McKnight Foundation. Thank you to MontiArts and all our Monti friends, especially Ali Yager and Jamie Randall, who read drafts upon drafts. Thank you to the Minnesota State Arts Board. Thank you to my Monticello Book Club.

Thank you to Karina Longworth, for making the greatest podcast ever made, and to Anne Helen Petersen, for writing that always reminds me to follow the trail that fascinates me no matter what. Thank you to Paul Lisicky for *The Narrow Door*.

Thank you to Mark and Rebecca Wiggs and the whole book club crew from Jackson, Mississippi, especially David Miller, who changed my life, always for the better, in ways you see reflected in this text as well as hundreds of ways you do not. Thank you to Chad Holley for devoting a year after college to teaching at the high school you graduated from. Every year of my life since has been better because you did.

Thank you to Union Congregational Church (UCC) and Northside Baptist and St. James Episcopal and St. Paul's for giving me hope and help.

Thank you to my extended family, all my aunts and uncles, especially my Uncle Richard and Aunt Judy, who have been encouraging me to finish this for the past twenty years, and who've told every writer they meet at Lemuria Books about their niece who's writing this book up in Minnesota. Thank you

ACKNOWLEDGMENTS

to all my Foster cousins, especially Brittany, who make coming home feel like home. Thank you as well to my Aunt Debbie, who encouraged me daily and whom I miss always. Thank you to her children, my cousins Deenie and Woody (and their spouses, Tim and Jen), for always understanding the thing in me that wanted to tell a story no matter what and for telling their stories too.

Thank you to Boystown and Story Studio and the Center on Halsted. Thank you to Unabridged Bookstore. Thank you to Nick Hurley, for carrying bags no matter what they looked like and for boxes of unprompted shoes, even my own personal ruby slippers.

Thank you to the friends who've become family from the Hyde Park house: Melissa, Katie, Reva, Phil, Chris, Ryan, and Chad. Thank you to Joel and Carlos, for rainy *Serpico* days.

Thank you especially to the housemate from Boston who's still my housemate: my second husband, Ben, the best person I've ever known. You made this book possible, and you keep making me possible. Cliché or not, I'd truly be lost without you, my phone friend.

Thank you to the Friendsgiving family: Kim, Marke, Chris, Amy, Nathan, Katie, Aaron, Mariko, Kristen, Colin, and all the kiddos. Thank you especially to Nathan and Katie for hundreds of hours of pep talks. Please, let's go back to Alinea now. Thank you to Zach and Nicole for making me feel like the book could actually be a book—for the drawings that helped it come to life, for hours of conversation that bolstered me.

Thank you to Ryan Berg and Juliet Patterson and Charlie Jensen.

Thank you to my Coven: Emily, Natalie, and Lisa. I survived the pandemic because of the three of you, and there are no words for the daily delight of knowing I can just reach out and text you any old time and hear right back. Thank you to my Marco Polo beloveds: Jen, Elizabeth, and Katie. Whether we are Split-Level Ghost Ranchers or Exsanguinated Horses, you tether me to the best of myself and you put up with the worst bits too. Thank you to Clint and to Nellie, honorary MPs.

Thank you to my students and colleagues (too numerous to name, but you know who you are) over the years: at Mississippi College, Jackson Prep (especially Anna and David), Loyola University Chicago, the Building Trnava, College of the Sequoias, St. Andrew's Episcopal School, Seattle Pacific University, and North Hennepin Community College. Thank you to the Bell and McCall families of Carnoustie, Scotland, and the Harkeys, who are fabulous. Thank you as well to the friends who appear in the manuscript only by first name or in previous versions but not this one, but who got me through the time depicted nonetheless: Amanda, Spivey, Lauren, HSK, Karoline, Christine, Jen and David, Joe and Wendy, LFR folks (especially Missy and Jolie and Cheryl), Kace and Dave, Sonja and Marshall, Bravo Jackson and Bravo Boston folks. The whole Brick Oven team.

Thank you to my in-laws, past and present. Thank you to Kathy, Denny, Andrew, Jen, Rachel, Matt, Izzy, JP, and all my Lundquist nieces and nephews: Kael, Elli, Beckham, Signe, Ren, Ansel, Kjell, Anders, and Elin. Thank you to Keith and Meredith, for taking care of my brothers so beautifully and for liking me too. Thank you to my Foster nieces and nephew: Emerson, Dean, and Polly. Thank you to my brothers, Colin and Craig Foster, my forever boys and anchors. I adore you both.

Thank you to my parents, David and Vicki Foster, for their unflagging support, both material and emotional. For teaching me to laugh. For teaching me to question. For being willing to change and to grow with me. For being still the easiest people in the world for me to be around. I love you so very, very much.

Thank you to my daughter, Ingrid Pearl, whose humor and fierceness in the face of injustice gives me hope. I love your guts. Bless your bones, my beautiful Pudding Pop.

For the people I'm probably forgetting, thank you!

Thank you to Kaye Publicity, for making me feel like I won the lottery.

Thank you to Kim and Marke Johnson, for the same.

Thank you to Eerdmans Publishing for all the support and to my editor, Lisa Ann Cockrel, who more than anyone else has taken the raw material of what I had and helped me transform it into a book I'm proud of. Thank you as well to Victoria Jones. I didn't know that copyediting is basically wizardry. But now I do. It was an honor and delight to work with you.

Thank you to all our Minnesota friends, especially Matt Horn and Kim Jakus. Thank you to Nick White, Ryan Berg, Charlie Jensen, Harrison Scott Key, Michael Kleber-Diggs, Hanif Abdurraqib, and Juliet Patterson, as well as my entire launch team. Thank you to the PFund Foundation.

Finally, thank you to Devin, without whose willingness to be depicted during one of the hardest periods of his life I would never have attempted any of this. We've had twenty good years of divorce-iversaries, my friend. Here's hoping the next twenty will be even better. I love you.

I'd like to dedicate this book to the memory of my grandfather, Richard Lawrence Foster. If there's an afterlife, I hope I am next to him in it: our feet sinking in sand, an eternal surf crashing before us, nothing left to do but take slow walks beside wide, blue water.

Notes

2   **"The Girl with No Gaydar"** "The Girl with No Gaydar," sketch from *Saturday Night Live*, season 27, episode 4, aired November 3, 2001, on NBC.

3   **"If you're a gay man looking for a beard"** *30 Rock*, season 1, episode 11, "The Head and the Hair," written by Tina Fey and John Riggi, directed by Gail Mancuso, aired January 18, 2007, on NBC.

3   **"Deal-breaker!"** *30 Rock*, season 3, episode 22, "Kidney Now!," written by Tina Fey, Jack Burditt, and Robert Carlock, directed by Don Scardino, aired May 14, 2009, on NBC.

4   ***Parks and Recreation* introduced the conservative character Marcia Langman** *Parks and Recreation*, season 2, episode 1, "Pawnee Zoo," written by Greg Daniels, Michael Schur, and Norm Hiscock, directed by Paul Feig, aired September 17, 2009, on NBC.

4   **later seasons of *The Office*** *The Office*, season 7, episode 9, "WUPHF.com," written by Greg Daniels, Aaron Shure, and Ricky Gervais, directed by Danny Leiner, aired November 18, 2010, on NBC.

5   **"What woman today"** Cindy Chupack, "Get This," in *Girls Who Like Boys Who Like Boys: True Tales of Love, Lust, and Friendship Between Straight Women and Gay Men*, ed. Melissa de la Cruz and Tom Dolby (Dutton Press, 2007), 164.

5   **"a sweet, quiet girl with short curly hair"** Tina Fey, *Bossypants* (Little, Brown, 2011), 35–36.

5   **"The Actress"** "The Actress," sketch from *Saturday Night Live*, season 44, episode 18, aired April 13, 2019, on NBC.

5   **Ann Harada plays Florence** *Schmigadoon*, season 1, episode 3, "Cross That Bridge," written by Cinco Paul, Ken Daurio, and Julie Klausner, directed by Barry Sonnenfeld, aired July 16, 2021, on Apple TV.

6   **"Dolly was short and plump"** Rebecca Makkai, *The Great Believers* (Penguin, 2019), 115.

6   **Tony Kushner's beautiful depiction** Tony Kushner, *Angels in America: A Gay Fantasia on National Themes* (Broadway Communications Group, 1992).

7   **Elizabeth Taylor threw a dinner party** Anne Helen Petersen, *Scandals of Classic Hollywood: Sex, Deviance, and Drama from the Golden Age of American Cinema* (Plume, 2014), chap. 12, EPUB.

8   **Clift survived** Karina Longworth, host, *You Must Remember This*, podcast, episode 20, "Liz <3 Monty," October 28, 2014.

22   **"I have heard the mermaids singing"** T. S. Eliot, "The Love Song of J. Alfred Prufrock," *Poetry* 6, no. 3 (June 1915).

23   **In the Andy Hardy series** Karina Longworth, host, *You Must Remember This*, podcast, episode 5, "The Lives, Deaths, and Afterlives of Judy Garland," June 9, 2014.

23   **"In a studio filled with glamour girls"** Anne Helen Petersen, *Scandals of Classic Hollywood*, 157.

24   **"She'll never be an actress!"** "The Ugly Duckling," *Silver Screen*, June 1940.

NOTES

24   **"You look like a hunchback"** Petersen, *Scandals of Classic Hollywood*, 174.

24   **And thus, she returned to her old lunches** Gerald Clarke, *Get Happy: The Life of Judy Garland* (Random House, 2000), 83.

51   **The first research essay I wrote in college** Tennessee Williams, *Cat on a Hot Tin Roof* (New Directions, 1955).

53   **"My hat is still in the ring"** Williams, *Cat on a Hot Tin Roof*, act 1.

98   **Among today's class reading** Mary Field Belenky et al., *Women's Ways of Knowing: The Development of Self, Voice, and Mind*, 10th anniv. ed. (Basic Books, 1997).

104   **"And from the time that it was revealed"** Julian of Norwich, *Showings*, trans. Edmund Colledge and James Walsh (Classics of Western Spirituality) (Paulist Press, 1978), 342.

104   **"At a time when the Last Judgment loomed heavy"** Janina Ramirez, "The Female Chaucer," *BBC History Magazine*, September 2016, 30–31.

137   **"Straight? What's straight?"** Tennessee Williams, *Memoirs* (New Directions, 2006), 54–55. Williams attributes this line to Blanche, though it does not appear in the play; the closest is in scene 9, where Mitch tells Blanche, "I was a fool enough to believe you was straight," to which she responds, "Who told you I wasn't—'straight'?" An abbreviated form of the above-quoted line appears in the 1951 film adaptation, for which Williams collaborated on the screenplay: "Straight? What's 'straight'? A line can be straight, or a street. But the heart of a human being?"

144   **a Christian woman on the cassette tape** Elisabeth Elliot, *Let Me Be a Woman* (Tyndale House, 1976).

150   "These are the things I know are true" Amy Tan, *The Bonesetter's Daughter* (Random House, 2001).

151   early selections of "Song of Myself" Walt Whitman, *Leaves of Grass: A Norton Critical Edition*, ed. Michael Moon (Norton, 2002).

156   "The indeterminacies of the 1855 Leaves of Grass also serve the purpose" Michael Moon, "The Twenty-Ninth Bather: Identity, Fluidity, Gender, and Sexuality in Section 11 of 'Song of Myself,'" in Whitman, *Leaves of Grass*, 856.

157   "The action of the passage" Moon, "Twenty-Ninth Bather," 857.

163   Like many now openly queer communities, Boystown came to be Steven Jackson and Jason Nargis, "Making Chicago's Boystown," WBEZ Chicago, May 7, 2017.

164   "heterotopia of deviation" Michel Foucault, "Different Spaces," trans. Robert Hurley, in *Aesthetics, Method, and Epistemology*, ed. James D. Faubion (New Press, 1999), 180.

169   as if we were Damon Wayans and David Alan Grier "Men on Films" is a series of comedy sketches that premiered on the first episode of *In Living Color* on April 15, 1990, on Fox, in which Damon Wayans and David Alan Grier play movie reviewers who are gay.

172   "Both critics and friends of Gender Trouble have drawn attention" Judith Butler, *Gender Trouble: Feminism and the Subversion of Identity*, 2nd ed. (Routledge, 1999), xviii.

173   what Paulo Freire calls the obscuring pedagogy of oppressors Paulo Freire, *Pedagogy of the Oppressed*, trans. Myra Bergman Ramos (Herder and Herder, 1970).

NOTES

173   "No deconstruction or dismantlement could really vitiate"   Eve Kosofsky Sedgwick, *Touching Feeling: Affect, Pedagogy, Performativity* (Duke University Press, 2003), 4.

173   "According to this fantastic logic, women are the token of a despiritualized materiality"   Judith Butler, "Desire," in *Critical Terms for Literary Study*, 2nd ed., ed. Frank Lentricchia and Thomas McLaughlin (University of Chicago Press, 1995), 374.

174   "Human knowledge is more independent than animal knowledge"   Jacques Lacan, *Mirror Stage*, trans. Alan Sheridan (Routledge, 1989), 77.

174   "Theory isn't difficult out of spite"   Thomas McLaughlin, introduction to *Critical Terms for Literary Study*, 2nd ed., ed. Frank Lentricchia and Thomas McLaughlin (University of Chicago Press, 1995), 2.

174   "No man for any considerable period can wear one face to himself"   Nathaniel Hawthorne, *The Scarlet Letter: A Romance* (Penguin Classics, 2002), 196.

175   **Stoker, himself a closeted gay man**   Talia Schaffer, "'A Wilde Desire Took Me': The Homoerotic History of *Dracula*," *English Literary History* 61, no. 2 (Summer 1994): 381–425.

176   **"Be assured of this, Walt Whitman"**   Bram Stoker to Walt Whitman, 18 February 1872, https://whitmanarchive.org/item/med.00004.030.

181   "I was driving down La Cienega"   "Interview with Liza Minnelli," *The Dick Cavett Show*, aired February 11, 1972, on ABC.

181   "Sally doesn't want to be beautiful"   "Interview with Liza Minnelli," from the 40th Anniversary Celebration of *Cabaret*, produced by the American Film Institute, aired February 13, 2012.

181 **"Behaving like some ludicrous little underage femme fatale"** *Cabaret*, directed by Bob Fosse (1972; Warner Home Video, 2013), DVD. Joe Masteroff wrote the stage musical script, adapting Christopher Isherwood's *The Berlin Stories* and John Van Druten's *I Am a Camera*, as well as the screenplay for the film adaptation.

183 **One biography of Vincent Minnelli** Emanuel Levy, *Vincente Minnelli: Hollywood's Dark Dreamer* (St. Martin's, 2009).

183 **Judy's father had slept with too many young men** Clarke, *Get Happy*, 13–14, 22–23.

184 **One of those sources is Judy's daughter Lorna Luft** Lorna Luft, *Me and My Shadows: A Family Memoir* (Gallery Books, 2015), 206.

184 **"Plain, ludicrously rather than pathetically plain"** Quoted in Frank Beaver, "Take That!," *Michigan Today*, March 10, 2015.

184 **"I don't know. I guess it's where I grew up"** Liza Minnelli, interview by Larry King, *Larry King Live*, CNN, October 6, 2010.

202 **Berlin didn't open until the early eighties** Naomi Waxman and Ashok Selvam, "What Led to the Demise of a Queer Bar Icon?," *Eater Chicago*, December 1, 2023.

261 **It's a special hour-long episode** Patricia Cornwell, "Inside the Mind of a Celebrity Stalker," interview by Diane Sawyer, *Primetime Live*, ABC, December 11, 2003.